D1617042

Migrants to Amazonia

Published in cooperation with
the Amazon Research and Training Program
Center for Latin American Studies
University of Florida

Migrants to Amazonia

Spontaneous Colonization in the Brazilian Frontier

Judith Lisansky

Foreword by Charles Wagley

Westview Press

BOULDER, SAN FRANCISCO, & LONDON

Westview Special Studies on Latin America and the Caribbean

All photos, including the cover photo, were taken by the author.

This Westview softcover edition is printed on acid-free paper and bound in softcovers that carry the highest rating of the National Association of State Textbook Administrators, in consultation with the Association of American Publishers and the Book Manufacturers' Institute.

Published in 1990 in the United States of America by Westview Press, Inc., 5500 Central Avenue, Boulder, Colorado 80301, and in the United Kingdom by Westview Press, Inc., 13 Brunswick Centre, London WC1N 1AF, England

Library of Congress Cataloging in Publication Data
Lisansky, Judith Matilda, 1950–
  Migrants to Amazonia : spontaneous colonization in the Brazilian
frontier / Judith Lisansky; foreword by Charles Wagley.
    p. cm.—(Westview special studies on Latin America and the
Caribbean)
  "Published in cooperation with the Center for Latin American
Studies, University of Florida"—Prelim. leaf.
  Includes bibliographical references.
  ISBN 0-8133-7495-2
  1. Santa Teresinha Region (Mato Grosso, Brazil)—Economic
conditions. 2. Santa Teresinha Region (Mato Grosso, Brazil)—
Population. 3. Land settlement—Brazil—Santa Teresinha Region
(Mato Grosso) 4. Land tenure—Brazil—Santa Teresinha Region (Mato
Grosso) 5. Migration, Internal—Brazil. I. Series.
HC189.S26L57 1990
304.8′811—dc20   89-37518
                                                                             CIP

Printed and bound in the United States of America

The paper used in this publication meets the requirements of the American National Standard for Permanence of Paper for Printed Library Materials Z39.48-1984.

10   9   8   7   6   5   4   3   2   1

This book is dedicated with love
to the two women who made it possible:
my mother, Edith Silverglied Lisansky Gomberg,
and my inspiring friend, Marisbela Vaitsman

Contents

Illustrations

Foreword

In 1939, when I first descended the Araguaia River by canoe en route to the Tapirapé Indians, I saw a small white chapel surrounded by perhaps four or five houses on a hill back from the river. I did not stop, for the back woodsmen who were my guides told me that Furo de Pedra was only "3 leagues" (9 kilometers) downriver. It was at Furo de Pedra that I was to meet my fellow anthropologist, William Lipkind; and it was there that I made my Araguaia River headquarters. There I was told that the chapel and the four houses were collectively called "Mouro de Areia" (Hill of Sand)—"a sad place to live." Both Furo de Pedra and Mouro de Areia were totally isolated settlements. They were about 600 kilometers from Leopoldina (now called "Arawana"), where a primitive motor road gave access to Goiaz, the former capital of the state by that name; and it was about the same distance to Conceição do Araguaia—a somewhat larger Brazilian settlement downriver, where riverboats provided occasional transportation to Belém at the mouth of the Amazon. Once a month, more or less, a small river boat ironically called the "Araguaia Express" plied between Leopoldina and Conceição, and every month two canoemen brought mail from Leopoldina to settlers along the same stretches of the river. The Araguaia River flowed through true *sertão* (back country), an area little explored and populated by Indians and a few subsistence farmers. In 1939 and 1940 I passed by Mouro de Areia several times on my trips to and from Furo de Pedra and the Tapirapé village up the Tapirapé River, an affluent of the Araguaia. I never stopped. There seemed little or nothing of interest.

In 1953, when I returned by airplane to visit the Tapirapé, who had moved their village downriver to the margins of the Araguaia, I landed at an airstrip at Santa Terezinha. I quickly recognized the small town as old Mouro de Areia. I was told that Furo de Pedra was being abandoned because of annual floods and that the people had moved to Santa Terezinha. A São Paulo corporation (probably CODEARA) had begun clearing forest back from the river. The company had opened the airstrip at Santa Terezinha and had persuaded a commercial airline to stop there once a week. There were more houses now, a small *pensão* for lodging company officials and technicians, and a general store. I met many of my old friends, who were refugees from Furo de Pedra.

In 1957 and again in 1965, I briefly visited Santa Terezinha—each time en route to the Tapirapé, whose village was situated some 30 kilometers upriver. The small town had grown rapidly. I heard considerable talk about Santa Terezinha and its problems during the time I resided in the Tapirapé Indian village. Padre François Jentel, the French worker priest who had settled with the Tapirapé, and the French missionary nuns (the Little Sisters of Jesus), traveled frequently to Santa Terezinha. These missionaries had extended their activities to the Brazilian peasant population of Santa Terezinha. On Sundays Padre Jentel celebrated mass in the chapel, which was now a church. He was organizing a cooperative among the small farmers and a small health clinic. The Little Sisters established a school and operated the health clinic. I learned that "the Company"—the ranching corporation—had claimed all of the surrounding lands, even the town of Santa Terezinha itself. The missionaries were appalled by the conditions imposed on the laborers contracted to clear the land for grazing, by the eviction of local people from land they occupied without title, and by the situation of migrants attracted to the area seeking land and work. Padre Jentel told me of unrest among the people of Santa Terezinha, adding that he feared violence. In 1972 violence did erupt in a gun battle between the displaced *caboclos* (back woodsmen) and "the Company." The federal government intervened by sending troops. The sad story of Padre Jentel, who was charged with subversion, imprisoned, and expelled from Brazil, is related in this book (see also Davis 1977). The resulting publicity did, however, force the Brazilian government to some action. The ranching company was forced to concede some land to long-term residents and to the town of Santa Terezinha itself.

In 1978–1979, when Judith Lisansky carried out her research for this study of Santa Terezinha, the social and economic problems of Santa Terezinha had not been solved. Other ranching companies had been attracted to the area. The small town had grown to about 2,000 people. It had become a *distrito* (subdistrict) of the enormous *município* (municipality) of Luciara, the seat of which is situated about 70 kilometers upriver. Migrants from northeastern Brazil, looking for work and/or land, continued to be attracted to the area; frustrated, they often moved after months, weeks, even days. People with land also continued to be evicted. The military government of Brazil had put down violence, but it had not solved the problems that produced violence. It was not a community in which an anthropologist could easily do fieldwork. Nothing seemed stable, even for a short time. One's friends of today might be gone tomorrow. Santa Terezinha exhibits many of the characteristics of a "wild west" frontier town of the mid-nineteenth-century United States. Judith Lisansky is to be congratulated for her study, undertaken in very difficult circumstances.

It has been a long-term dream of Brazil to develop its vast Amazonian territory. In 1940 President Getúlio Vargas made his famous Amazonian address in Manaus in which he announced the determination of Brazil to develop the Amazon. But World War II intervened, and it was not until 1965 that the isolation of the region from the rest of Brazil was ended by the completion of the Belém-Brasília Highway. Until then, access to Amazonia from the more populated and economically developed Brazil to the south had been by slow coastal steamers—or by air. In the 1970s Brazil extended the Amazon highway system by building the Transamazon Highway as well as other roads such as the Brasília–Porto Velho, the Porto Velho–Manaus, the Manaus–Boa Vista, and the Belém–São Luis. For the first time, one could travel by land to the cities of the northeastern coast such as São Luis, Recife, Fortaleza, and Salvador (Bahia) and to the industrial parks of the south.

Brazil took up its effort to develop the Amazon with enthusiasm. This effort has been marked by two seemingly opposing policies. On the one hand, the government has made enormous land concessions to corporations, both Brazilian and foreign. It also made credit and tax incentives available to the large undertakings. CODEARA and the other cattle-raising ranches in the Santa Terezinha vicinity are examples of such enterprises. On the other hand, the Brazilian government sponsored a plan and an effort to stimulate colonization. The states of northeastern Brazil have been plagued by periodic droughts, poverty, and *latifúndio*. Colonization in the Amazon might relieve this situation. Accordingly, in 1970 the military president of Brazil, Emílio Garrastazú Médici, spoke of the Amazon program as an effort to bring "men without land to land without men." The early 1970s also saw the establishment of the National Institute of Colonization and Agrarian Reform (INCRA), a federal agency charged with colonization by millions of small farmers of Amazon land. A plan was presented to provide 100 hectares (250 acres) of land along the Transamazon Highway to colonists from the northeast and from south Brazil; and INCRA carried out smaller, less ambitious projects elsewhere in Amazonas. The Transamazon scheme met with little success due to problems of transportation, lack of technicians, and selection of recipient colonists (see Moran 1981). Thus the government supported "a grandiose scheme to encourage individual colonists and providing favorable conditions for large capitalistic enterprises which wanted to enter the game" (Wagley 1974:10).

In any case, the two policies attracted hordes of migrants from the rural zones, the small towns, and even the cities from the states east of Amazonia. They came looking for land, for work—anything to improve their economic misery. A small number were incorporated into planned communities. The majority of these so-called voluntary migrants had been pushed out by eviction from the land they occupied in their home states as well as by other economic circumstances. These migrants added to the population of existing Amazon settlements and in some cases formed entirely new communities. Santa Terezinha is one such "spontaneous" frontier community—an example of a population attracted to a locality offering both land and work. The presence of corporation-owned cattle ranches provided the stimulation for growth. The conflict between the opposing policies of Amazon development is clearly summed up in this book by Judith Lisansky. The corporations gobble up the available land, but they need temporary labor to clear the forests to plant pasture.

As Judith Lisansky correctly states in Chapter 1, she does not argue that "Santa Terezinha is perfectly representative of all spontaneous colonization. The objective of a case study [such as this book] is partly to make concrete and alive the on-the-ground situation of real people involved in larger transformational processes." Certainly one community cannot be representative of such an extensive region as the Amazon. Each community has its own history, and none has witnessed the entire gamut of events and problems of the region. Yet the story of Santa Terezinha is hardly unique. Other observers have reported land conflicts, outbreaks of violence, and economic exploitation in Amazonia (see Casaldáliga 1978; Ianni 1978; Martins 1975; and Schmink 1982). Judith Lisansky has been most successful in documenting the human suffering, frustration, and disruption in the lives of the inhabitants. In fact, her picture of the situation in Santa Terezinha makes a mockery of President Médici's 1970 statement. INCRA was able to distribute some land formerly claimed by the cattle ranch (it claims 100 grants of 250 acres each), but many of the recipients had already sold their holdings.

The majority of people of Santa Terezinha "expressed frustration to the point of despair," states Judith Lisansky. Yet she goes on to add that, "despite much despair and feelings of hopelessness, most people were far from the point of giving up the struggle to secure a better life for themselves and their children." This says something, I think, about the Brazilian national character. "God is a Brazilian" and "Brazil is poor but Brazil is large." But on a more practical level, Brazilians also say that, when faced with danger, "believe in the Virgin but run." Thus, they have devised "survival strategies" that allow them to persist and to keep their hopes alive. By "survival strategies" Judith Lisansky means those arrangements and activities that provide at least temporary but modest solutions to poverty. They include cooperation and mutual aid of kin and *compadres* (co-godparents); ties of individuals as clients to protective patrons; diversification of occupation, as when a small farmer works part of the year as a wage laborer; and, if all else fails, migration—moving on to other localities to look for jobs and/or land. This is not to say that Santa Terezinha is made up entirely of a floating population of poverty-stricken people. Some inhabitants, such as the owners of commercial enterprises and those with salaries from the cattle ranches, provide stability to the community. But the overall picture of Santa Terezinha is not one of a developing frontier town with a bright future. In fact, Judith Lisansky interprets the growth of Santa Terezinha since I first saw it in 1939 as a distribution point for river-transported merchandise and as a way-station providing temporary accommodations to rural migrants seeking jobs and/or land. She predicts that with the completion of a federal road some 100 kilometers inland, river transportation along the Araguaia will become obsolete and Santa Terezinha will decline as a regional center.

Finally, it should be said that Lisansky's excellent study of Santa Terezinha is part of a larger program on the Amazon Frontier undertaken by the Center for Latin American Studies at the University of Florida. In 1974 the Center embarked on a modest program of research along the new Transamazon Highway. Emilio Moran's study of a planned colonist community (an *Agrovila*) on the highway near the small city of Altamira was the result of this early research. Then in 1980 an extensive program known as the Amazon Research and Training Program, with a grant from the Andrew Mellon Foundation, was launched. Thanks to this program, and to funds from the Mellon Foundation and research fellowships from diverse sources, a series of M.A. theses and Ph.D. dissertations based on field research in the Amazon basin have been completed. Most of these are listed in the bibliography of this book (see Butler 1985; Gomes 1977; Jones 1980; Lisansky 1980a; Darrel Miller 1979; Linda Miller 1982; Picchi 1979; Poats 1975; Stocks 1978; and Wilson 1985). Members of the faculty have done fieldwork in the Amazon as well (see, for example, Schmink 1977, 1980, and 1982; Wood 1980). In addition, two international conferences on Amazon problems have been planned and carried out, along with published papers (Wagley 1974; Schmink and Wood 1984). A newsletter reporting ongoing research by social and natural scientists from the United States, Europe, and Latin America, including a roster of scholars actively researching in the Amazon, is regularly distributed. A program of scholarly exchange with the Museu Paraense Emílio Goeldi and the Núcleo de Altos Estudos Amazônicos of the University of Pará has also been maintained. Scholars from the University of Florida have undertaken research with the co-sponsorship of these Brazilian institutions, and visiting lecturers and visiting scholars from Brazil frequently visit the University of Florida. This book by Judith Lisansky, although it was written after her graduate student days, is indirectly a product of this program. It is an important book—one that should be of interest to all of us interested in the future of the Amazon, in the study of Brazil and Latin America generally, in frontier societies, and in the field of social anthropology.

Charles Wagley
Graduate Research Professor
Emeritus of Anthropology
University of Florida

Acknowledgments

My greatest debt is to the people of Santa Terezinha, without whom this book would have never been written. Despite the very real hardships of their lives, they welcomed me and responded with grace, humor, insight, and incredible patience. They taught me new meanings for the concepts of dignity and courage. I truly hope that the telling of their story will contribute to improving their lives and the lives of other migrants. I especially want to thank my dear friends Raimunda, Dona Marcionilha, Nazaré, Rosaria, Dona Oda, Dona Luisa, Vilka, Dona Anna, Maria das Neves, Delmina, Leo, and Dona Tapuya. I am also indebted to Felicissimo, Doca, Pedro, Ben, André, Luis, Pedrão, Edna, Albino, Txawanété, Terezinha, Tadeo, Cesar, Aluisio, Arquimedes, Nayi, Procópio, Dona Cosma, Francisco de Sales, Ron and Darla Key, Sasaki, the Little Sisters of Jesus, and Bishop Pedro Casaldáliga. Please note that the names and minor details in the case studies in the book have been altered to maintain the anonymity of the informants.

I am very grateful to my family for support, encouragement, and tolerance for my choice of an undependable career. I also want to thank the other members of my Brazilian family, Bina and the late Julio Vaitsman of Salvador, Bahia. At the University of Florida, I had the great good fortune to have had Charles Wagley as a doctoral adviser. I am also grateful to other Florida faculty, particularly the late Solon T. Kimball, Anthony Oliver-Smith, Maxine Margolis, and Paul Doughty. Marianne Schmink and Chuck Wood deserve a very special thanks.

It is a pleasure to thank my dear friends, especially Margaret Andrews, Sandy Parker, Elaine Elisabetsky, Sandra Powers, Susan Carol Rogers, Rigoberto Lopez, Linda Girdner, Darrel and Linda Miller, Larry Hunter, and Anthony Stocks. I am also indebted to other good friends and comrades, including Debra Picchi, Susan Poats, John Wilson, Arlene Kelly, Carmen Arrue, George Vollweiler, John Butler, Kenneth and Elaine Konyha, Samuel and Elisa Sá, Lawrence Carpenter, Mercio Gomes, Anabela Viana, Ulli Pfeil, Darrel Posey, Cricket Dadian, Mary Karasche, and Eric Pederson.

Research in Brazil was facilitated by many people and institutions. I would like to especially thank Raymundo Heraldo Maués, Auriléa

Abelem and other faculty and students at the Núcleo de Altos Estudos Amazônicos at the Federal University of Pará. I would like to acknowledge help from the Museu Emílio Goeldi, the Brazilian Indian Foundation (FUNAI), the Conselho Nacional de Desenvolvimento Científico e Tecnológia, and the Brazilian Air Force. None of the work would have been possible, of course, without grants. I was fortunate to have received funding from Fulbright, the Foundation for Lowland South American Studies, and the Amazon Research and Training Program of the University of Florida. Of course, any errors in facts or interpretation are the sole responsibility of the author.

Judith Lisansky
Washington, D.C.

Brazil in Its Regional Setting

1

Forests for Farming

Introduction

I met Raimundo one overcast afternoon in December 1978. I was surveying the Rua da Palha side of the town of Santa Terezinha, a Brazilian frontier settlement of almost 2,000 people located along the Araguaia River in the northernmost portion of the state of Mato Grosso. I had arrived in Santa Terezinha that past March and was planning to stay until the following March to collect data for my dissertation on Amazon frontier life.

I approached a flimsy-looking thatch hut and politely clapped my hands in front of the doorway to let the people inside know I wanted to enter. A grey-haired woman came to the door and beckoned me inside. Her brother, also old and white-haired, sat quietly on a stool braiding reeds into rope. A hammock was hung directly across the main room, and I could see a man inside, obviously sick, wrapped in a grey blanket.

The *dona* of the house answered my survey questions in a perfunctory manner and then her brother spoke up and asked my purpose. I explained that I was a student, studying the region and the people so that one day I might write a book about Santa Terezinha. It was then that Raimundo, shivering from malaria attacks in the hammock, began to explain how things were with the people of this place.

"The *bandeira verde*[1] you were asking about just now," he said, "it means the forests. *Bandeira verde* are the forests for farming."

"We were told, many years ago," he said, "that there would be a war and much fighting in Goiás and that we should hide ourselves over here in the forests of Mato Grosso."

Referring to the droughts in northeastern Brazil in the 1930s, he continued, "There were many difficulties there, you know. The difficulties of the drought, in the northeast, when people had no resources, no aid of any kind. The plants died for lack of water. The animals died."

1

"The older people," he explained, "thought they ought to leave that place where things were bad and go out to the forests. They said they needed to search out a place with conditions where poor people could survive. The rich had bought it all," he added, referring to the land.

"So those people left there and went off to Mato Grosso, to Goiás, and to Pará, where today they are all peons. The old people said, 'Let's go. Let's go to the forests over there.' But the *fazendas*[2] took everything! Mato Grosso and Pará are all shut off, all fenced off. The poor have no choice but to be peons where on payday they get almost nothing and oftentimes end up still owing money to the *fazenda*."

"You realize, don't you," he said, lifting himself up painfully in the hammock, "that there is no place for the people who came here to go. So they become peons. The men have to leave their wives and children in a settlement like this one, and go out to be peons, fighting and struggling to earn just a little bit."

"If we enter any piece of land around here, they throw us out," he said bitterly. "There is no land for us. So we have to work as peons. But while you're working as a peon, you use up all your pay—buying food, buying medicine, and everything—and so at the end you make almost no money. Goods are very expensive at the *fazendas*, and so you are left with nothing."

"I am sick now with malaria, and I have no money. We live sick like this, sick and suffering. We can only work as tenants or hired hands because there is no longer any way to work for oneself. I was working for this cat[3] named João Preto and people say he's a good cat but the *fazenda* didn't pay him and so the cat couldn't pay the peons. Instead they gave us little pieces of paper, but the stores here won't accept those pieces of paper. So I'm broke now," he said and paused.

"The people in the northeast, they said, 'Let's go to Pará and Mato Grosso because over there is plenty of rain.' And maybe too they left because they were scared of the fighting. They thought there would be a revolution because there were so many suffering people. They wanted to go where it rained a lot. So the people came here. But there is no land."

"Look at me," he said. "I never made any progress. Here I am poor, and when I work it only serves to feed myself alone. In 1932, there was a drought all over. My family left. My father left there with his burro and his cart loaded with all our things, and we went to Maranhão and Piaiu looking and looking for a better place. We were scared of the hunger and of revolution. There were so many hungry people."

"So Padre Cicero Rumão Batista," he continued, referring to a famous popularly sainted folk hero of northeastern Brazil, "Padre Cicero explained to the people that we needed to go to the forests, to the places with mountains that catch the rain. Padre Cicero explained everything. He said that from 1970 onward there would be good times for everyone in the regions that had water. So, the northeasterners came here. Our land over there, it's still there but it was all dried up. All our animals died, and there was nothing left to eat. The older people said we should go to the forests of Mato Grosso, and so they left and wandered and walked for months and months, traveling, all those thousands of hungry people." The grey-haired woman silently handed us small glasses of hot coffee. Raimundo refused his, in a hurry to finish his story before the fever returned.

"Now we're in that era that Padre Cicero said would be a good time for everyone," he continued urgently. "But the land is all taken. It's all claimed. The poor aren't able to enter a single spot. The *fazendeiros*,[4] they're the ones with the money and the education. The poor can't fight them, so we become their employees. The poor live only to work. We have no rights and no place of our own."

"Now, of course, a man likes to work hard," Raimundo said. "If he has his own place he works hard and plants manioc, sugar cane, beans, and rice and even grows enough to have some leftover to sell. And so he buys a few things, maybe an animal. Maybe in ten or fifteen years a man might have something built up. But the *fazendas* don't allow him! No! They don't let us!"

The white-haired man asked me a question about government policies for farmers, and we spent some time discussing this topic. I explained about the fiscal incentives used by the government to encourage companies to invest in Amazon development projects.

"It's the rich who get all the help," Raimundo exclaimed. "They get all the help, credit and machines. The machines do a lot now, you know. Because of the machines there are almost no jobs. The *fazendas* are using machines to clear the forests, so jobs are getting even more scarce. It's getting harder to find a job. A peon can even less afford to complain about anything because the *fazendas* can easily find other men."

"I myself have been eight years away from where my mother lives. I can't return. Maybe I earn 1,000 cruzeiros,[5] but I need to buy some clothes, some shoes, food, and maybe a hammock and instantly the money is gone. I am ashamed to return to my people in São Paulo the way I am now. I am a broken man. A man with nothing."

"You see all these men in the streets here drinking *cachaça*?"[6] he asked, motioning with his arm toward the street. "These peons drink because they live disgusted with life. Because they don't have anywhere to go. When a fellow is so far away and he doesn't have the money to go home, he drinks to distract himself. They'll go on drinking until a cat appears. No one will help them," he said sadly.

"What Mato Grosso needs is a large, good area for us to cultivate. Look at me! I know almost every job there is to know on a farm and I have no place to go. Brazil has so many men, so many, many men—some even with some education—but they don't know what to do. They have no place . . . and they can't go home anymore."

I never met Raimundo again after that afternoon though I cannot forget him. When I returned to the thatch hut several days later, he had already left to join another work gang on a large *fazenda* about 250 kilometers to the south. He was still sick when he left, the grey-haired woman said, but he was broke and needed a job. The owners of the thatch hut, it turned out, did not know Raimundo well. Even though they didn't have enough to eat for themselves, they had allowed him to hang his hammock in their house because they saw he was sick and penniless. Raimundo, sensitive to the frontier rules of hospitality, had left before he overstayed his welcome.

Santa Terezinha, the frontier settlement I lived in between 1978 and 1979, was always full of men like Raimundo. Sometimes the transients were men—seeking work, on paydays, or recovering from jobs—and sometimes they were wives and children who had been hastily left behind when a man went off to a distant *fazenda* with a cat. Very often, too, I encountered transient families, bewildered and disoriented, who had recently been evicted from their forest homesteads and had made their way to Santa Terezinha, where they either threw up a temporary shelter or rented a hut while they considered their situation and hunted for alternatives. Each time I met these people, in the streets, at bars, at gatherings, or in their own homes, their refrain was always the same: "We came here seeking forests for farming. We thought there would be land here. But there is no more land. So we will have to manage as best we can."

The initial focus of my research project was an investigation of the dynamics of rural-rural migration. Massive rural-urban migration, already acknowledged as a major socioeconomic problem and relatively well researched, had resulted in incredibly overpopulated urban centers in which jobs, housing, and services were insufficient, a proliferation of *favelas* (shanty towns), and a tremendous amount of human suffering.[7] Policymakers in Brazil, and other Latin American countries as well, increasingly came to view the resettlement of people in remote rural areas as a potential solution for decreasing the rural-urban migration flood.

The question, then, was how to encourage people from relatively densely populated rural zones, such as northeastern Brazil, to resettle in more remote and less populated rural zones in the interior of the country. National attention for this resettlement, particularly from 1970 onward, focused increasingly on the vast and sparcely populated Amazon region. Thus my research objective, in its simplest form, was to try to understand how settlement in remote rural areas of the Amazon might be best encouraged.

The exploitation and settlement of the vast Amazon region has long been a cherished Brazilian goal. Amazonia today still constitutes one of the earth's last major frontiers. Brazil's portion of the region, referred to as Amazonia Legal (Fig. 1.1), encompasses some 5 million square kilometers, an area larger than Western Europe and equal in size to approximately one-half of the United States. Although Amazonia Legal constitutes almost 60 percent of the Brazilian national territory, it contained only 7.3 percent of the nation's population in 1960; by 1980 this share had increased to 9.2 percent of the total (Kleinpenning and Vobeda 1985:12).

The initial model selected for resettlement was planned agricultural colonization along the proposed Transamazon Highway, a major east-west road to be built across the region.[8] However, in the surge of enthusiasm for planned colonization, one important aspect of Amazonian settlement patterns was largely ignored. For many years, migrants from other rural areas had been coming into the Amazon region on their own. These pioneers, unofficial colonists in many people's eyes, had already created numerous little communities scattered throughout the region.

These spontaneous communities, particularly in eastern and south-eastern Amazonia, were usually formed by landless peasant farmers from Brazil's impoverished northeastern region. Many of these migrants had been moving westward for generations. These so-called spontaneous migrants, such as Raimundo and other inhabitants of Santa Terezinha, ended up totally outside the orbit of government-sponsored colonization efforts. Settlements such as Santa Terezinha received almost no attention from state or federal development agencies and precious little by way of supportive programs or services. They were strictly on their own.

Ironically, despite the knowledge that most Amazonian migration has occurred (and continues to occur) outside of official channels, many planners dismissed spontaneous colonization as a valid or reasonable model for development. In addition, most research carried out in Amazonia has focused on the planned agricultural colonizations. Far fewer studies have been conducted among *coboclo*[9] or migrant settlements unconnected to official government programs.[10]

The basic assumption underlying the planners' dismissal of spontaneous colonization is that it will come to nothing because the unofficial migrants are riff-raff—that is, ignorant and illiterate peasants. The underlying assumptions of my research project were two: that there might be

6

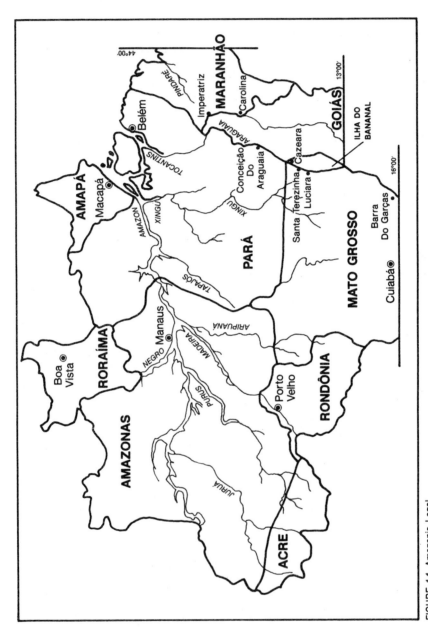

FIGURE 1.1 Amazonia Legal

valuable lessons to be learned as to how best to encourage settlement by examining how people accomplished it on their own; and that planners might be "blaming the victims"—that is, by attributing their relative lack of economic success in the frontier to the quality of the human resources without also examining the social, political, and economic constraints of frontier expansion.[11]

During the first phase of my project, I looked at migration patterns and decisionmaking. On one level, the conclusions of this part of the research became distressingly obvious. Migrants to Santa Terezinha left other places because they felt that their livelihood alternatives were impossibly constrained. They came to Santa Terezinha because of a glimmer of hope that the new location would enable them to improve their economic situations. Most of the migrants came with a strong desire to find unclaimed land for farming. They came from rural areas and moved to even more rural areas. They often expressed a healthy skepticism about their ability to make it in an urban context, noting their lack of skills and training. They also expressed a decided preference for a life described as *sossegado*—referring, that is, to the peace, tranquility, and self-sufficient abundance of the rural homestead.

As the research proceeded, however, it became increasingly clear that, for the majority of Santa Terezinha residents, the dreams of a better life were largely unobtainable because of seemingly insurmountable obstacles, such as the inability to gain access to land or the inability to depend on the farm for livelihood even with access to land. Although a small number of individuals in the community had improved their situations, principally those who ran the most successful stores or boarding houses, the majority of the frontier inhabitants expressed frustration to the point of despair.

The main objectives for research thus became two. One was to arrive at a better understanding of the obstacles confronting the frontierspeople. This entailed a study of Brazilian development policies, of the means by which these policies were translated into support for corporate cattle-raising projects in northern Mato Grosso, and of the impacts and implications of this type of development strategy for the region's small farmers.

The second objective was to explore the ways in which individuals and households in the frontier responded to increasing livelihood constraints. For it was clear that, despite much despair and feelings of hopelessness, most people were far from the point of giving up the struggle to secure a better life for themselves and their children.

This book, then, is the story of one Amazonian community located along the middle Araguaia River in the northeastern corner of the state of Mato Grosso. The first six chapters focus on the situation in the late

1970s and are based on fourteen months of fieldwork in 1976, 1978, and 1979. The epilogue, which documents more recent changes, is based on research conducted in the autumn of 1987.

Some of the material presented here is unique to Santa Terezinha, but most—if not all—of the most crucial social and economic problems encountered there are all too common throughout Amazonia. I do not argue that Santa Terezinha is perfectly representative of all spontaneous colonization. The objective of a case study is partly to make more concrete and alive the on-the-ground situation of real people involved in larger transformational processes. On a certain level, to understand the story of Santa Terezinha is to comprehend the dilemma and tragedy of Amazonian development. But Santa Terezinha is also a portrait of the human costs in social and economic change. One can only continue to ask whether the stories of people like Raimundo are simply the inevitable price paid for change—or might there be a better way?

Public Policy in Amazonia

Interest in exploiting the Amazon had been longstanding in Brazil, but little was actually accomplished toward this goal until the late 1950s.[12] Several events in the late 1950s and 1960s helped set the stage for the renewed national effort to develop Amazonia. First, the federal capital was moved into the center of the country; and, second, a highway was constructed between Belém do Pará at the mouth of the Amazon River and the new capital of Brasília. The Belém-Brasília Highway, completed in 1960, provided the first major overland transportation link between northern and southern Brazil.[13]

In the 1960s, and particularly after the military coup of 1964, the government sought to respond to mounting national social and economic problems by creating regional development agencies charged with the mandate of designing and implementing regional development plans. It was during this decade that the Superintendência de Desenvolvimento do Nordeste (SUDENE), the northeastern regional development agency, was created, and a previous Amazon regional development agency (SPVEA) was reorganized to become the Superintendência de Desenvolvimento da Amazônia (SUDAM), headquartered in Belém, the capital city of Pará located at the mouth of the Amazon River. SUDAM immediately became active in approving corporate investment projects in the Amazon. For example, between 1966 and 1970, SUDAM authorized and helped finance sixty-six agribusiness projects in northern Mato Grosso, including many of the large cattle *fazendas* that later came to threaten the way of life of the farmers of Santa Terezinha (Davis 1977:144).

A major drought in northeastern Brazil in 1970 marked a turning point in Brazilian national development policies. President Medici visited some of the drought areas and, according to the media coverage, was so moved by the suffering he witnessed that he vowed "to take a people without land to a land without people!" Thus, the first National Integration Plan (Plano de Integração National, or PIN) was launched.

One of the main goals of the PIN was a renewed effort to develop, exploit, and settle the Amazon region. To accomplish these ends, the government commenced the construction of an extensive road network across Amazonia, beginning with the Transamazon Highway. A second aspect of the plan was an ambitious colonization scheme designed to resettle thousands of landless northeastern farmers in agricultural colonizations along the 100-kilometer wide strips of land on either side of the new federal highway.[14] The Institute for Agrarian Reform, reorganized and renamed Instituto de Colonização e Reforma Agrária (INCRA), was given the mandate of designing and implementing the colonization.

The main objectives of the PIN colonization were (1) to provide a safety valve for emigration from the more densely populated northeast region, where highly unequal landownership patterns and the drought had contributed to growing social unrest, and (2) to increase agricultural production by small farmers for the benefit of Amazonia and the nation as a whole (Moran 1975:145). Yet, despite large financial investments and the involvement of numerous government agencies coordinated by INCRA, the colonization program was soon criticized by many observers over the next few years as falling far short of projected goals. The implementation of the colonization became snarled in bureaucratic delays and confusion, credit and marketing plans backfired, and far fewer than the anticipated number of colonists were actually settled.[15]

Throughout this period of policy commitment to small farmer colonization in Amazonia (1970–1974), the government also continued to support and encourage companies interested in Amazonian development projects (Wagley 1974:8). Fiscal incentives for corporate investment, originally designed for northeastern Brazil, were extended to apply to Amazonia as early as 1963. These incentives included a 50 percent reduction of corporate income taxes destined for Amazon investment, full tax exemption for approved projects up to 1982, exemption from import duties for raw materials, exemptions from export duties for certain commodities, special credit arrangements, and matched funding (Kleinpenning 1977:301; Panagides and Magalhães 1974:249). In short, as Charles Wagley (1977:10) observed, the Brazilian government appeared to be "playing both ends against the middle," as it continued to support corporate investment projects and, at least briefly, showed a commitment to encouraging small farmer settlement in the Amazon

The implications of governmental development policies for northern Mato Grosso were several. Since this area was not a designated official colonization area, frontier migrants received no attention, aid, or support from INCRA or related agencies. However, corporations planning investment projects in the area did receive excellent support and services from SUDAM, the Amazon development agency.

Shelton Davis (1977:114) has documented the fact that, by the end of 1970, "the amount of fiscal incentives invested in these two counties (sic) [Luciara, the municipality in which Santa Terezinha is located, and the neighboring municipality of Barra do Garça] alone totalled nearly 300 million *cruzeiros.*" In short, the small farmers in northern Mato Grosso received no government support whereas the large companies entering the region received many special and elaborate support and financial services from government agencies. The deck was clearly stacked against the small farmer.

To a large extent, Brazilian development policies for Amazonia have been characterized by self-fulfilling prophecies and implicit contradictions. For example, although government planners assumed that in the long run spontaneous colonization would be the main force in Amazonian settlement, many still considered "official colonization a necessary first step to spontaneous colonization" (Panagides and Magalhães 1974:248). The implicit assumption of the planners was that spontaneous colonization would *not* lead to desired development goals because self-selected pioneers were somehow inherently deficient; they were considered incapable of creating stable communities.

Translated into action, this policy assumption meant an official lack of support and encouragement for unplanned communities. They were assumed to be nonviable; therefore, nothing was done to help them become viable communities. At the same time, official policy assumed that corporate development projects would fulfill various development objectives; therefore, companies increasingly received major governmental support. Policy analysts Panagides and Magalhães (1974) document the accelerating expansion into Amazonia, since the mid-1960s, of mining, forestry, and cattle companies. They also note that this type of development strategy will result in the creation of "economic enclaves" within regions; that is, the labor absorption of the large enterprises will be minimal, and "they will tend to remain economic enclaves with minor linkages within the region."

Since 1974, Brazilian development policies for Amazonia have shifted away from official colonization and toward greater support for large-scale investment projects (Davis 1977; Kleinpenning 1977). The Second National Integration Plan, covering the period 1975–1979, considered the Amazon region primarily a "resource frontier" and selected fifteen locations as "growth poles" (Programa de Polos Agropecuários e Agrominerais da Amazônia, or POLAMAZÔNIA) designed to "stimulate investment in key sectors and areas for development purposes" (Schmink 1980:4). Official colonization efforts were cut back and private colonizations, organized and run by large firms, were encouraged. Spontaneous colonization, as before, was largely ignored.

The Third National Development Plan, formulated in 1979 for the next five years, varied little from the course charted in the Second Plan (Kleinpenning and Volbeda 1985). Subsequent plans followed similar trends; indeed, Marianne Schmink (1986:16) documents how, despite critical debate about the economic and ecological rationality of large-scale cattle ranching, "the incentives for livestock ranching have remained fundamentally unchanged."

Thus, current Amazonian development policies continue to be heavily weighted in favor of large-scale and corporate projects. Spontaneous colonization, which accounts for the majority of settlers entering Amazonia, has never received development specialists' attention (Panagides and Magalhães 1974). Small farmers, even within official colonizations and particularly outside of them, continue to receive minimal governmental encouragement or support.

Frontier Expansion

Many theoretical attempts to conceptualize frontier expansion in general tend to portray it as the movement of entrepreneurial pioneers into "empty" zones, which they then transform. A key element of most of these frontier theories is the assumption of abundant land to which most of the pioneers have access. Critical features of the frontier are then discussed in terms of spatial dispersion, labor scarcity, inadequate infrastructure, and communication problems. Many of these older frontier theories, reviewed by Thompson (1973), have been criticized as deceptively simple, cross-culturally inappropriate, and inapplicable to Latin America and specifically to Amazonia (Martins 1975).

The theme that repeats over and over again in the current literature on Amazonia is not land abundance but, rather, intense and bitter conflicts over control of land.[16] This struggle for land is sometimes difficult for outsiders to grasp, since the region is generally—and correctly—perceived as geographically vast and sparsely populated. Three more recent theoretical formulations of frontier dynamics, developed specifically in the Brazilian context, are useful for understanding frontier expansion in Amazonia and the seemingly incongruent fact of land conflict.

The first is the "boom-and-bust" model. Most observers concur that, prior to the 1950s, it was correct to characterize the Amazonian economy within the framework of the "boom-and-bust" cycles of the larger Brazilian economy. The boom stage begins when one natural resource or product—such as rubber, coffee, or sugar—coupled with a strong but temporary demand from the world market, stimulates intensification of extractive or productive activities for the commodity within one region. This stage is generally accompanied by large-scale emigration to the region of people seeking opportunities related to increased economic activity there. Later, when world demand for the product falls off or the Brazilian monopoly is broken, the activities slow down or cease and the people leave the region. This is the bust stage. Some writers have characterized what is left over after the cycle as a "hollow frontier."[17]

The rubber boom in the Amazon fits this pattern. The boom ended because of competition from Asian rubber plantations and, later, synthetic rubber. Most of the people attracted during the boom left the region afterward, although some did settle down permanently in the region (Cardoso and Muller 1978).

Policies, economic activities, and migration patterns since the 1950s, however, exhibit some fundamental differences from the "boom-and-bust" cycles. Migration into the region was spurred on by publicity about road building, colonization, and land distribution. At the same time, government encouragement to companies seeking investment opportunities supported projects with a somewhat longer-term orientation rather than projects characterized by the more "get rich quick" mentality of the booms. While the large-scale projects in timber, mining, and cattle have been described as economic enclaves, they are not typical of the predatory and rapidly disintegrating structures of boom enterprises. The firms now established in Amazonia—such as Volkswagen and Banco de Credito Nacional—are of a significantly different order of organization than previous forms described and analyzed for Latin America and Brazil, such as the *aviamento*[18] system during the rubber boom (Ianni 1978; Wagley 1976) or traditional plantation society (Hutchinson 1957; Wagley 1976; Willems 1975).

The second theoretical formulation of Amazonian frontier dynamics is oriented toward the post-1950s period. It is Brazilian sociologist José de Souza Martins's (1975) typology of the "demographic frontier" versus the "economic frontier." Martins defines the "demographic frontier" as the settlement of remote areas by petty commodity producers such as small farmers, artisans, and commercial middlemen. The "economic frontier" refers to the movement into the frontier zone of capitalist enterprises, primarily southern Brazilian and multinational companies. The two types of frontiers inevitably clash, according to Martins, because the *sine qua non* of capitalist enterprises is the appropriation and control of the means of production. During the period of expansion of only the "demographic frontier," land may continue to be abundant. However, when the "economic frontier" arrives, conflict ensues, and land and other resources become scarce.

Briefly applying this typology to events in Santa Terezinha, we should note that the initial settlement of the area by small farmers since the turn of the century can be considered the expansion of the "demographic frontier." When the cattle companies arrived in the region in the mid-1960s, one of the first consequences was an intense and protracted conflict between the companies that tried to evict local people from their homesteads and the town, and the farmers who attempted to maintain their claims to land by squatters' rights.[19]

The third formulation is Joseph Foweraker's (1981) three-stage scheme for frontier expansion in Amazonia. He defines the three stages as (1) noncapitalist, (2) precapitalist, and (3) capitalist. The stages are heuristic concepts rather than precisely operationalized sequences that can be sharply differentiated one from another. The critical distinguishing features of each stage are not only the extent and nature of the links to outside markets but, more important, the mode of production dominant in each stage.[20] The model also takes into consideration the fact that a number of quite different, though interconnected, types of production can coexist simultaneously.

The first (noncapitalist) stage is the earliest stage, during which the regional economy is relatively isolated and largely extractive. The sphere of exchange of the market is quite limited, with perhaps only one or two products sent out to the national market. Relations of production are mainly servile, according to Foweraker, with direct coercion of labor as in debt peonage, although some relatively independent petty commodity producers (such as subsistence farmers) can coexist. Otavio Velho (1972) and others have emphasized the interstitial nature of the rural poor in Amazonia. These people became rubber collectors or laborers during the boom periods and returned to subsistence farming during the bust periods.

The second (precapitalist) stage sees an intensification of extractive activities, increased immigration, and the buying and selling of land with the emergence of institutionalized private property. Capitalist enterprises begin to appropriate land, and conflicts, often violent, occur. During this stage, capitalism is not yet the dominant form, and the relations of production are mixed and may include both servile relations and the beginnings of wage labor. The links to outside markets are strengthened by fairly regular commodity production by capitalist enterprises and petty commodity producers. This transitional stage is frequently heterogeneous and complex.

The third (capitalist) stage is reached when the capitalist enterprises have become the dominant form of production. Land prices rise, private control over land is further institutionalized, and landownership becomes increasingly concentrated. Population movement increases, depending in part on what types of commodities large enterprises are producing; and both immigration and emigration may increase as people enter the region looking for work and commercial opportunities, and farmers who have lost land leave for other places. Relations of production, during the third stage, are mainly characterized by the growth of a free labor market, whereby workers are employed in wage labor. This stage, however, does not preclude other types of production, such as the continuation of some peasant farmers. Small farmers may be allowed to remain if, as Bryan Roberts (1976:100) noted in his study of the Mantaro area of Peru, the large enterprises have periodic labor needs for which it is convenient that "a substantial part of their labor needs should be temporary workers who continue to farm land." Lowly paid workers who provide their own foodstuffs and remain nearby serve as a reserve pool of cheap labor.

Applying Foweraker's model to Santa Terezinha, we see that although it deviates somewhat because there was no boom product there in the early period (i.e., no rubber and few nut trees), in most other ways the history of the area conforms to the basic outlines of the model. The noncapitalist stage in Santa Terezinha, dating roughly from the turn of the century until the 1950s, saw the settlement of the region by small farmers who engaged in subsistence produce and sold or bartered a few commodities to river traders who connected them to outside markets. Land was held and exchanged by usufruct; private property was not institutionalized.

Santa Terezinha began to enter stage two in the late 1950s and early 1960s, when land development companies began to activate titles and the first cattle companies began operations nearby. It was during this early period of the establishment of the cattle *fazendas*—approximately a decade—that debt peonage was the major method by which companies obtained their labor. Immigration intensified and, as predicted, by the mid-1960s a conflict situation had developed between the farmers who claimed the land by squatters' rights and the companies that claimed the land by deeds. This period of Santa Terezinha's history witnessed an institutionalization of private property and a great concentration of landholding patterns.

By the late 1970s, Santa Terezinha was entering stage three, the phase in which the capitalist enterprises become the dominant form of production. The *fazendas* controlled most of the land; and the immigration of people seeking land and work, as well as the emigration of people unable to obtain access to land or other livelihood opportunities, increased as predicted by the model. The coercive debt peonage system was replaced by a system of labor gangs run by crew leaders on contract to the *fazendas*. The impact of large-scale enterprises on a region depend on what kinds of productive activities the firms are engaged in—in this case, cattle. As predicted by many analysts, the cattle *fazendas* of northern Mato Grosso in the late 1970s were becoming economic enclaves with minimal linkages within the region. Food, tools, machinery, skilled labor, and other inputs were imported by the *fazendas* from southern Brazil, thus bypassing the local economy. Another important point about large-scale cattle production is that it requires very little labor in the long run. Labor is needed for the initial forest clearing and establishment of pastures; but after the pastures are formed, very few workers are needed to run a cattle operation. Thus, cattle *fazendas* neither stimulate local producers nor create many long-term employment opportunities. Small farmers are not needed even on an occasional basis for these kinds of agricultural enterprises.

By the mid-1980s, Santa Terezinha can be considered to have fully entered stage three; however, the regional development equation also shifted somewhat because of *fazenda* diversification into other agricultural enterprises and several other factors. These factors and their implications are examined in Chapter 7, which is based on fieldwork carried out in 1987.

Survival Strategies on the Frontier

Living within a research situation often profoundly changes the research agendas of anthropologists. My work was no exception. The realities of an Amazonian frontier town are quite different from a textbook exercise. As I continued working in Santa Terezinha, the focus of my research changed. I went beyond my initial concern with the push-pull model of migration (see, for example, Butterworth and Chance 1981). There is something remarkably self-evident about the observation that people leave a place because they feel economically constrained (push factors) and move to another location because it seems to offer somewhat improved livelihood opportunities (pull factors).

In short, my research came to focus on both the constraints faced by frontier households and the responses or adaptations made in the effort to surmount these constraints.[21] This kind of research is similar to Larissa Lomnitz's (1976:141) call to investigate "the survival strategies used by marginals," Bryan Robert's (1976:114) stress on the importance of understanding the "informal economy," and Anibal Quijano's (1970:18) emphasis on the need to examine the "survival structures."

The term *survival strategy* perhaps best conveys the idea because it conjures us an image of fighting for one's very life. The word *survival* connotes seriousness, and the term *strategies* suggests both the multiplicity and the purposiveness of the methods used. The strategies, as I have conceptualized them, are largely cultural. This is not to say that they are not shaped by larger forces but, rather, that they consist of what human beings have perceived as possible and feasible. They are abstractions because the informants themselves did not always see the patterns in their behavior. I have chosen to avoid the term *adaptations* because this word carries such heavy baggage, and also because it tends to imply a positive assessment or prognosis for success.

Survival strategies is used here to mean patterned activities that help ensure the continuation of the social group. It means livelihood activities, but it encompasses such concepts as informal economic activities, dyadic and group cooperation, and alliances through co-parenthood, local organizations, and the like. Some of the frontier strategies identified and discussed further in Chapter 6 include immigration, intensification and diversification of household labor, various types of reciprocity, and emigration.

There are several reasons for which research on survival strategies is a valid and useful area for investigation. One reason is inherent in the nature of anthropological research methods, which are better suited to the intermediate level of analysis, such as the household or community, than to either individuals or national or international systems (Lomnitz 1976; Shoemaker 1981; Steward 1955). Essentially, the anthropological case study method provides an ethnographic social impact statement, thus allowing for the exploration and understanding of how larger forces and policies actually affect people (Chambers 1977; Kimball 1978).

Second, an examination of survival strategies provides scientific evidence against social disintegrationalists and proponents of the vulgarized version of the culture-of-poverty concept (Lomnitz 1976). It is important to remember here that Brazilian planners largely dismissed spontaneous colonization as a worthwhile option because of strongly held prejudices against peasant farmers. Such prejudices, which portray the peasant farmer as ignorant, irrational, tradition-bound, and backward, are part of the overly simplified culture-of-poverty notion that blames the underdogs for their disadvantaged social and economic position. Relatively few studies of Brazilian small farmers have emphasized either adaptive strategies or more positive and creative responses to socioeconomic marginalization. Brazilian policy- and decisionmakers tend to be educated urban elites whose familiarity with rural people is based only on hearsay or popular images. Indeed, their stereotypes often substitute for realistic appraisal.

A third reason for focusing analysis on survival strategies is that it is critical to assess and attempt to explain the differential impact of forces of change on different types of rural zones and communities. As Norman Long (1977) points out in his book on the sociology of rural development, most theorists of the historical-structuralist school (and the modernization school, too, for that matter) have tended to downplay or even ignore internal factors (i.e., within countries, regions, and communities) and the roles they play in the maintenance or change of systems. In Long's attempt to empirically test the validity of the propositions and hypotheses set forth by Andre Gunder Frank (1969) and Julio Cotler (1976), he concluded that they underestimate the impact of lower-level organizations on national and international structures, and fail to comprehend the complexity of the local rural systems they are describing. Macro-level generalizations, then, must be examined in light of the findings from specific rural settings.

A fourth and related reason for studying survival strategies is to provide empirical data to support or dispute propositions regarding the nature of socioeconomic change. For example, the satellite-metropole model of Andre Gunder Frank (1969) has been criticized both theoretically (Leclau 1979) and empirically (Long 1977). One problem with Frank's assumptions is that he posits change in the countryside as totally dependent on forces emanating from both national and international metropoles. Similar to the dualistic models of the modernization school, which posit most change as deriving from a modern industrial and urban sector moving into and transforming an archaic, traditional rural sector, this formulation tends to deny any dynamic role at all on the part of the so-called satellites.

Finally, I think that the intermediate level of analysis of community and household dynamics has a largely untapped potential for reshaping policies designed to ameliorate rural poverty. While policy formation is not the central topic of this book, nor is it generally the main focus of most anthropological research, it seems reasonable to suggest that a better understanding of frontier constraints and the ways people respond to them constitute a useful body of knowledge that could significantly strengthen development planning. In short, as David Pitt (1976) and others have suggested, a grass-roots approach to development that builds on the existing strengths and assets of a population can be expected to be far more effective than plans formulated from afar that do not take into account the synergistic effects of different kinds of development efforts, cultural values and preferences, typical ways of cooperating, and indigenous organizations and institutions.

Describing and analyzing the situation of the Amazonian frontier of Santa Terezinha does not in itself provide either an automatic or a simple solution to the critical problems faced by the small farmers there. But many of the people of Santa Terezinha—people who unstintingly gave their time and energy and patiently answered my endless questions—felt quite hopeful that if the outside world knew of their plight, it would be moved to help them. I can only hope that this book will be a small beginning toward this end.

Notes

1. *Bandeira verde* is literally translated as a "green band" but is used here in the sense of the green promised land.
2. *Fazendas* means ranches. In this context, the term refers to the large ranches owned by companies or very wealthy individuals.
3. "Cat" (or *gato* in Portuguese) is a slang term for labor contractor or crew leader.
4. *Fazendeiros* are owners of the *fazendas*.
5. In 1978–1979 there were an average of 20 cruzeiros to the U.S. dollar.
6. *Cachaça* is raw rum.
7. See, for example, Perlman (1976), Connell et al. (1976), Butterworth and Chance (1981), Portes and Browning (1976), and Roberts (1978).
8. Additional material on the planned agricultural colonizations along the Transamazon Highway can be found in Kleinpenning (1977), Mahar (1979), Miller (1979), Moran (1975, 1981), Poats (1975), Smith (1982), Wagley (1974), and Wood and Schmink (1979).
9. *Coboclo* is a word with many meanings; in this case it refers to long-time Brazilian inhabitants of Amazonia.
10. One recent excellent exception is Parker's (1985) recent collection focused on the *coboclo* in Amazonia.
11. For a more complete analysis of the tendency to blame the small farmers for the delays and failures in the colonization, see Wood and Schmink (1979).
12. Material on the history of Brazilian efforts to develop the Amazon prior to the 1950s can be found in Cardoso and Muller (1978), Davis (1977), Mahar (1979), Miller (1979), and Wagley (1974, 1976).
13. Material on the effects of the Belém-Brasília Highway can be found in Hebette and Acevedo (1979) and Velho (1972).
14. One hundred kilometers on each side of any federal road, built or merely projected, is automatically transferred to the public (federal) domain to be administered by INCRA.
15. For evaluations of the Transamazon colonization program, see Bunker (1979), Kleinpenning (1977), Mahar (1979), Moran (1975, 1981), Poats (1975), Schmink (1977), Smith (1982), Wagley (1974), and Wood and Schmink (1979).
16. There is an increasing amount of information available on land conflicts in the Amazon; see, for example, Branford and Glock (1985), CNBB-CEP (1976), Foweraker (1981), Ianni (1978), Schmink (1977, 1982).

17. For additional information on the "boom-and-bust" cycles of the Brazilian economy, see Cardoso and Muller (1978), Margolis (1973, 1977), Reis (1974), and Wagley (1971).

18. *Aviamento* refers to the trading-post debt-peonage system common during the rubber boom.

19. Squatters' rights are technically referred to as usufruct or rights by use. The Portuguese term is *posse*, which refers to possession by occupation and use. Squatters' rights are protected under the 1964 reformulation of Brazilian land law, *Estatuto da Terra*—on paper, at least.

20. What is meant by *mode of production* is based on Long's (1977:96) clarification of the Marxist term and is defined as the forces of production (technological rules, resources, tools, and labor power) together with the social relations of production, which refer to the ownership and/or control over the means of production and the deposition of the value of the commodities produced.

21. For conceptual clarity, it is useful to point out the difference between the terms *family* and *household*. Family refers to individuals (kinsmen) who are linked together through ties of marriage and descent. Household refers to the people who live together in one residential unit. In Santa Terezinha most households are composed of nuclear families, although some households are headed by females with an absent male, some contain members of the extended family, and a few contain nonkin members. The term *marriage* as used in this book refers to several types of marriages, including church and/or state sanctified unions, common-law unions, and unions sanctified by folk rituals (e.g., "marriage of the fire").

2

Santa Terezinha, Mato Grosso

The Town Behind the Sand Hill

In 1931, Catholic missionaries who had been working in this remote region for several decades built a modest church on a sandy hill overlooking the Araguaia River, a tributary of the Amazon. Shortly afterward, frontier families from tiny hamlets and forest homesteads began building their homes behind the church. At first the settlement was known as Moro de Areia, or sand hill. Later it was named Santa Terezinha in honor of its patron saint, Saint Teresa.[1]

Seen from the air in the late 1970s, Santa Terezinha forms a large U shape. The main streets wind around several small hills in the center of town that appear as green mounds from above. As the plane flies lower, one can easily observe that the more permanent-looking buildings, those plastered and painted white, pink, and blue with orange roof tiles, cluster toward the bottom of the U nearest an inlet of the river where the boats dock. Farther from this "center" of town, the houses are more consistently the dull browns of mud, thatch, and sun-dried adobe. The homes on the outskirts of town are half-hidden by brush and trees.

The road from the dirt airstrip to town, like all the roads in the region, is dirt—a sea of mud in the rainy season and deeply rutted in the dry season. Entering town, one usually sees a few people on the road, walking or on bicycles, often clutching paper-wrapped parcels from shopping. It is not uncommon to see small groups of men gathered in the shade of a large mango tree in front of a bar and, less frequently, small groups of women, chatting and crocheting while sitting on stools on the shadey side of a house. Children play in the streets and chickens run loose. The passing of a vehicle always draws stares because it is an uncommon event.

In the dry season, with the sun always overhead, the town seems a somewhat forlorn outpost—quiet, dusty, and half-deserted. Soldiers and *fazenda* managers assigned to the region receive "hardship pay" to compensate for the difficult living conditions. *Fazenda* workers, overheard in bars, refer scornfully to the town as "Santa Terezinha, the chamber pot of Brazil"!

Behind the main streets that form the U, the roads taper rapidly into paths that wind through overgrown brush. It is difficult at first to realize that approximately 1,930 adults and children live in the settlement. There are no poles and wires because the community has no electricity. There is no postal service either.

Local people divide the town into four named parts or neighborhoods (see Fig. 2.1). At the bottom of the U is the downtown area known as Rua do Comercio (Commerce Street); the right side of the U leads to an airstrip known as Rua do Campo (Airstrip Street); the left side of the U is known as Rua da Palha (Thatch Street); and the red light district is known as the *cabaret* or *zona*, somewhat separated from the town proper by another small hill.

Consistent with the Brazilian urban ethos so well described by Marvin Harris (1971), Santa Terezinha is often proudly referred to, especially by the local elite, as an "urban nucleus," even though to North American eyes it appears to be a village or, at best, a town. Similar to other Brazilian and Latin American "urban places," the downtown is easily identified by the central plaza (*praça*), even though in Santa Terezinha's case it is only an open muddy area graced by two scrawny trees and a wooden bench. Proximity to the plaza confers status and prestige. Santa Terezinha's downtown area contains six of the town's seven boardinghouses, the mission health clinic, the agricultural cooperative, the largest stores, the homes of the town's more illustrious citizens such as the sheriff, tax collector, and director of the elementary school. Of the fifty-two structures in the area generally considered as downtown, twelve are homes, ten are businesses, and twenty-four are combined business-and-residential units. Although Rua da Palha actually has more stores, Rua do Commercio remains the downtown. People frequently visit this part of town to shop at the larger stores, including one run by the cooperative and another by the neighboring *fazenda*, to conduct business with officials, or to buy medicine or seek treatment at the mission clinic.[2]

The two halves of the U shape—that is, the two long main streets and the residential areas behind them—are similar in many respects. One difference, however, is that Rua do Campo is the more settled and permanent side of town. It is here that the original settlement behind the sand hill was located. Rua da Palha is the newer side of town and has a more raw frontier flavor. It also has more businesses, many of which are small bars and kiosks, more nightlife, more drunks in the street, and far more recent arrivals and transients. It got its name from

22

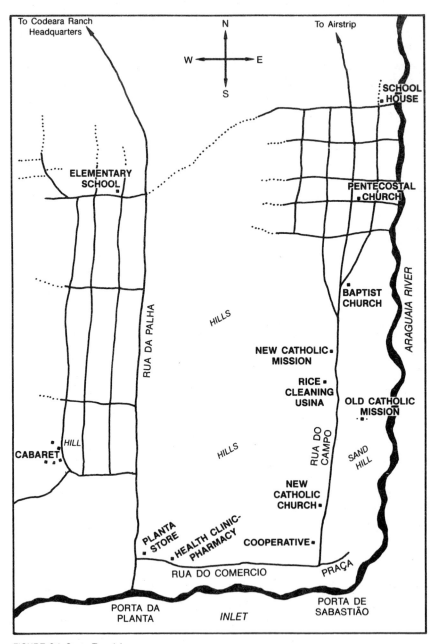

FIGURE 2.1 Santa Terezinha

the thatch huts that newcomers have built as temporary homes. Rua da Palha also derives some of its rough-and-tumble character from its proximity to the *cabaret* area with its houses of prostitution and "discoteques" that cater to ranch workers.

In 1979, I counted 222 structures of the Rua do Campo side of town, of which 211 were homes and 11 were combined business-and-residential units. Generally speaking, the farther one walks from the main road, the poorer and more temporary-looking the buildings are. This is so partly because, as people arrive in Santa Terezinha, they obtain lots farther and farther from the main street. Roughly speaking, proximity to the main street correlates with the amount of time a person or family has lived in Santa Terezinha. This is true for both sides of town.

The residential areas behind the main streets, on both sides of town, are laid out in rough rectangular blocks. The centers of these blocks, much like all of the thoroughfares in town, are overgrown with weeds, and residents complain that their streets are ugly, a *vergonha*.[3] However, the public-private space distinction in Latin American shapes the assumption that common space, being in and of the public domain, is the responsibility of the government rather than of the citizens (Harris 1971).

In sharp contrast to the untended streets, the areas directly in front of houses and behind, considered private space, are kept tidy and immaculate. The dirt is swept daily, and the fronts of homes are often decorated with brightly colored plants in tin cans. The backyard, or *quintal*, is frequently fenced and is an integral part of the home. It is almost always planted with fruit trees, a bean patch, sweet manioc, peppers, corn, okra, sugar cane, and other cultigens. Many yards also have a well, a thatch bathing hut, a wooden rack for doing dishes, and a slanted board for beating laundry. Privies are not common.

Dona Flora and her family will serve as an example of the kind of people living on the Rua do Campo side of town. I did not meet Dona Flora until I had lived in Santa Terezinha for three months because she and her husband had been living at the *roça*.[4] Their house in town had been closed.

One morning at dawn there was a knock on my door. I opened it and Dona Flora stood there, a short wiry dark-skinned woman wearing a shapeless cotton dress, rubber flip-flops on her feet, her hair tied in a tight knot on her head. She was forty-seven years old. She had come, she explained, to ask me if she could do laundry for me because she needed money to buy salt, oil, tobacco, and medicine to take back to the *roça*. She said that she had run out of tapioca flour to sell and that she could not earn money sewing because her eyes were too weak. She wanted laundry customers.

Dona Flora is an uneducated woman; only with difficulty could she write her name. But she is intelligent and articulate, and soon became a friend and an informant. Whenever she spent time in town, she would come over and work with me, patiently answering my questions into a tape recorder and providing me with a vivid picture of her life and childhood growing up in the region.

Dona Flora and her husband Francisco had received land during the 1972 land distribution, a virgin plot of forest some six hours walk from town. From thirteen pregnancies, Dona Flora had five living children, the youngest a two-year-old daughter—"an afterthought," she explained. The two sons, one married and one still at home, worked as peons at *fazendas* and occasionally helped their parents farm. The oldest daughter had married, and the young couple lived and farmed at Flora and Francisco's *roça*. Frequently broke, the young couple lived at home, but there was mounting tension in the house because of the young man's drinking and unwillingness to do household chores.

Their modest white house situated directly on Rua do Campo had three rooms, a small main room and two bedrooms. Cooking was done in a lean-to attached to the back of the house, and much time was spent in Dona Flora's immaculate *quintal*. The house had a dirt floor. They had considered making a cement floor in the main room but decided to wait because they were considering moving and building a new house next door to their son's home some ten minutes walk away. In the main room there was a simple wooden table, a few stools, and a calendar on the wall.

Both Dona Flora and Francisco had been born and raised nearby. Dona Flora's maternal grandparents had been from Maranhão. In 1905, they had migrated to an area near Araguacema, Goiás, and from there to northern Mato Grosso in 1925. Dona Flora's paternal grandparents, from Piabanha, Goiás, had moved to Mato Grosso in the 1920s. Dona Flora was born in 1931 in Antonio Rosa, an area of scattered *roça* homesteads 84 kilometers north of Santa Terezinha. When she was five years old, her family moved to Furo de Pedra, a village directly north of Santa Terezinha and the forerunner settlement before Santa Terezinha formed behind the church. Her parents had a home in the village and farmed in the forests nearby. In 1950, Dona Flora married Francisco, a local man and a farmer. They spent their first two years of married life tending cattle on the interfluvial island of Bananal and in 1952 moved to Santa Terezinha. By the 1950s Santa Terezinha was growing and the other village, Furo de Pedra, often inundated by flood waters, was in the process of being abandoned. Santa Terezinha, Dona Flora explained, stayed dry throughout the rainy season and, in any case, already had most of the commerce and a couple of boardinghouses where women could find work cleaning, cooking, or washing clothes.

With the money they earned from the sale of the calves they had earned in payment for two years of tending other peoples' cattle, Dona Flora and Francisco purchased squatters' rights to a piece of forested land only fifteen minutes walk from town. They built their house in Santa Terezinha and could easily walk to work in the *roça* nearby. For twenty years they developed their *roça* homestead, planting fruit trees and even experimenting with a few hectares of pasture grasses for cattle. The nearby location was very convenient, as it allowed them to live in town where their children could study. But in 1972, when the Institute of Agrarian Reform organized the land distribution in Santa Terezinha, Flora and Francisco lost their nearby farm to a more prominent local citizen. They received land in the distribution, but this time it was a piece of virgin forest some six hours away by foot.

They began all over again, now living more permanently at the *roça* where they grow mainly rice and manioc. Dona Flora feels they were fortunate to have received land in the distribution, but she dislikes the distance from town and the isolation in the forest. Most of their neighbors in the forest, she explained, have either moved to town or sold out. Francisco worries when he comes to town to shop, because if Dona Flora has an emergency there are no neighbors at the *roça* to call for help. There is no road to the *roça*. Carrying supplies and produce is difficult; usually it is done by hand or on the one bicycle they own. Dona Flora pointed out that the reason she has no chickens or pigs is because it would be too difficult to move the animals between the two places, the *roça* and the house in town. All in all, she explained, she would prefer to live in one place; but they need to tend their *roça*, and they also need to come to town to buy and sell and visit relatives. Dona Flora keeps hoping for a neighbor to move in within several kilometers of their new *roça*.

Until 1977, people obtained town land either by settling an unclaimed spot or by purchasing the "rights" from the previous inhabitant. Property rights and what might be called ownership (more precisely a form of stewardship) are overwhelmingly conceptualized by most rural people in terms of *posse*, variously translated as usufruct, possession, squatters' rights, or use rights.[5] *Posse* is an especially crucial notion to understand if one is to comprehend Amazonian frontier expansion and land conflicts, because it helps clarify the differing world views of peasants, operating by rules of *posse*, and of private and corporate companies in the Amazon, operating by rules of institutionalized private property.

Essentially, *posse* refers to a philosophically different type of property possession. It is not ownership of the land itself but, rather, a set of rights to the benefits of the land. Possession by *posse* is established by virtue of using the land, with the original rights going to the first user. This user, in turn, can "sell" his or her rights to use the place to a second party. The second party pays for the "rights" established by the first party and any improvements made, such as the addition of fruit trees, fences, or buildings. Holding or transferring land held by *posse* almost never refers to a legal deed or title. It is not illogical, then, that land held by *posse* tends to sell for well below the price of land held as private property with a title.

Posse is most frequently established on land thought to be without owners (i.e., pertaining to the nation [*terra devoluta*]) or land held by rich private landlords who live in far-away cities and take little active interest in what they own. Of further relevance is the fact that folk notions of "rights by virtue of use" have been reinforced by various versions of Brazilian land law (*Estatuto da Terra*)—particularly the 1964 version, which offers a way (albeit a highly complex and infrequently used way) for squatters to press their claims against an absent landlord if they have lived on the land for sufficient time, demonstrated that they actually use the land while the owners neglected it, and notified the owners by public declaration (*uso capião*). Encouragement of squatters' aspirations to obtain land pertaining to the nation (*terra devoluta*) were, of course, further reinforced by the publicity surrounding the federal government's claims to 100 kilometers of land on either side of new federal roads in Amazonia, and the subsequent distributions of land in official colonizations along the Transamazon Highway. Ideologically, the codification of squatters' rights in law signifies, in part, an official acknowledgment of the injustice and waste of the *latifúndio-minifúndio* complex, whereby very few hold title to vast amounts of land and the majority has access to little or no land. Efforts to integrate *posse* into federal land law reflect an ideological commitment, at least, to the notion that the land should belong to those who work it, rather than to those who let it remain idle while waiting for speculative gain. In reality and actual practice, however, the law is very rarely used successfully by squatters.

Until 1977, no one in Santa Terezinha paid much attention to transactions relating to town property. However, in 1977, the municipal government announced that it would begin to regulate town properties. People were informed that from now on all townspeople would be required to pay to have their property surveyed, to "buy" their property from the municipal government, and to undertake expensive trips to the municipal (Luciara) and judicial (Barro do Garça) seats to process papers for definitive title.[6] Needless to say, most townspeople were furious when they heard about the new regulations. Some households complied, but most desisted. In the resulting confusion, a few families lost their town properties. Interestingly enough, those who lost properties tended to be those with prime locations, and these lots somehow ended up being owned next by the municipal councilmen. Public outcry continued, and local government officials let efforts to enforce the policy die. However, newcomers to Santa Terezinha are frequently told they must purchase empty lots from the municipality for between 1,000 to 2,000 cruzeiros (US$50 to $100), which is very often a large part, if not all, of the nest egg with which they arrived in town.

The Rua da Palha side of town, including the *cabaret*, has 147 structures, of which 104 are homes, 19 are businesses, and 24 combined business-and-residential units. In other words, there are 43 commercial establishments in this side of town; 12 of these are in the *cabaret*. Businesses range widely in size, from combination boarding houses and houses of prostitution to tiny little kiosks that sell coffee and *cachaça*. The long main street of Rua da Palha becomes the road to the neighboring *fazenda*, CODEARA, when it leaves town. CODEARA is about 2 kilometers to the northwest of Santa Terezinha. There is also more traffic on this side of town as ranch personnel come in to shop, mainly at the *fazenda* store, and workers are picked up and dropped off here. On weekends and pay days this part of town, especially the *cabaret*, becomes very lively, and it is not unusual to see drunks staggering or sleeping in the streets at any hour. Tales of robberies, stabbings, and shootings filter out from the *cabaret* to the rest of town.

Like Raimundo (described in Chapter 1), many of the residents behind the main street of Rua da Palha are recent arrivals to Santa Terezinha. Dona Raimunda and Antonio are another fairly typical Rua da Palha story. I met them while conducting my survey on that side of town. They had been in Santa Terezinha only two weeks and were rapidly depleting their small savings with rent for the dirt-floored thatch hut and purchased foodstuffs. They were in their late 30s and had several young children. When I arrived near lunch time, they were all eating bowls of rice and sharing a small tin of sardines among five people. They politely offered me food, but I refused. By then I had learned the frontier rules of etiquette, which compel the host to offer food but require the guest to refuse at least three times. If the host continues to repeat the offer, then the guest may assume the host genuinely wants to share food.

Dona Raimunda and Antonio were both from Goiás. Their parents had migrated there from Ceará in the 1930s. Hearing about unclaimed land to the west of the Araguaia River, Raimunda and Antonio decided to try to buy a small farm. In 1972, they arrived in a small settlement some 80 kilometers to the southwest of Santa Terezinha and purchased the squatters' rights to a forest homestead. They used their entire savings from almost a decade of work to buy the land. They settled down there, working hard to improve it, planting fruit trees, making a well and fences, and so forth. But then one day after they had been there six years, they were visited by representatives of a nearby cattle *fazenda* who informed them that they were living on company land and must leave. They resisted for a while, but finally, thoroughly intimidated, they accepted a modest payment for the farm and left the area. They decided to come to Santa Terezinha, hoping to get work as tenants on someone else's *roça*. But as they knew no one in Santa Terezinha, all they had accomplished since arriving was to find shelter in their rented thatch hut. With their resources rapidly disappearing and no tenant farming opportunities to be found, Antonio had begun considering joining a work gang leaving Friday for a month's work at a distant cattle *fazenda*. However, he was worried about leaving Raimunda and the children without support for a month in a strange town. When I returned a week later to visit this family, the shabby hut was empty. No one seemed to know where they had gone.

For a town of only 1,930 inhabitants, Santa Terezinha has a rather extraordinary number of stores, bars, pool rooms, and boarding houses. Clearly, it is not the predominantly small farmer, local population that supports this commerce. Rather, the proliferation of businesses is linked to the presence of the *fazendas* in the region. Bryan Roberts (1976) correctly identifies the evolving roles of provincial urban places like Santa Terezinha, which have been marginalized by the rapid penetration of industrial capitalist firms into the countryside. These urban places thus come to serve as distribution centers for imported goods and as way stations for a transient population of uprooted landless farmers and workers. An examination of the types of commerce found in Santa Terezinha confirms this pattern. For example, the majority of Santa Terezinha businesses either retail imported goods (from southern Brazil) or shelter or entertain the increasing numbers of transients—such as Raimundo, and Dona Raimunda and Antonio. Many other kinds of businesses normally found in provincial towns or even villages, such as bakeries, beauty parlors, garages, restaurants, and even a farmers' market, are *not* found in Santa Terezinha.

A second reason underlying the proliferation of commercial activities is the high cultural value and prestige attached to the occupation of merchant (Harris 1971). Given the relatively limited range of livelihood options available in the frontier town, the aspirations of many of the people I interviewed focused on trying to enter commerce (*tocar comercio*). Not only is it seen as a route for upward mobility, but it is considered a pleasant occupation—white collar, social, and leisurely. This dream of becoming a merchant helps account for the high degree of redundancy in the town businesses and the pride with which the owner of even a broken-down one-room hut stocked with one shelf of tinned goods will state his occupation as "merchant."

Santa Terezinha, like the rest of Brazil, is predominantly Catholic. Many of the small farmers and other regional inhabitants practice a folk Catholicism described in detail in other books (e.g., Forman 1975: Queiroz 1977; Wagley 1968, 1976; Willems 1975). In addition, there were two evangelical Protestant groups present in the town, the Assembly of God (*Assembleia de Deus*) and a small Baptist congregation. The core of the Assembly of God congregation consisted of several families, whereas the Baptist group consisted of ten people, mostly children. The differences I observed about Protestant converts are consistent with Sydney Mintz's (1974) observations in Puerto Rico; converts to Protestantism tend to be somewhat better off than the rest of the population, subscribe more fully to the Protestant work ethic and related values, support the status quo, manifest a higher degree of respect for "the authorities," and, in general, are oriented toward upward social mobility.

The fourth religion represented in the town is called Vovo Rosa (Granny Rosa), a rather unusual evangelical version of Catholicism disseminated by radio from São Paulo. The name comes from a popularly sainted miracle worker in São Paulo who was referred to as "Granny Rosa." The adherents explain Vovo Rosa as a kind of fundamentalist Catholicism that is a reaction against what they see as trends toward a decadent liberalization of the Catholic Church. It appears to be less a reaction against liberation theology than a reaction against changes such as priests wanting to marry or the Protestant-like simplicity of some rural churches. Members adhere to strict behavioral and dress codes and forswear drinking, dancing, smoking, gambling, and swearing. A very important feature of this religion is the believed curative powers of the blessed water, which adherents can obtain by placing a glass of water on the radio during Vovo Rosa broadcasts. This blessed water is thought to cure a wide variety of ills, although one of my friends in this group who had malaria hedged her bets by using my malaria medication in addition to this water. In 1979, the religion had fifteen members in town, all converted by the radio and by the other adherents. It is interesting to note that thirteen of the fifteen were women, all of whom had similar small farm (*roça*) backgrounds and most of whom worked as the town's laundresses.

No one writing today about the Brazilian Amazon should ignore the truly pivotal role played there by the liberation theology branch of the Catholic Church. As Shelton Davis (1977) so eloquently illustrated in his study of the impact of development policies on Amazonian Indians

and peasants, it is primarily the members of Catholic organizations—
priests, nuns, and lay workers—who have acted as advocates for Indians
and the rural poor.

The Catholic mission in Santa Terezinha was forever changed by a
French "worker priest" whose dedication and advocacy for the Indians
and small farmers led to his deportation from Brazil in the early 1970s
(Davis 1977; Wagley 1977). It was this mission that helped organize the
agricultural cooperative in the mid-1960s as part of its efforts to aid
local farmers and help provide them with an organizational basis to
their land claims against the demands of the *fazenda* CODEARA (Shapiro
1967). It was the mission that created and staffed the first school in
town. It also established a health clinic, organized some welfare services
for destitute transients, started a regional newsletter, raised protests
when Indian land claims and health needs were neglected, and brought
(and continues to bring) news of regional events in Amazonia to the
attention of the national and international news media.

Although the activities of this and other Catholic activist groups are
very important in numerous respects, the role of the Catholic mission
does not receive direct attention in this study. This is not because its
role was unimportant but, rather, because its position was politically
sensitive: The mission appeared to be under continual surveillance and
investigation by the government during the time I lived in Santa Terezinha.
It also seemed reluctant to allow many of its grass-roots activities to
be observed. These factors led to my research decision to minimize
participation in and investigation of the mission's activities. I should
add, however, that I agree with Shelton Davis (1977) and others who
have praised the work of these grass-roots activists and advocates,
because the disinherited of Amazonia have often had no other voice,
no other defenders who confronted the power structure and got the
stories of. what was occurring in Amazonia out to the outside world.

It should not be surprising that the Catholic mission was continually
at loggerheads with the local and regional power structure. It was viewed
with great antipathy by regional *fazenda* managers. When the state
government took over the running of the town school from the mission,
the mission continued to run the adult literacy program (Movimento
Brasileiro de Alfabetizacào, or MOBRAL) and to provide some of the
best trained teachers to the school. School administrators, however, were
political appointees of the military government's party (Aliança Reno-
vadora Nacional; ARENA) and repeatedly tried to fire the mission teachers
who outspokenly supported the opposition party (Partido do Movimento
Democratico Brasileiro, or PMDB) and used Paulo Freyer's educational
methods to raise consciousness and politicize students. The mission also
provided leadership during the protests against the registration of town

properties and helped found two new organizations in 1978–1979—namely, the "Committee for the Emancipation of Santa Terezinha," which sought to make Santa Terezinha the seat of its own municipality, and the Rural Workers Union.

The political orientation of the mission and its very active advocacy and grass-roots organizing roles have drawn, like a lightning rod, the wrath of various authorities, officials, and defenders of the status quo. The Santa Terezinha mission is part of the diocese of the outspoken Bishop Pedro Casaldáliga of São Felix do Araguaia, whose writings and speeches on the oppression and exploitation of Indians and the rural poor in Amazonia have become internationally known (e.g., Casaldáliga 1971, 1978). The bishop, a Spaniard, is frequently threatened with deportation from Brazil. Both the diocese and the Santa Terezinha mission are viewed by many government officials as "subversive" and "communist."

The formal political structure of Santa Terezinha in 1979 was relatively new. In 1976, the governor of the state of Mato Grosso designated Santa Terezinha as a district (*distrito*) within the county-like municipality of Luciara. The town of Luciara, 90 kilometers to the south, is the municipal seat. It runs the municipal government and controls the revenues, activities that are deeply resented by many who are quick to point out that Santa Terezinha is larger than Luciara and also contributes more in state taxes. Accordingly, Santa Terezinha has been trying to become a separate municipality.

Meanwhile, the mayor of Luciara, five out of the seven elected municipal councilmen, and the *camara* (legislative body) are in Luciara. Two councilmen live in Santa Terezinha, and the mayor assigns a vice-mayor (*subprefeito*) to the town. These officials, however, are viewed by Santa Terezinha residents as largely powerless. The vice-mayor sells the town controlled properties but spends most of his time leasing his truck and services to cattle *fazendas* to transport work crews. The *delagado* (sheriff), a local man, is appointed by state authorities and has a somewhat uneasy relationship with state soldiers (who are not locals) posted to the town. The tax collector, whose job it is to issue permits to commercial establishments and to extract the state's share of the profits, is not overly popular. Many small businesses, especially those operated out of homes, have no permit. Santa Terezinha has no lawyers or judges of any kind; nor does it have registries for obtaining documentation, such as birth and marriage certificates or deeds to property. Since most residents cannot afford the costly trips to offices in Luciara and Barro do Garça (the judicial seat), they lack most of the legal documents required by Brazilian law. This is a disadvantage, to say the least

Finally, the urban area of Santa Terezinha is 517 hectares (roughly 1,292.5 acres). The nearby *fazenda*, CODEARA, ceded this land to the town in 1976. A significant portion of the land, obstensibly intended for "urban expansion," was rapidly sold by municipal officials as *chacaras*, prime garden lots ranging from 5 to 10 hectares on the perimeters of town. Some fifteen *chacaras* were purchased by the more well-to-do residents. This transfer of the land around the town from the public to the private domain meant that the nearest "common lands" for gardening or grazing animals became unavailable to the poorer residents and new arrivals. It also left the town with minimal land for future growth.

The Middle Araguaia Region

Santa Terezinha is like a tiny boat in a large ocean of surrounding *fazendas* (see Fig. 2.2). Starting in the mid-1960s, vast areas of the state of Mato Grosso were sold to national and multinational companies. According to government sources, there were 192 *fazendas* in Mato Grosso by 1978. Seventeen of these were said to be located in Santa Terezinha's municipality of Luciara (SUDAM 1978). However, an environmental group, checking official figures by actually counting *fazendas* on satellite maps and by making on-site inspections, documented seventy-five to eighty-five large fazendas in the two municipalities of Luciara and Barro do Garça (CNDDA 1978).

The small farmers of the region, claiming land by *posse*, were unaware of the land transfers until representatives of the neighboring *fazenda*, CODEARA, arrived in the mid-1960s and told them to clear out. Between 1966 and 1972, CODEARA tried with threats, intimidation, and harassment to convince regional inhabitants to leave. Fields were burned. Animals were found castrated. Father Jentel, the French "worker priest," tried to negotiate with the *fazenda*, asking if it would perhaps be willing to "sell" the local farmers their homesteads and the town its land. However, the ranch refused to consider such options. Sporadic violence occurred and continued to escalate until, in 1972, there was a gun battle between the farmers trying to build a health clinic in town and the company men sent to bulldoze it down. Only then did the government intervene. Subsequent publicity and pressure forced the *fazenda*, at this point, to return some of the land to the local people.

CODEARA, the *fazenda* that tried to eliminate Santa Terezinha, is owned by a corporation whose major stockholder is the Banco Credito Nacional de São Paulo. This corporation holds title to 320,000 hectares— some 9.5 million acres—with a riverfront width on the Araguaia River of 17 kilometers and a length of 100 kilometers. Between 1967 and

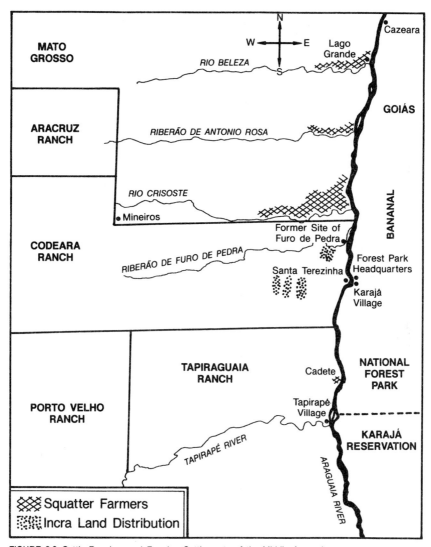

FIGURE 2.2 Cattle Ranches and Farming Settlements of the Middle Araguaia

1978, the *fazenda* deforested more than a half-million acres to make "improved pastures" for cattle raising.

The CODEARA headquarters, about 2 kilometers from Santa Terezinha, constitutes a small town in itself, with central offices, machine, and carpentry shops, housing for upper-echelon personnel, a boarding house for unmarried workers, a luxury cottage for visiting corporate officials, a zoo (containing regional animals that are becoming increasingly rare), electrical generators, corrals and an insemination station, radio towers, and its own airstrip. The ranch also has nine *retiros*, or range areas, each with an outpost station for cowboys and workers. In addition, it operates a sawmill and a small company village about 25 kilometers from the headquarters. In 1978, the CODEARA herd numbered 30,000 head, with 8,000 calves born that year. Employees of the *fazenda*, who actually appear on its payrolls, number about 160 persons, but this figure does not include the so-called indirect labor made up of work crews (peons) hired by labor contractors.

Under pressure in 1972, CODEARA agreed to distribute land to local residents and to cede land to the town. The land transfer was organized and directed by the Brazilian Agrarian Reform Institute (Instituto Nacional de Colonização e Reforma Agrária, or INCRA), which claimed to have distributed 110 rural modules (100 hectares) to long-time residents.[7] The land distribution, which was not completed until 1976, created three "islands" of homesteads ("rural modules") located in forested areas within the *fazenda* itself.[8] After a great deal of work, I was able to verify the existence of only 76 of the supposed 110 lots given out to local farmers.

The land distribution resulted in a complete reshuffling of homesteads such that the families who had already built up farms, cleared land, constructed buildings, planted fruit trees and pasture, and generally improved their places lost them and were given virgin forest lots at considerable distances from town. Lot distances vary from one to six hours walk (4 to 35 kilometers). The closest ones are considered the most desirable because farmers prefer to have relatively easy access to town. Access to the school and health clinic is also highly valued, as is the shorter distance to haul produce and carry supplies back to the *roça*, generally done without the aid of vehicles of any kind. While the closest *roças* were all being used by owners, their relatives, or tenants, almost a third of the more distant lots remained unworked. Considering the lack of roads, vehicles, and services, it is not difficult to understand the farmers' reluctance to reside 20 to 35 kilometers away in the wilderness. Many of the more distant *roças* were worked by men alone while their families lived in town and were visited by their menfolk on weekends.

Both the farmers on INCRA lots and others scattered in the countryside think of Santa Terezinha as their central place, their city. Conversely, Santa Terezinha, in its bid to become a municipality, started to define the rural areas that constitute "her interior." Settlements that look to Santa Terezinha as their "urban center" include Cadete, Crisoste, Antonio Rosa, and Lago Grande. The Cadete, a scattered settlement of about twelve squatter farm families 20 kilometers to the south of town, was in land disputes with both the neighboring *fazenda* (TAPIRAGUAIA) and the Tapirapé Indians, whose village is 10 kilometers farther south. The Crisoste, sometimes referred to as João Goulart for the former president of Brazil whose family is said to legally own the land, is an area of about 40,000 hectares located 25 kilometers to the north of Santa Terezinha. It is settled by approximately seventy to eighty squatter families. Land is bought and sold by *posse*. Antonio Rosa, about 50 kilometers to the north of town, contains another twenty-five to thirty-five families who were beginning to dispute land rights with a *fazenda* starting operations there. Lago Grande, 80 kilometers downriver (north) is a village ringed with farms. It has a population of approximately 1,500 persons and is also in dispute over land with a neighboring *fazenda*. In addition, Indians, more isolated *roça* dwellers, and illegal squatters from across river frequent Santa Terezinha.

Three Indian villages (one Tapirapé and two Karajá villages) and thousands of squatter farmers located across river in the national forest preserve or inside the Karajá reservation are within 5 to 50 kilometers of Santa Terezinha. The situation across river on the interfluvial island of Bananal in the state of Goiás is particularly difficult to ascertain with precision. The southern two-thirds of the island was declared an Indian reservation, although the Karajá Indians do not inhabit the interior of the island. The northern third of Bananal was declared a national forest preserve and squatter farmers were subsequently prohibited from using it.

Nonetheless, the Brazilian population of Bananal is estimated at 15,000 persons, most of whom practice slash-and-burn agriculture in gallery forests and graze cattle on the natural savannas.[9] The National Indian Service (Fundação Nacional do Indio, or FUNAI) tries to discourage Brazilian settlers by charging cash rentals to nonindigenous land users.[10] The approach of the Park Service (Instituto Brasileira de DeSenvolvimento Florestal, or IBDF) is more straightforward. It simply prohibits agriculture, livestock raising, hunting, and fishing (except to Indians) and brings in agents to enforce the regulations. Many farmers, who had been buying and selling *posse* rights for generations, have been forced out of the park. The Park Service told these families that it would pay them compensation, but, as of 1979, no payment had ever been made to any of them. Most of the families forced to leave Bananal moved west across the river and settled nearby or in Santa Terezinha.

Since the 1960s, however, the potential areas for squatter settlements around Santa Terezinha have shrunk. Aside from the neighboring *fazenda* CODEARA, with its 9.5 million acres, there are numerous other, mostly corporate, cattle projects. To the south of CODEARA and roughly of equivalent size are *fazendas* called TAPIRAGUAIA, PORTO VELHO, TAPIRAPÉ (no relation to the Indian tribe), BRASIL CENTRAL, FREY NOVA, and PIRACUAÇU. To the north of CODEARA are ARACRUZ, SERVAP, and PORTO AMAZÔNIA. Directly to the west is *fazenda* BCN, another enormous tract owned by the same bank that is the major shareholder in CODEARA. Almost all of these ranches are sufficiently well established to have herds of between 20,000 and 40,000 head.

It is important to realize that, apart from airplanes, the main connections of this region to the outside continue to be the Araguaia River. For a time it seemed as though road building was surging ahead, and many riverboat operators sold their boats and bought trucks. But progress on regional roads has gone extremely slowly and is continually set back by annual floods and downpours that wash away large sections of road and many bridges. In 1978, people were again busy building and buying boats.

Almost all goods from cloth to sugar to beer, sold in the many stores of Santa Terezinha, are imported from southern Brazil. Many goods are purchased by merchants in Goiania and brought north by trucks on the Belém-Brasília Highway, which is paved. At Paraiso do Norte, the goods are transferred to smaller trucks for the trip west on a dirt road to Cazeara, a small town along the Araguaia River. In Cazeara, the goods are loaded onto boats or barges for the trip upriver (south) to Santa Terezinha. The largest barge operating on the river, and the only one capable of transporting trucks and large machinery, belongs to CODEARA.

The first road into the area, a dirt one not even reaching Santa Terezinha, was officially opened in 1975. This road runs from Goiania northwest to Barro do Garça, where the road becomes BR 158. It then goes north, to the west of the Araguaia River. In the vicinity of São Felix do Araguaia, the road is some 50 kilometers inland from the river. Farther north and parallel to Santa Terezinha, the road is approximately 100 kilometers inland. Santa Terezinha remained unconnected to the BR 158 until 1976, when *fazenda* CODEARA finished a dirt connecting road to this dirt federal highway. Unfortunately, these roads are extremely rudimentary and often impassable. Each rainy reason, portions of the road and many bridges wash away. The Araguaia River, then, remained the most reliable link. Future plans for the BR 158 are that it is to eventually serve as a main road linking northern Mato Grosso and southern Pará.

Meanwhile, the majority of people and goods traveling in the region use the river, with Cazeara serving as the funnel point out to the paved Belém-Brasília Highway. Airplanes are also extremely important in the region; private pilots with small planes for hire charge about 2,000 cruzeiros (US$100) an hour. Many *fazendas* have their own planes and airstrips. In 1978–1979, a small private airline company made almost daily flights between Belém and Brasília, with myriad stops at almost every major frontier outpost along the way, including Santa Terezinha. In addition, the Brazilian Air Force makes a weekly run through the region with a two-hour layover in Santa Terezinha. This visit is important to inhabitants because the Air Force doctors not only treat the sick but frequently also arrange to transport dangerously ill people free of charge.

In summary, such infrastructural considerations are crucial to understanding both the region's links to the rest of Brazil and Santa Terezinha's central role in the transportation system. Little leaves the region except for people and cattle. Almost all goods and many foodstuffs sold are imported with Santa Terezinha as the distribution point. As the river provides the town with its *raison d'être*, the town's future does not look promising. It is likely that the road system will eventually become more functional. Indeed, even in 1979, some of Santa Terezinha's most successful merchants were already considering trying to obtain property along the BR 158, some 100 kilometers to the west farther inland from the river.

Notes

1. Most maps of Brazil made prior to the mid-1980s do not show Santa Terezinha. The way to locate this spot on a map is to find the Araguaia River; look for Bananal Island, formed by the two branches of the river; locate the Tapirapé River, which flows into the Araguaia from the west; and mark a spot 30 kilometers to the north of the Tapirapé River on the west bank of the Araguaia River. This is where Santa Terezinha is located.

2. *Mission clinic* is a somewhat misleading translation. The mission runs a pharmacy and usually has one or two practical nurses who provided medical care to the population. It is called "*A Unica*," meaning "the only one," because it is the only medical service available to most people. The state government has a health post in Santa Terezinha as well, but during the year I spent there I remember it being opened only twice. In punishment for the municipality voting for the opposition party, the government party–controlled state government cut off state medical services provided previously by a visiting medical team. This state outpost was empty and always locked. The Brazilian Air Force medical team also visited the town for approximately two hours almost every week, providing some medical services and medicines, and flying out critical emergencies.

Because the medical services in Santa Terezinha are so rudimentary, most families with a seriously ill member try desperately to raise the large sums of money necessary to hire a private plane to fly the sick person to a hospital, if they cannot wait for the sporadic visits of the Brazilian Air Force. Sometimes families sell everything they own to pay for rapid transportation of a sick member to a hospital.

3. *Vergonha* means a shame or disgrace.

4. The word *roça* refers broadly to the country, rural regions, or backwoods farms. It is also used more narrowly to mean swidden fields.

5. The Brazilian term *posse* is usually used to refer to possession of the land as opposed to legal ownership by definitive title. Brazilian land law does recognize certain rights of owners by means of *posse*, although these are rarely implemented. The best English translation appears to be "squatting." People who possess land by *posse* are referred to as *posseiros*.

6. Exchanges of land held by *posse* may be formalized by a *declaração*, a homemade document "declaring" the transaction. Any literate person can make a *declaração*. A paper of this type is not really a legal document, although in certain cases it might help establish a party's claim to land. Part of the complication and confusion of land conflicts in Amazonia derives from the bewildering variety of homemade, fraudulent, semilegal, and legal documents with which parties claim various rights to land ownership. Peasants, who rarely have sufficiently convincing kinds of documentation, are usually the losers in cases of conflicts over land. See Octavio Ianni (1978), Joseph Foweraker (1981), and Marianne Schmink (1982) for more extensive discussions of the dynamics of Amazonia land conflicts.

7. INCRA sent personnel to Santa Terezinha to conduct surveys and evaluations determining who was to receive land in the distribution. Later, they also assisted in processing the titles to the land. The criteria used by INCRA to evaluate farmers' claims to land included an evaluation of the length of residency at a particular location (minimum time to qualify was one year and one day) and the number of improvements and fields the farmer had made. The process of evaluation looks reasonable and fair on paper, but inequities always enter into the actual distribution of free land. Some small farmers interviewed felt they had received a raw deal. A number of farmers who had *roças* close to town lost them in the distribution to more powerful residents. Other families who had left during the years of violence returned but received no land because they could not prove their prior residence. Bananal residents, for example, and farmers who had fled down river because of CODEARA's pressure, were not considered for the lots. However, despite some influence-peddling and other inequities, most of the recipients were local squatter farmers.

8. Each state in Brazil determines what constitutes a "rural module" in that state. In Mato Grosso a rural module is 100 hectares (about 250 acres) in size. The exact locations of the distributed lots were difficult to determine with precision because both INCRA and CODEARA, when contacted, were unable to provide me with maps showing the distribution. No maps were available in Santa Terezinha either. The seventy-six INCRA lot owners identified during the

research interviews provide the basis for generalizations regarding locations, land-use patterns, and ownership.

9. This population estimate is based on a report prepared by a Catholic mission team that spent three months in 1977 conducting a survey of Bananal by horseback, and on data provided by Superintêndencia do Contrôle da Malária (SUCAM), the government health teams that travel throughout the countryside spraying houses with antimalarial chemicals. SUCAM records are very useful for estimating the size of the population in areas of Amazonia for which no census data is available. The spraying teams travel to quite remote places and carefully record the number of structures they spray. The only caution, however, is that SUCAM's records do not distinguish between homes and other types of buildings. Therefore, the estimate of 15,000 persons on Banal may be somewhat inflated; 10,000 might be a more realistic guess.

10. FUNAI divides cattle raisers into two categories: (a) temporary residents who use the savanna for grazing three to five months a year, and (b) permanent residents who exploit and live on the island of Bananal full-time. Taxes are supposedly much higher for permanent residents, to discourage them from remaining on the island. Confusion about taxes is widespread, however—both in the countryside and at FUNAI headquarters, where the structure of tax collection and income generated were described as "unknown" by the department in charge (FUNAI 1978).

3

Frontier Expansion

Stage One—Common Lands

"I am going to tell you how it was that I came to be here," my neighbor Pedro said to me one rainy afternoon. "The people always used to go to Joazeiro. They used to call it Romeiros. They used to go see Padre Cicero, who was a very famous padre. Everyone believed in him a lot. Everything he said, everyone believed it. He had a mysteriousness about him like God. Everything he spoke came to pass."

"He always used to say to the people that there would come a time when we would all be in a tight spot. There would be war. So he told the people to buy pots and salt and hide them away deep in the forests. Because later the people would not be able to go to the city to buy things. He told them to put foodstuffs in these pots in the forest. There would come a time when people would eat only by stealing, and those who wanted to escape should follow these instructions."

"This was in Ceará," Pedro explained. Pedro, now in his 40s, had grown up in Ceará, moved to Goiás with his parents, and then lived almost two decades on a *roça* near Santa Terezinha. He had left his *roça* in 1969 because of *fazenda* harassment, stolen animals, and mysterious fires in the fields. "Padre Cicero said a war would come and so the goods should be hidden away because later on we wouldn't be able to go out into the streets."

"The *bandeira verde* the padre used to speak about, it's an isolated place where there aren't any people. A place that has only forests. That was where the people could hide themselves, right? Which is to say the *bandeira verde* doesn't exist anymore. There are still a lot of forests left, but there are so many airplanes above them. Those binoculars don't allow anything to escape! Today, there is just no way, no way at all for things to work out. . . . The people used to hide themselves in the forests, but today it doesn't work because they have this apparatus, you know, for finding everything. Right? There just isn't any more *bandeira verde*. It's over and done with," Pedro said. And the other people in the room nodded in agreement. I asked some questions about the old days when people were just beginning to arrive in the region, near Santa Terezinha.

"The land was common," Pedro explained.[1] "That is to say, it was the government's. One could make *roças* wherever one wanted to. There weren't any companies then, no *fazendas*, no cattle of the *tubarões*."[2]

"If you found a place pleasing to you, well, you made a house and a *roça*," he said. I asked if it thus became your own place.

"Some remained on their places," he answered, "and others, like me, the *fazenda* threw out. They dragged us out. They bought it! They bought the land of our nation! It must have been God who let them. The land was ours! It was ours!" Pedro had left his *roça* near Santa Terezinha because he was afraid of the conflict with the *fazenda*. He had moved temporarily to Lago Grande downriver and returned in the year of the land distribution. But officials had decided that he had no proper and legitimate claims to land, even though he had lived there almost twenty years. He currently made his living doing odd jobs.

"The land that didn't have owners by deeds, before," he continued, "that land was excess. That land was the government's, right? This land all around us here in these parts where everyone was arriving. People came to live and work. We didn't used to pay anything and we were also the owners, because we didn't used to have this business of deeds. Afterwards," he added sadly, "from Goiás all the way over here, everything was changed and we were called *posseiros*."[3]

Another neighbor, Zeze, a tenant farmer in town that day to sell a sack of manioc flour, added his opinion. "That land," he said vehemently," was the government's. No one paid it any attention back then. One could say thus: This land is mine. Whoever wanted to could put in a *roça* of two hectares. If you wanted to put in one or three, four, or even five hectares, however much you wanted, that's what you did. Whatever place seemed promising to you, that's where you put your *roça*. One simply put it there. Now, after they've twisted the screw, now all the land has owners. The land is owned by deeds."

"The government," Pedro said bitterly, "they sold it to the *tubarões*, and then left. Everything became impossible for us. There was no way out of the dilemma. Now everything has an owner."

"At first," Zeze explained, "there were only the distant uninhabited forests. There was only wild game. One person lived over here and another maybe way over there. There were few people in these parts in those times."

"They never fought over the land," Pedro said in response to my question about land disputes. "In that time they never used to fight. Old Alderão, for example, used to live here," he said waving his arm, "and I lived a league from him. I'd call him to come live closer by and he would say, 'No, no, I won't abandon my place. No, young man, I would rather stay on my place alone.' Nowadays people say, 'Don't come anywhere near my place,' and soon a fellow is assaulting you . . . ah, ya . . . that's the way it is now."

We talked for several hours that wet afternoon, sitting on hide stools in Pedro's dirt-floored front room. We talked about the details of inheritance, landownership, and how sharecropping used to be done in northeastern Brazil. Both men made the point that tenants in the northeast were sick of giving half of the harvest to the landlord and that's why they came west, seeking a way to be their own boss.

"Ah, yes," Pedro said in summary of our discussion. "The people were hunting a way to become proprietors. But we found out that it is us that is in excess. We're the overflow. We ended up without anything. And now, now it's finished, over and done with. It's finished! Because the government sold the land to the *fazendas*. Now everything in Brazil is used up. Everything has owners now."

One cannot say with certainty, but it is very likely that the first Brazilian settlers to the Santa Terezinha area were northeasterners drawn to the Amazon during the rubber boom in the mid-nineteenth century. Once the process of vulcanization was discovered, there was a rush to exploit the Amazon's rubber trees, then the only known source of rubber in the world. The population of the Amazon, which, in 1800, had been around 100,000 persons, grew to 340,000 by 1872 and to 700,000 by 1900; it reached 1.4 million by 1920 just before the boom collapsed. It is estimated that a half-million people immigrated to Amazonia during the boom years (Cardoso and Muller 1978).

The rubber boom, which made great fortunes for a few, brought to the Amazon a cruel system of servile labor generally referred to as *aviamento*.[4] Rubber trees naturally grow at some distance from each other throughout the forests. Tappers were needed to walk miles through the forests every day, first making cuts in the trees and affixing a small bucket to catch the dripping latex, and then, on the same trail, collecting the latex which they then coagulated in smoke over fires. Although slavery was not abolished in Brazil until 1888, slaves were not used for rubber collecting. Rather, large numbers of desperately poor peasants from the backlands of northeastern Brazilian were encouraged, and often tricked and conned, into coming to the Amazon to work in rubber. Once in Amazonia, most workers were trapped by the debt-peonage system. Powerful individuals who, by force of arms, controlled rubber trails and the trading posts, informed the workers that they were in debt for their transportation to the region, their tools, and their medicine and food. Frequently forbidden to plant a garden to grow some of their own foodstuffs, workers had little choice but to buy supplies at the trading post at highly inflated prices. Thus, they entered a never-ending cycle of debts to traders who controlled the prices tappers received for delivered latex. Tacit agreements between traders helped discourage workers who thought of fleeing to try their luck somewhere else. The traders, in turn, were frequently in debt to rubber dealers in Manaus and Belém, and the dealers were indebted to the foreign companies purchasing rubber (Ianni 1978; Wagley 1976).

Rubber trees, however, are not evenly distributed throughout the Amazon. Some places—for example, Conceição do Araguaia, which is situated some 300 kilometers north of Santa Terezinha, became practically boom towns overnight when rubber trees were discovered nearby (Ianni 1978). The tiny settlements near Santa Terezinha did not experience a boom because rubber trees were not found there. It is very likely, as supported by informants' accounts, that the earliest settlers to Santa Terezinha were either former rubber collectors (i.e., primarily northeastern migrants) or displaced small farmers from the rubber areas.

The first inhabitants of the region were, of course, the Indians. The two tribes who lived there, the riverine Karajá and the interfluvial Tapirapé, had very different contact experiences. The Karajá, a fishing people who lived along the Araguaia River, were first contacted by eighteenth- and nineteenth-century expeditions and missionaries (Baldus 1944/1960a, 1948/1960b; Ehrenreich 1891/1965; Lipkind 1963).

Early population figures are unclear, but Krause (1911/1966) estimated the 1908 Karajá population at 10,000. In 1939, the anthropologist William Lipkind (1963) counted 1,510 Karajá; and in 1976, FUNAI (1976), the Indian Service, calculated that there were only 1,200. The Tapirapé Indians, living farther back from the river, deep in the forests, remained uncontacted until shortly after the beginning of the twentieth century. But new diseases, carried by other Indians and travelers, took a heavy toll even before sustained contact was made with outsiders. Charles Wagley, an anthropologist who has studied the tribe since the 1930s, estimated that the Tapirapé population at the turn of the century numbered between 1,000 and 1,500 persons. When Wagley first encountered the tribe in 1939, there were only 187 Indians left. By 1947, there were 100, and by 1957, there were only 55 (Wagley 1977). Extinction looked imminent but was narrowly averted by the combined efforts of a dedicated Indian agent, Padre Jentel, and the Little Sisters of Jesus, an unusual order of French nuns.[5]

Both the Karajá and the Tapirapé were peaceful in their relations with their new Brazilian neighbors, unlike the Kayapó to the north and the Xavante to the south. Both tribes had dwindling populations, and neither competed directly with Brazilian settlers for resources, particularly land.

Jumping ahead in the story for a moment, I should note that the Tapirapé were not concerned about tribal lands until the 1960s, when a neighboring *fazenda* claimed traditional Tapirapé lands and put up no trespassing signs to keep the Indians out. After intense lobbying in Brasília by the tribe and their advocates, the *fazenda*, under pressure, "donated" 9,000 hectares to the Tapirapé. This land, located 30 kilometers to the south of Santa Terezinha, is largely of inferior quality, unsuitable for gardens. Somewhat ironically, the Karajá, primarily fishermen relatively uninterested in agriculture, were given the southern two-thirds of the interfluvial island of Bananal as a reservation. However, even this much larger area on Bananal is mostly savanna and best suited to livestock raising. The Karajá, despite the educational efforts of FUNAI, have resisted becoming cattle raisers. Also present in the reservation are large numbers of Brazilian settlers who are ostensibly paying "rent" to the Indians through FUNAI.

During the first three decades of the twentieth century, a number of Brazilian settlements were established in the middle Araguaia region. Five settlements are described in early documents. Macauba, located directly across river from Santa Terezinha, was originally a leper colony run by Scottish missionaries. About 90 kilometers to the south of Santa Terezinha was a small settlement called Mato Verde, which later became Luciara, the municipal seat. Mato Verde was founded in the early 1930s by an outlaw named Lucio da Luz, who had fled to the remote Araguaia region to avoid arrest. Anthropologist Herbert Baldus (1948/1960b) described Mato Verde in the 1940s:

> When, a few years ago, all regular boat transportation on the middle Araguaia came to a stop after the dissolution of the enterprise that handled the service with motor launches, life in those . . . locations deteriorated to the point of despair, for there was no longer any outlet for local products. In the entire region, there remained but one man who bought them: Mr. Lucio. He was and remains the chief supplier of the principal goods needed by the frontiersmen: salt, and some fabric for clothing. Furthermore, he gives them credit. They sell to this man, who owns an outboard motor, a house covered with tiles, and thousands of head of cattle, what little rice and manioc flour they have left over and an occasional cow out of the half-dozen that constitute their wealth. They speak well of the man and regard him as their greatest benefactor. (pp. 3–4)

The third settlement, located about 100 kilometers to the southwest of Santa Terezinha along the Tapirapé River, was a hamlet of eight families called Porto Velho. Baldus (1944/1960a) notes that the residents of Porto Velho "came from the state of Pará and had lived previously at various spots along the Araguaia."

Twenty kilometers to the north of Santa Terezinha was the village of Furo de Pedra, described by Charles Wagley (1977) as the largest non-Indian settlement along the middle Araguaia in the 1930s. Furo de Pedra was really the forerunner of Santa Terezinha. In the 1930s and early 1940s, the Furo de Pedra families began moving to the settlement at Santa Terezinha because of the church on the hill, the school, and the medical services provided by missionaries. Santa Terezinha was also on somewhat higher ground and was less threatened by flooding than Furo de Pedra. Charles Wagley (1977) described Furo de Pedra in 1939 as follows:

> It contained about 35–40 illiterate frontier families who made a living from grazing a few cattle on the semi-flooded grasslands back from the river and from subsistence gardens. There were two miserably stocked stores which served more as trading posts, receiving hides and skins . . . as well as salted pirarucu (large fresh water fish) in exchange for manufactured goods and tinned food. . . . There was a perennial shortage of cloth, agricultural implements, and other more basic items. . . . [The people] had seen few foreigners except for a Dominican priest who lived over 200 miles downriver at Conceição do Araguaia, and the Scottish missionaries, who maintained a ranch at Macauba, not many miles away, as a refuge for lepers. (pp. 11–12)

Finally, there was Santa Terezinha itself. Different sources provide different dates for the founding of the settlement, but the Dominicans were apparently present there between 1910 and the 1930s. The church on the sand hill was built by priests from Conceição do Araguaia in 1931. During the following decade, the settlement seems to have remained small, just the church and a handful of houses behind the hill. At the same time, however, other settlers, estimated by Wagley at 50 to 120 families, lived on *roças* scattered throughout the forests surrounding the two settlements of Santa Terezinha and Furo de Pedra.

Brazilian settlers who arrived in the area during the 1920s and 1930s were predominantly northeasterners or children of northeasterners who had moved westward to the neighboring states of Goiás and Maranhão. To understand why the northeasterns left their region of origin, it is necessary to understand the conditions of chronic poverty, skewed land tenure, and periodic droughts of northeastern Brazil. Charismatic leaders, such as the prophetic and beloved Padre Cicero mentioned by Raimundo and Pedro in previous passages, addressed themselves to the problems that concerned the rural poor (Queiroz 1977). Padre Cicero's message, in its most basic form, was that in order to save themselves, the rural poor of the northeast should go west to find unclaimed land in places of more reliable rainfall. It is no coincidence that almost every person in Santa Terezinha over 45–50 years old remembered this message of Padre Cicero from the 1930s.

The land tenure system of northeastern Brazil has been characterized since colonial times in terms of the *latifúndio-minifúndio* complex (Feder 1971), consisting of few very large and many tiny landholdings. Large holdings were worked by slaves until abolition in 1888. Later, peasant families with small farms worked at plantations and ranches to augment their incomes, and landless people became *agregado*, or tenants, for larger owners. Arrangements varied from sharecropping to the *sorte* system (whereby each cowboy received every fourth calf born to the herd) to allowing peasants to farm on estate lands in return for certain services. Small farm owners were often hard-pressed to sustain themselves on tiny plots with inferior soils. In addition, major droughts, which occurred every ten years on the average, drove people out of the northeast.[6]

Since the 1930s, the situation of small farmers, tenants, and landless peasants in rural areas of the northeast became worse. The factors that contributed to this intensification of rural poverty include (1) a growing population and increasing fragmentation of already small plots because of inheritance patterns; (2) increasing commercialization in marketing to supply growing urban centers, leading, in turn, to increases in size and mechanization of food production—hence, to larger farms; (3) continued agricultural production for export; and (4) the changeover from family-owned and -managed plantations to manager-run corporate-type farms (*usinas*), which did not allow payment in kind. Other problems frequently mentioned by informants were land taxes and ruin caused by drought. All of the above contributed to the heavy emigration from northeastern Brazil.[7]

The migration data collected in Santa Terezinha consist of hundreds of intergenerational life stories. The majority follow a similar pattern of step migration over three generations. As noted, many families left the northeast in the 1930s. Most of these people then moved as far west as western Maranhão or northern Goiás (to the east of Santa Terezinha, Mato Grosso), which in the 1930s and 1940s were still quite remote areas. The small farmer migrants settled and claimed the land by *posse*. In most locations, deeds and land taxes were unknown. However, during the 1950s and 1960s, these more remote areas of Maranhão and Goiás were "opened" by the construction of the Belém-Brasília Highway, which passed through these two states. Land speculation and the processing of titles to land increased, and many small farmers felt compelled to move farther westward in their search for land without owners. Thus, they arrived in Bananal, northern Mato Grosso, and southern Pará.

TABLE 3.1
Birthplaces by State of Three Generations in Santa Terezinha

State	Percentages		
	Grandparents	Parents	Children
Northeast			
Bahia	6	4	0
Pernambuco	2	1	0
Parnaiba	1	1	0
Ceará	4	2	1
Piauí	10	7	2
Maranhão	31	17	7
Mato Grosso and			
Adjacent States			
Mato Grosso	2	10	43
Goiás	23	43	35
Pará	4	7	9
Rondônia	0	0	1
Center South			
Minas Gerais	2	2	1
Espirito Santo	1	0	0
São Paulo	1	1	1
Paraná	0	1	1
Total Number	396	198	192

The movement westward can be easily seen in Table 3.1, which shows the birthplaces by states for three generations of frontierspeople: (1) Santa Terezinha elementary school children, (2) Santa Terezinha household heads and their spouses, and (3) the parents of Santa Terezinha household heads (grandparents). For the oldest generation, birthplaces are clustered in the northeastern states, including 10 percent in Piauí and 31 percent in Maranhão; 23 percent were born in Goiás, the state just east of Santa Terezinha. The movement westward can be seen in the birthplaces of the next generation of current household heads. Far fewer of these were born in the northeast; many more (43 percent) were born in Goiás, directly across the river from Mato Grosso. The children column again shows the movement westward, with the least born in the northeastern states, 35 percent born in Goiás, and the largest proportion, 43 percent, born in Mato Grosso. In addition, between 3 and 4 percent sampled in any generation came from center southern Brazil; this migration trend, however, is far less common. The predominant pattern, as reconstructed, was movement into Maranhão and Goiás during the 1930s and 1940s, and from there westward into Mato Grosso.

TABLE 3.2
Dates of Migration to Santa Terezinha, by Decade

Decade	Number of Persons	Percent
1920 to 1939	7	4
1940 to 1949	13	7
1950 to 1959	25	13
1960 to 1969	73	37
1970 to 1978	66	34
Totals	196	100

The Santa Terezinha area is defined as the town itself plus the forest and settlements within a radius of approximately 50 kilometers.

Table 3.2 shows the years in which 196 persons arrived in either Santa Terezinha or the forests nearby. Together with the birthplace data, these figures present a more complete picture of intergeneration migration. Only about one-fourth of those sampled had arrived prior to 1959; the majority of these were probably living in Maranhão and Goiás until they moved westward. The largest number entered Santa Terezinha in the 1960s and 1970s. This observation is consistent with the "push" small farmer migrants felt because of development in states to the east and the "pull" toward Santa Terezinha they experienced because of increasing accessibility.

In my effort to get a sense of how life was lived in the early days of frontier settlement, I have based the following account on both written sources and oral histories.[8] During the 1930s and 1940s, the region was populated primarily by small farmers who often raised a few head of cattle on the natural savannas. Some small shopkeepers and traders lived in small villages (such as Furo de Pedra), but most trade was carried out by itinerant river traders utilizing both barter and cash. Lucio da Luz, the outlaw, and the various missionaries were probably the wealthiest inhabitants of the region. Subsistence farmers sold small amounts of surplus, dried fish, and animal pelts to traders who carried them downriver to Conceição do Araguaia and from there to Belém at the mouth of the Amazon. There were no direct conflicts over land between Indians and frontierspeople because there was enough land for everyone. Both Indians and pioneers hunted for wild game in the forests and fished in the rivers. The Indian population continued to decline rapidly from diseases, and in 1947 the one last Tapirapé village was attacked and burned by a war party from the Kayapó (a tribe farther to the north). The surviving Tapirapé moved to nearby Brazilian settlements temporarily (for several years).

Both Indians and Brazilian small farmers used the forests for slash-and-burn agriculture. Nothing was surveyed, and no one had deeds or titles to the land. The land worked by an individual or family was considered theirs by *posse* or squatters' rights. Subsequent owners then based their "claim" on the "rights" of the first homesteader. The pioneers considered the land around Santa Terezinha to be "common lands," or *terra devoluta* (federal land). The small farmers were relatively unaware of the exact provisions for squatters' rights as codified (since the 1950s) in Brazilian land law. As late as 1978, the informants interviewed did not know the legal stipulations for establishing claims by squatters' rights. Deeds, registries, and taxes played no part in the lives of the early pioneers. Most transfers of property were not even written down on paper.

The economy of the region during this early period was one primarily of subsistence agriculture and some extraction of forest and river products. Cattle were (and continue to be) the main form of accumulated savings. The sale of a head or two to a local butcher or a traveling cattle buyer would be used to generate the money needed to buy land rights (*posse*), for use in an emergency, or to finance a move. Items such as dried fish or pelts were bartered or sold for the cash needed to buy manufactured goods. Although there were river traders who bought merchandise on credit from merchants downriver and who may have extended some credit to frontierspeople, the *aviamento* system of debt peonage did not exist in the Santa Terezinha area because there was no boom product (such as rubber) and no need to coerce local labor.

The early pioneers grew manioc, some rice, sweet potatoes, corn, squash, cotton, sugar cane, beans, and various fruits. Brown sugar (*rapadura*) was produced from sugar cane. Cotton was spun and woven into hammocks. Cooking oil was obtained by rendering pig fat or from the nuts of the macauba palm; and when kerosene was hard to get, lights were fueled with castor oil or bees' wax. The early economy had to have been characterized by a rather high degree of self-sufficiency.

The connection to outside markets, via Conceição do Araguaia and Belém, was clearly a sporadic and marginal one. Profits from river trading were not especially lucrative; indeed, one woman interviewed, who had worked for years with her husband as a trader since the mid-1930s, explained that they eventually decided to settle down in Furo de Pedra to farm and raise cattle. Young adults, seeking adventure and improved opportunities, sometimes left for the *garimpo* (mining) in Goiás or southern Mato Grosso; they rarely accumulated any wealth, however, and usually returned home to Furo de Pedra after several years.

Exact population figures for this early period are impossible to obtain, but it appears that the pioneer population was rather sparse and spread out. Furo de Pedra, in 1939, probably contained 300 persons at most, and Wagley (1977) has estimated the forest population nearby at approximately three times that of the village.

In summary, this period of early frontier settlement fits rather well with what Foweraker (1981) has defined as the noncapitalist stage of frontier expansion in Amazonia. The regional economy was relatively isolated and extractive. The linkages to national markets were quite rudimentary. Property was held in terms of usufruct rather than as private property. The major respect in which Santa Terezinha does *not* fit the definition of this stage is that the predicted servile relations of production (such as debt peonage) were absent. The reason is that there was no boom product, such as rubber, during this period. In Santa Terezinha, the servile relations of production appear during the second stage of frontier expansion.

Stage Two—The Cattle *Fazendas*

During the 1950s, the topic of the development and exploitation of Amazonia received renewed attention and emphasis in Brazil. A second minor rubber boom there between 1940 and 1945, coinciding with World War II and the Allies' inability to obtain Southeast Asian rubber, had brought an additional 25,000 northeasterners into the region but had not resulted in any real development or infrastructural change (Cardoso and Muller 1978). A severe drought in the northeast in 1958 again underscored the acute poverty and misery of the peasantry there. Social unrest spurred on the formation of Peasant Leagues for collective action that were viewed with concern by government leaders (Moraẽs 1970).

During the 1950s, the national drive to develop the interior of Brazil and to better integrate the country began to be translated into concrete action. In 1957, construction of the Belém-Brasília Highway was started. This paved road, completed in 1960, provided a critical link between northern and southern Brazil and had many effects on transportation, communication, commercialization and marketing, supply centers, development projects, and migration patterns (Hebette and Acevedo 1979; Velho 1972). The highway, which passed through the middle of the states of Goiás and western Maranhão, also spurred on land speculation and investment in these areas.

The effects of the highway on Santa Terezinha were twofold. First, many small farmers in Goiás and Maranhão felt compelled to move to more remote locations, and, in fact, many moved to northern Mato Grosso. Second, the supply lines and routes to northern Mato Grosso changed radically. No longer were goods brought from Belém to Conceição do Araguaia to Santa Terezinha, as previously described. Now, with the highway, the goods were purchased in Goiania or Anapolis (both in

Goiás) and sent north on the highway by truck to Paraiso do Norte, where they were transported on a dirt road to Cazeara on the Araguaia River and from there upriver to Santa Terezinha by barge or boat. In other words, access to the area had improved.

The new programs and policies of the federal government and regional development agencies spurred on land speculation and investments in Amazonia by national and multinational companies. Unknown to the Indians and farmers of the middle Araguaia, much of the land they considered their own was being sold by the state of Mato Grosso to real-estate companies, which then sold it again to various companies and individuals. In the rush to sell the land, many areas were not surveyed or were improperly registered; some pieces of land were sold several times to several different parties. Companies often had to hire lawyers to help press their claims, sort out confusion, and obtain definitive titles to purchased land. Meanwhile, the people in Santa Terezinha did not become aware of these events until representatives of the corporate owners began arriving in the region in the 1960s.

In 1964, the military took over the government of Brazil. This new government, concerned about economic development, social unrest, and peasant organizing in the northeast, swiftly passed a series of decrees designed to alter and intensify development efforts. For example, federal land law (*Estatuto da Terra*) was revamped in 1964—a move ostensibly designed to help break up the *latifúndio-minifúndio* pattern and to better defend squatters' rights. Regional development agencies were reorganized—Superintêndencia de Desenvolvimento do Nordeste (SUDENE) for northeastern Brazil and Superintêndencia de Desenvolvimento da Amazônia (SUDAM) for Amazonia. Fiscal incentives to encourage corporate investment in Amazonia, introduced in 1963, were continued and expanded.

The changes occurring in Santa Terezinha itself during this time were relatively slow paced until the mid-1960s, when representatives of the large cattle *fazendas* arrived to begin operations. Prior to the arrival of the cattle companies, however, immigration of small farmer migrants into the area increased. The regional dependence on trade with the north was broken. The former village of Mato Verde became the new municipality of Luciara.

Another event of the 1950s that had serious consequences for the small farmers of the region was the arrival of the Forest Park guards who had been sent to protect the environment of the Bananal Forest Preserve. The first park agents arrived in 1958, sent out by the Institute for the Development of Forests (Instituto Brasileiro de Desenvolvimento Florestal, or IDBF) in Brasília. The northern third of Bananal had been declared a national biological preserve several years previously, although no one in Santa Terezinha knew anything about it until the first guards appeared. The southern two-thirds of the island had also been set aside as an Indian reservation for the Karajá. The Forest Park Service, in an effort to stop exploitation of the environment and to encourage Brazilian squatters to leave the park, began to implement a series of regulations regarding the legal use of the natural habitat in the park. They forbade hunting and fishing (except to Indians) and banned agricultural activities, the cutting of trees, and the construction of permanent buildings. Many small farmers with herds on Bananal decided to leave the park at that point. Many of these families, however, had purchased squatters' rights (*posse*) to their homesteads and wanted compensation. There was talk of making payments to evicted farmers, but as of 1979 this money had never materialized. Many of the Bananal families moved across the river to Santa Terezinha, where they again purchased squatters' rights from local owners. Other Bananal residents moved their herds to the southern part of the island, where Indian Service controls on squatters were more loosely enforced.

During the late 1950s and early 1960s, almost all the families living in Furo de Pedra just to the north of Santa Terezinha moved to Santa Terezinha proper. There were three main reasons why Furo de Pedra died and Santa Terezinha grew. First, Furo de Pedra was periodically inundated during the rainy season, whereas Santa Terezinha was located on higher and drier ground. Second, the changes in transportation and supply routes made the deeper docking area available at Santa Terezinha more critical. Santa Terezinha was becoming the main commercial outlet in the region. Third, the Catholic mission had established both an elementary school and a health post in Santa Terezinha and people wanted to be close to them. As the cattle companies began to arrive in the 1960s and Santa Terezinha began to develop as a center for commercial goods and a way station for workers, more jobs became available for local people in the town. The women informants, in particular, often mentioned that they have moved from Furo de Pedra to Santa Terezinha because of the availability of jobs as maids or laundresses.

During this period, the Karajá Indian population decline seems to have leveled off. The Karajá continued to make their gardens in the river bank forests and to fish in the rivers. Because the Forest Park Service did not try to regulate Indian fishing, the Karajá became enmeshed in a system of commercial fishing for Brazilian middlemen (traders) who illegally exported dried fish from the region to Brazilian urban centers. Frequently, the Indians were cheated by these middlemen. There was no regulation or supervision of trading because the trade was illicit. Some documentation of Indian exploitation in fish trading is available in an article by Christopher Tavener (1973). Tavener has also noted that the formerly independent and proud Karajá had begun to settle more permanently around various mission stations and Indian Service posts, attracted by medical and educational services, opportunities to earn money, and availability of manufactured goods.

The Tapirapé village, as mentioned previously, was abandoned in 1947 after a Kayapó attack. In 1950, a dedicated agent of the Indian Service who had also previously worked as an assistant to anthropologist Charles Wagley, helped the remaining Tapirapé to reorganize and begin a new village. He even managed to provide the necessary money and food to tide them over during their first year while they were waiting for their fields to begin producing. The new village, however, was located at the mouth of the Tapirapé River (where it joins the Araguaia River) and far from the forests where the Indians must make their *roças*. In 1952, the first group of Little Sisters of Jesus arrived from France to provide a mission for the Tapirapé. They have remained to the present day, providing medical, educational, and other support services to the tribe.

Shortly after the Little Sisters of Jesus arrived, a French priest named Padre Francisco Jentel also arrived from France to work with both Indians and Brazilian settlers. Jentel arrived in 1954 and for a time maintained a part-time residence in the Tapirapé village. Later he moved to Santa Terezinha. Padre Jentel was a key figure in founding the elementary school, in bringing in a nurse to establish a health post, and, later, in establishing an agricultural cooperative. He traveled a great deal throughout the region, holding services, conducting marriages and baptisms, and providing help and advice to families in even the most remote locations. His energy and dedication were warmly remembered by all who knew him in the region.

In the mid-1960s, the cattle *fazendas* began to make their presence known in the region. In 1965, CODEARA started operations in the vicinity of Santa Terezinha. They claimed to hold title to 9.5 million acres that included the farms of local farmers and the land of Santa Terezinha itself. Another company, TAPIRAGUAIA, at approximately the same time, began installing a ranch to the south of CODEARA. The TAPIRAGUAIA *fazenda* claimed ownership of the Cadete, a small settlement of Brazilian farmers, and the land on which the new Tapirapé village was located. Additional *fazendas* (see Fig. 3.1) began ranching operations in other locations in the region at approximately the same time.

The cattle *fazendas* intended to raise beef cattle on "improved pastures." To make these pastures they began a program of deforestation and subsequent planting with special African pasture grasses. The labor requirements for making pastures of this kind are initially quite high

54

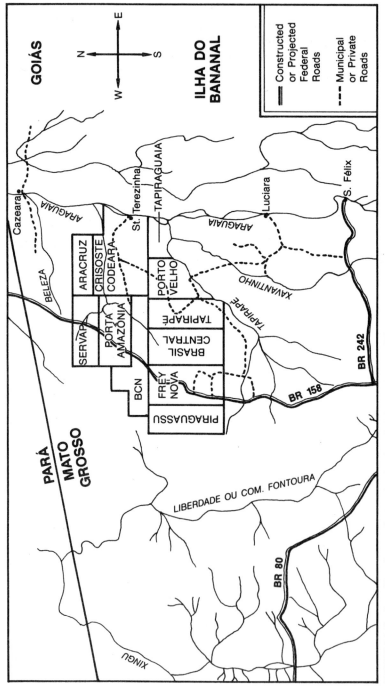

FIGURE 3.1 Northern Mato Grosso. *Source:* Landsat (satellite) image, August 1976.

because the clearing of the forest is generally done by gangs of men rather than by machinery.

Since the local population was rather sparce and generally quite unwilling to work for the *fazendas*, the ranches relied on a servile system of labor not unlike the *aviamento* debt-peonage system previously described for the rubber boom. The way it worked was as follows. Recruiters worked in Brazilian cities to gather poor unemployed men into labor crews to bring out to Mato Grosso and other areas. The men were lured with promises of good living conditions, high pay, and other benefits. Once they had arrived in a remote location, however, they found the conditions quite different. They discovered they were already in debt for their trip, tools, and food. Living conditions were generally squalid, with no medical services. Wages then went to pay off workers' debts, but these debts kept growing because workers were forced to buy their provisions at the company or contractor's store. It was a never-ending cycle of debt and exploitation. Malaria took a tremendous toll. Because workers would sometimes try to escape, companies hired gunmen to keep them in line and to prevent flight. During my fieldwork I often heard stories of local settlers or Indians who had sheltered fleeing workers in the fashion of an underground railroad. From the point of view of the *fazendas*, this system helped compensate for regional labor scarcity (local people were even more unwilling to work for *fazendas* upon seeing the cruel conditions of the outside workers), helped keep labor costs down, and compelled workers to remain on location. Bishop Pedro Casaldáliga (1971), of the regional Catholic mission, however, called this system "white slavery."[9]

Immigration into the region during the 1960s increased dramatically for several reasons. First, some of the workers brought in managed to free themselves from the *fazendas* and settle down, and others came to the region of their own accord because they needed jobs and had heard rumors about high wages. Second, the region was easier to get into and out of because of the changes in transportation routes previously described, and because of increased airplane service. *Fazendas* immediately built airstrips in many locations. Third, the migrants were increasingly under pressure to leave other places. For example, many of the small farmers I interviewed reported that they felt compelled to leave places in Goiás and western Maranhão because of land taxes, eviction, and other problems. In addition, many families were forced to leave the Bananal Forest Park during this period. Others moved out of the Indian reservation as well when the Indian Service began charging a yearly tax per head of cattle. Still other families were evicted from locations to the north and west of the Araguaia River. Many of these migrants then came to Santa Terezinha in the hopes of finding unclaimed land on which to farm.

A fourth reason why immigration increased during the 1960s had to do with the development of the town and its commerce, which, in turn, was linked to the increasingly active presence of the cattle *fazendas* in the area. As Santa Terezinha's role as a commercial outlet and a way station for displaced farmers and workers grew, more people were attracted by a variety of related job opportunities. Most of these jobs involved cooking, cleaning, and washing clothes. Finally, people came because they wanted to be near the school and medical assistance available in Santa Terezinha.

This stage of Santa Terezinha's history conforms to Foweraker's (1981) second stage of frontier expansion, which he labels as the precapitalist stage. It is characterized by an intensification of extractive activities, increased immigration, and the buying and selling of institutionalized private property. When capitalist enterprises begin to appropriate land, violent conflicts often occur. Foweraker also notes that the relations of production can include both servile relations (as in debt peonage) and the beginning of wage labor. The violence predicted by this formulation did in fact occur in Santa Terezinha.

The mid-1960s brought many disappointments both to the old inhabitants and to the more recently arrived migrants. The CODEARA *fazenda* began operations in 1965, built its headquarters only 1.5 kilometers from town, and started clearing forests close to the town and local farms. The company gave notice to local farmers that they were living on company land and must get off. The farmers tried to ignore the *fazenda.*

CODEARA increased pressure on the farmers and local population between 1966 and 1972. They hired gunmen and thugs to harass local people. Farmers would return home to find their fields destroyed or their animals dead or castrated. Fruit trees were cut down. At the same time, some of the indebted workers were trying to escape from *fazenda* labor camps and were sometimes aided by local families and Indians who hid them and helped them with food and transportation. The cattle *fazendas* would periodically call on the state militia to help them come and "put down rebellions." On one occasion, a military unit armed with submachine guns invaded the Tapirapé Indian village where some escaped *fazenda* workers were hiding (Shapiro 1967).

Padre Francisco Jentel tried to organize the farmers and to inform them of their rights as squatters under the law. He also tried hard to negotiate with CODEARA, at one point even suggesting that the small farmers might be able to "buy" back their farms from the company. CODEARA ignored such overtures (Wagley 1977). The priest also urged farmers to join the agricultural cooperative he had organized in 1962 so as to have a corporate institution to represent their legal claims to their places and the town. By 1967, an anthropologist working in the region reported that about 92 families had joined the cooperative (Shapiro 1967).

The Tapirapé tribe was also under pressure from its neighboring *fazenda*, TAPIRAGUAIA, which wanted the Indians to leave their village and fields. In 1967, the Indian Service, under increasing pressure from Brazilian and foreign anthropologists, museums, agencies, and the Catholic Church, initiated negotiations with the *fazenda* about the land. After several years of discussion, TAPIRAGUAIA finally "donated" 9,000 hectares of land at the mouth of the Tapirapé River to the tribe. This land, however, is inadequate because most of it is marshy and full of grassy areas unsuitable for slash-and-burn agriculture; in addition, the amount of forest is insufficient to support a growing population. The Tapirapé continued to negotiate for more land in the vast areas to the west of the Araguaia River that used to be their own; but as of 1981, they had not made any progress (Anthropology Resource Center 1981).

Meanwhile, the tensions of the escalating conflict between CODEARA and the Santa Terezinha farmers was about to erupt into violent confrontation. Anthropologist Judith Shapiro (1967:8) described the situation in 1967:

> The company has the complete support of the state in its attempts to dispossess the settlers. The Secretary of Justice of the State of Mato Grosso has led the farmers to believe that they have no rights in the matter, presenting them with the ultimatum of either working for the company or leaving their lands. The farmers were told . . . that [the] squatters' rights provisions had been done away with in the new constitution. . . . The state government has provided the company with a permanent police force to overcome resistance to the company on the part of the local population. . . . The position of the company in Santa Terezinha is like that of an occupying army: the local inhabitants, rather than being incorporated into its activities, are considered enemies to be subdued.

In 1972, the confrontations came to a head. A number of company men entered Santa Terezinha and destroyed the construction site of a new health clinic, ramming the walls with a tractor and demolishing the well, the garden, and a large supply of costly building materials (Davis 1977). Padre Jentel and the group building the clinic began construction again. The CODEARA men were again sent out to destroy the building. This time, however, local men who had remained behind to guard the construction site opened fire on the *fazenda* men. According to the information gathered by Shelton Davis (1977:125) and corroborated by many of my own informants, "seven people were wounded in this incident, and the town of Santa Terezinha was placed under military control." The government considered Padre Jentel responsible for the incident.

Charles Wagley summarizes the events that took place after the violence (1977:294–295):

> The outcome was a sad one. Padre François Jentel was denounced to the Minister of the Interior, to the Minister of Justice, and to various state authorities as a "communist agitator." Despite the support of his bishop and other Catholic authorities, he was tried and sentenced to ten years in prison. He served part of this term in a prison in Mato Grosso, and it was not until 1974 that he was released and exiled from Brazil. By then his case had been widely reported by the press in the United States and Europe.

In part because of the national and international attention focused on events in Santa Terezinha, the CODEARA *fazenda* bowed to pressure and agreed to distribute some land to local farmers and to the town. The National Agrarian Reform Institute (INCRA) was asked to supervise the land distribution. According to INCRA, between 1973 and 1976 approximately 110 lots were distributed to local farmers, and the town was given 517 hectares of land as well.

Stage Three—The Current Era

The beginnings of the third stage of frontier expansion in Santa Terezinha are the subject of the subsequent three chapters, which focus on the impact of the *fazendas* on the frontier settlers in the late 1970s. Following Foweraker's (1981) formulation, it is during stage three that the capitalist enterprises begin to achieve dominance, institutionalized private property becomes increasingly concentrated, immigration increases as people enter a region looking for land and jobs, and emigration increases as landless farmers leave for other places. The full impact of stage three is explored in the new final chapter, based on a revisit to the region in 1987.

Notes

1. Rural people use the expression *terra comum* to refer to land without owners.

2. The word *tubarões* translates as "sharks" but means "landgrabbers" in Amazonia.

3. *Posseiros* are squatters, or people owning land by *posse*.

4. *Aviamento* is literally translated as a system of provisioning.

5. The Little Sisters of Jesus are a very unusual order of nuns and missionaries in that they do not proselytize and are committed to helping their target populations retain as much of their traditional culture and lifestyle as possible. The presence of the Little Sisters in the Tapirapé village, according to most observers, has made a critical difference to the survival of the tribe as a people.

6. For further details regarding the situation in northeastern Brazil, see CIDA (1966), Feder (1971), Forman (1975), Forman and Riegelhaupt (1970), Gross and Underwood (1971), Hutchinson (1957), Johnson (1971), Morães (1970), Queiroz (1977), and Wagley (1971).

7. These dynamics are documented further in Forman (1975), Forman and Riegelhaupt (1970), and Johnson (1971).

8. The written sources I used to reconstruct early frontier life include Baldus (1944/1960a, 1948/1960b), Ehrenreich (1891/1965), Krause (1911/1966), Lipkind (1963), and Wagley (1977).

9. Further documentation of worker abuses in the Santa Terezinha area can be found in Shapiro (1967) and CNDDA (1978); regarding Brazil in general, see Saint (1981).

4

The Small Farmers of Santa Terezinha

Introduction

The folk typology of socioeconomic categories in Santa Terezinha reduces the complexity of frontier social structure to three occupational types: (1) *lavrador* (peasant farmer), (2) *peão* (peon or farm hand), and (3) *comerciante* (merchant, trader, or businessman). Farmers are those who have remained in agriculture, peons work for the cattle *fazendas*, and merchants are those who engage in any kind of commercial activity from a coffee stand to a dry goods store. Although people frequently engage in more than one of these livelihood activities, they are generally classified in terms of only one of the three categories. For example, a farmer who occasionally works in a labor crew at cattle *fazendas* will be referred to as a farmer, although his son who rarely helps at the farm and mostly works at *fazendas* will be referred to, somewhat derogatorily, as a peon.

The vast majority of people I interviewed in Santa Terezinha identified themselves as peasant farmers (*lavradores*), although in many cases they had ceased farming. The critical limiting factor in most of these cases was access to land and productive resources. For example, one woman interviewed said:

> Everything is so difficult! The *fazenda* has money and can do jobs of any type in any way, but a poor person doesn't have any money. Many people here are without land. People get upset and they sell out. There are people living here and there, all screwed up, without a place to live.

She was referring to the pressures brought to bear against small farmers holding land by *posse* by cattle companies intent on displacing them. Eventually, the squatter farmers become intimidated, accept the compensation offer (usually a token sum), and leave the homestead. Very often the same displaced farmers arrive in settlements like Santa Terezinha, disoriented, almost broke, looking for a way to reestablish

TABLE 4.1
Types of Landownership and Access in Santa Terezinha

Type of Access	Number of Households
Type of landownership:	
INCRA title land	10
Squatters' rights to land (*posse*)	8
Own no land	81
Total	99
Access to land of the 81 nonlandowning households	
Use of INCRA lot owned by relatives	8
Use of *posse* lot owned by relatives	3
Sharecrop on other INCRA lot	8
Sharecrop on other *posse* lot	1
No reported access to land	61
Total	81

themselves in agriculture. But farming begins to seem only a remote possibility. A middle-aged former farmer turned cattle *fazenda* worker explained the situation as follows:

> You see, the land sharks are grabbing everything. The poor people will be left on the moon with their hands on their heads. All this here belongs to CODEARA, and we, we will end up as her tenants. What we need is our own land! That's all we need. I am of the forest. With land we could muster our energy and raise cattle, pigs, chickens, make a pasture. With land we could make an abundance!

Despite the INCRA land distribution described previously, many aspiring farmers remain without land. In a survey of 99 randomly selected Santa Terezinha households, only 10 percent reported owning what is commonly referred to as "INCRA land" (see Table 4.1). Eight households indicated that they owned land by *posse*, and 81 reported that they owned no land at all. Of these 81 without land, 20—one-fourth—had arranged access to land as tenants. However, 61 households reported no access to land at all.

Therefore, although immigration into the area is heavy and most of those arriving continue to be small farmers seeking land, the actual number of people with access to land and actually farming appear to be declining annually. For example, while 86 percent of the grandparental generation in two surveys were reported as farmers, only 61 percent of the sampled Santa Terezinha household heads had actually farmed in the last five years, and of these only 25 percent were actually found to be preparing fields to plant in 1978.

This chapter focuses on the farming livelihood as it was practiced in Santa Terezinha in 1978–1979. It also highlights some of the problems and obstacles faced by local farmers. The farming system is described primarily from the farmers' perspective and in terms of the farmers' goals and aspirations. Attention is directed in turn to the production system, marketing, and consumption patterns. The final section reviews the complex series of constraints that impede agricultural production and, ultimately, the small farmer livelihood itself. Wage labor opportunities at *fazendas* and commercial activities, the two other main livelihood categories, will be explored in Chapter 5, and survival strategies will be covered in Chapter 6.

Production

The type of farming practiced in Santa Terezinha is shifting cultivation or slash-and-burn agriculture, which has been extensively described for Amazonia (e.g., Meggers 1971; Moran 1974, 1975; Wagley 1976). Each year, new fields are made by clearing forested land that is later burned and planted shortly before the winter rains begin. Farmers concurred that the land here "tires easily" when stripped of forest cover and cannot be productively planted for more than two years. Fields are then allowed to return to secondary growth (*capoeira*) and will be used again only after a rest of five to fifteen years. This type of agriculture thus requires relatively large amounts of land to allow sufficient time for regrowth and renewal of soil fertility during very long fallow periods.

Farmers prepare new fields during the dry season from May to September, during which the most active months for clearing are June, July, and August. Men, using axes, scythes, and knives, do the heavy work of felling trees and clearing the brush. They usually do the clearing work alone or in small groups of two to four. These work groups most frequently consist of the "owner" of the land and relatives such as brothers, sons, and sons-in-law. The men usually do the clearing together but divide the field into separate plots before planting. Sometimes other family members—women, children, and elderly relatives—help in the lighter chores of clearing.

The *multirão* (traditional communal work party), in which a large number of people come together to work at each farm and are rewarded with a feast and a party, was not present in Santa Terezinha, although the Catholic mission had actively encouraged farmers to organize one. Of 44 households questioned in one survey, 39 had never participated in a *multirão*. Four had participated in other places (southern Mato

Grosso and Goiás), and only one family had participated in Santa Terezinha in a *multirão* organized by the priest. Families interviewed who had participated in or observed the priest's *multirão* stated that, although they liked the idea of communal work parties, they would not participate in any future ones. The reasons given by informants were that (1) it was too expensive to feed so many guests, (2) some families' fields were cleared too late, thus throwing off planting schedules, and (3) many felt that they worked harder at their neighbors' fields than their neighbors had worked in theirs. The conclusion they reached was that "we are too disunited for *multirão* here."

A far more common form of cooperative labor exchange is the custom of "trading days" (*troca de dias*) or "trading jobs" (*troca de serviço*). Trading days is a short-term temporary arrangement usually made between two relatives or friends. Each man spends several days working in the other's fields; the host provides shelter and food for the worker. Interestingly, the trading of days is very common for clearing work but is quite rare for all other types of agricultural work. It is important to realize that neither money nor large amounts of food are needed to do this kind of exchange.

Some of the better-off farmers or men with other occupations occasionally pay laborers to do their clearing for them. Cash will be paid for the work if it is the only work done by the employee. If the worker goes on to plant and harvest, he or she is considered a tenant and pays the "owners" either by delivering half the harvest or by leaving the field planted in pasture grass.

The areas cleared for *roças* are relatively small and normally range from half a hectare to 1.5 hectares. The cleared field is left to dry in the sun of the dry season for a month or longer. It is burned sometime between late August and early October.[1]

September to November are the months for planting all cultigens except rice and pasture grass, which are planted later. Major cultigens include sweet and bitter manioc, corn, several varieties of beans, sweet potatoes, two varieties of pineapples, several varieties of squash, sugar cane, and watermelons. Rice, manioc flour (*farinha*), and beans are the main components of the population's diet. Corn is eaten green (fresh) but is grown mainly in small quantities as animal food. Other useful trees and plants are cultivated; some of the more important ones are several varieties of bananas, mangoes, papayas, several varieties of oranges, lemons, *limas* (sweet limes), several varieties of passion fruit (*maracujá*), cotton, hot peppers, gourds, avocadoes, guava, castor oil beans, and *atá* (sugar apple). A small number of farmers were experimenting as well with coffee and tobacco, but since these crops require better soils and fertilizers, few farmers considered the possibilities very good.

Men also do most of the actual planting, although other family members sometimes help. Most men plant their *roças* alone unless their families are staying at the fields or they have a tenant working with them. The only "machine" used in planting is a wooden rice seeder. All planting, except for rice, is done with knives, hoes, and hands.

All planting, harvesting, and cutting of wood are done in accordance with the phases of the moon. All of the Santa Terezinha farmers I interviewed, regardless of their migration histories, believed that "the moon governs the land" and that agricultural activities must be properly coordinated with the appropriate phases of the moon.[2]

Fertilizers are neither used nor available locally. Many farmers had heard of them and expressed great interest. However, the lack of technical information, access, and financing has effectively blocked the adoption of fertilizers. The present method of farming requires almost no capital investment. Most farmers pointed out that innovations and expansion of production would necessitate some sources of credit. But there are no credit facilities in Santa Terezinha.[3] Most farmers buy and use insecticides, which they mix with rice, corn, and sometimes beans before planting. Seeds to be planted are saved from the previous year's harvest, although some farmers do sell seeds. Manioc, on the other hand, is never planted with insecticide, and the cuttings (to plant) are never sold. Any farmer with manioc in his fields will provide cuttings at no charge to anyone who asks for them.

Rice is usually planted in December and January, during the rains. The reason for this delay is that the rice matures in four to five months and farmers prefer to harvest rice well after the winter flood waters have receded. Rice is known to do well in damp ground (locally called "cold ground"), and farmers usually plant rice in the lowest-lying part of their field and near streams. Rice planted in especially "cold ground" will produce a second smaller harvest following the first one.

Farmers prefer to plant rice late so that they can harvest it in the (usually) dry month of May. If the rice is planted earlier, in October or November, farmers will likely have to harvest it while wading through water or from a canoe. Effort must be expended to keep the harvested rice dry during the rainy season or it will start to grow mold. Some farmers, however, do plant a portion of their rice early so they can harvest in late January, February, and April. This is done because January and February are the leanest months in Santa Terezinha, when most households are already out of last year's rice. Rice that sold at harvest time for 300 cruzeiros (US$15) a sack (60 kilos) in 1978 went as high as 800 cruzeiros (US$40) a sack in February 1979. Wage labor opportunities tend to decline during the rainy season as cattle companies reduce their work forces; and although foodstuffs are imported into Santa Terezinha during the wet season, money is extremely tight at a time when food prices are at their highest. Therefore, an early rice harvest, while troublesome and problematic, is considered worthwhile by some enterprising farmers.

Rice, an important crop in Santa Terezinha, constitutes a major item in the diet of all but the poorest families. Manioc flour (*farinha*), while a staple, is considered to be and is insufficient alone as it provides calories but little protein or other nutrients (Roosevelt 1980). People described times of suffering as times when they had only *farinha* to eat for months on end. Estimates provided by my informants indicate that an average adult ideally consumes between 1.5 and 2 sacks of rice per year (90 to 120 kilos), or approximately one-fourth to one-third of a kilo of rice a day (about three-quarters of a pound). The goal of most family members interviewed was to have at least 10 sacks (600 kilos) of rice in storage for home consumption for one year.

Farmers measure rice production in terms of the number and productivity of *linhas* (meaning lines, of which there are 4 in each hectare) and the yield in sacks (60 kilos a sack). Each *linha* cultivated ideally should produce about 15 sacks (900 kilos). The number of *linhas* planted varied between 1 and 10. The goal of most farmers who plant rice on about five *linhas* is to harvest between 40 and 60 sacks so the household can reserve 10 to eat and sell the rest.

Other factors enter in and alter these production goals, however. Problems with the quality of land selected for cultivation, problems with weather changes, late arrivals of rains, excessive flooding, and rain during harvest time have significantly reduced farmers' yields.[4] Examples of disappointing yields in 1977 include one family who planted 1 *linha* with a goal of 15 sacks but harvested only 1 sack, and another family who cultivated 10 *linhas* but harvested only 38 sacks. Further problems in obtaining harvest labor and in transporting the rice to town contribute to losses in rice production. Fluctuations in local rice prices also affect farmers' decisions about how much to plant. The low 1977 harvest price for rice of 50 cruzeiros (US$2.50) a sack dissuaded many farmers from planting for surplus production the following year. The next year, however, there was an acute local rice shortage because farmers had planted less and then lost much of the harvest to unseasonable weather. Prices for rice soared, and farmers began to consider expanding the areas for rice cultivation.

Before the arrival of the cattle *fazendas* in the mid-1960s, many small farmer families raised a few head of cattle and allowed them to graze on the natural savannas. Some of the more successful small-time "ranch-

ers" even achieved herds of several hundred head: A man with a herd
of a thousand was considered to be a "wealthy rancher" (*fazendeiro*).
These small farmer ranchers or their resident "cowboys" (*vaqueiros*)
continued to practice slash-and-burn agriculture and identified themselves
as farmers. The economy was basically a subsistence economy, and cattle
represented a form of savings. Cattle roamed freely on the "common
lands," and only fields were fenced to keep animals out. During the
last ten to fifteen years, however, local cattle raisers have lost access to
most of the common grazing areas. Bananal, as described previously,
was divided into an Indian reservation and a Forest Park, and the
corporate cattle *fazendas* moved into the land to the west of the Araguaia
River.

The majority of Santa Terezinha families who own some cattle have
been unable to create sufficient areas of improved pastures for their
upkeep—that is, pastures prepared, planted with African pasture grasses,
and fenced. Therefore, the custom in the late 1970s was for the local
cattle raisers to allow the animals to graze on the *varjão* (flood plain)
to the north of town, which was exposed during the summer months,
and to bring the cattle into town during the rainy season. During the
winter, then, cattle roam the streets of Santa Terezinha eating brush
and garbage and even breaking into kitchen gardens. In 1978, the
situation became acute when CODEARA began laying claim to the
grazing area to the north of town and fenced it in to make it off-limits
to local people. Local animals found outside the town's borders were
occasionally seized by *fazenda* personnel and were difficult for local
farmers to get back.

Local farmers thus became increasingly interested in planting and
maintaining improved pastures in the same way as the corporate *fazendas*
had done. However, the process is expensive and land-extensive. The
farmers buy the special grass seeds used by the large companies.[5] The
most common way of making improved pastures is to clear the forest
and prepare the land for regular crops. Annual crops are then planted
on the burned field, and after they have begun to grow, the grass seed
is planted in the same field. After the farmer has completed his harvest,
he allows cattle into the field to graze and trample the area, thus
scattering the grass seeds for further replanting. Approximately one year
later the entire field is burned, "to clean it," and the field spontaneously
regenerates a fresh cover of pasture grass.

The changes toward modern cattle production have a number of
implications for the local small farmers. First, fields that will be turned
into pastures are planted only with short-term crops, such as rice, beans,
and corn. Manioc, the most dependable cultigen that produces for three
to four years after planting, is *not* planted in areas earmarked to become

pastures. The result has been a decrease in the planting of manioc that was reflected in periodic shortages in town of locally produced manioc flour, a dietary staple.

Second, the newly created pastures must be kept fenced to control access of the animals to the fodder and to keep out neighbors' animals. The best fencing material is wire, which entails a large expense for the farmer. Third, the pasture requires upkeep, periodic burning, and weeding so as to decrease the number of invading plants.[6] Finally, and perhaps most important, a field that has been planted as pasture is extremely difficult to return to agricultural production. Even neglected, it tends to remain as grass and does not return to the secondary growth necessary for future cultivation. So, over time, the amount of land suitable for agriculture is decreased as forests are turned into pastures.

The majority of the small farmers of Santa Terezinha found the creation of improved pastures too expensive an undertaking. Many farmers expressed serious doubts about the enterprise and asserted that their neighbors who were making pastures were "foolish." It had become increasingly common for tenants to be asked to pay rental in the form of leaving the fields planted in pasture grass rather than delivering a portion of the harvest, as had been traditional.

Landowners with definitive titles are usually the ones most interested in the investment in pastures. Some farmers who had made pastures in the past on land owned by *posse* (squatters' rights) expressed bitterness and frustration at having been forced to move on and lose their pastures.

Land holdings, whether by deed or *posse*, tend to be about 100 hectares each—but not all 100 hectares are of equal value to the farmer, since the type of terrain and soil can vary. Some lots contained only a relatively small proportion of the forested land considered to be optimal for farming and pastures. Farmers who have continued to carve out new areas of pastures each year are effectively eliminating these portions of their land from future food production and are making a calculation that cattle production, in the long run, will eventually provide a more secure livelihood.[7]

Harvesting begins in December when some of the cultivated fruits, water melons, mangoes, and pineapples begin to mature. The rainy season is the time of fruits, both cultivated and wild. Almost all Santa Terezinha households, whether farmers or not, collect and eat wild fruit. Some families even collect fruit and sell it door to door. Some of the most important wild fruits collected are the palm fruits *buriti* (*Mauritia vinifera* Mart.), *buritirana* (*Mauritia martiana* Spruce) and *bacaba* (*Oenocarpus distichus* Mart.); *murici* (*Myrosonima crassifolia* [L.] Kunth) and *pequi* (*Caryocar* spp.) are also important. All, except for *pequi*, are made into beautifully colored gruels sweetened with sugar. *Jenipapo* fruit (*Genipa americana* L.), used as a black dye by Indians, is also found in these regions but is eaten less often.

Collecting is an important subsidiary activity for most households.[8] Families collect not only wild fruits but also fruits and other products planted and abandoned by people. During the rainy season, people make trips to the abandoned settlement of Furo de Pedra, for example, to harvest the fruit trees still there.

Three types of beans are cultivated by farmers: *fava*, or broad beans (*Vicia faba*); "*trepa-pau*," or climbing beans (probably *feijão de espanha* or *Phaseolus multiflora*); and *andú*, a pigeon pea (*Cajanus cajan*) that is called *feijão de Madeira* in the northeast. *Fava*, *trepa-pau*, and *andú* have an advantage in that they can be harvested continuously rather than all at one time. Thus, small-scale harvesting of these beans occurs sporadically throughout the year. Usually the amounts picked are small, perhaps several liters total, and they are always used for home consumption and never sold. Indeed, bean production overall is quite small. All the stores in town carry *mulatinho* beans (*Phaseolus vulgaris*), imported from southern Brazil, as these are the most popular for eating. At 40 cruzeiros (US$2) a kilo in 1978, however, *mulatinhos* were more expensive than some of the cheaper cuts of meat throughout most of that year, until meat prices doubled. Most households in Santa Terezinha, including farmers, purchase *mulatinho* beans if the budget permits; beef was so scarce during 1978 that beans (and fish) were the main sources of protein for most families.

Manioc or cassava (*Manihot* spp.) is a crop of central importance not only in Santa Terezinha but in the entire northern region of Brazil as well. This starchy root formed the mainstay of the diet of the indigenous population of the Amazon Basin and today is a basic staple for most Brazilians (Moran 1974; Wagley 1976). It is extremely well suited to humid tropical conditions and soils, and the sturdy plants require no protective insecticides or fertilizers to achieve yields of up to 10 tons per hectare. It is planted by taking cuttings from the stalks of other manioc plants. Mature roots are ready for harvesting in about six months and can be left in the ground for long periods of time, although after as many as four years the roots become fibrous and prone to diseases and pests.

Manioc is consumed mainly in the form of manioc flour (*farinha*), a by-product that results from processing the root. *Farinha* has excellent storage capacity. It is eaten every day, at meals and in between meals. It is usually mixed with almost all other foods; for example, it can be sprinkled on rice and beans or added by the handful to mashed avacadoes or palm fruit gruel. An average household in Santa Terezinha consumes between 1 and 2 kilos of *farinha* a day, or approximately 548 kilos a year.[9] *Farinha* is the most constant item in the population's diet because it is cheaper and more available than any other food.

The folk system classifies manioc into two varieties. Sweet manioc (*Manihot aipi*) contains the least poison (prussic acid) and can be eaten without processing; the roots are boiled, baked, or fried. Poisonous or bitter manioc (*Manihot esculenta*) contains more prussic acid, which must be removed before the root can be eaten. It is from the more poisonous variety that *farinha* is made. Two main kinds of *farinha* are produced: *farinha branca* (white manioc flour) and *farinha puba* (water processed or fermented manioc flour); the latter is the more popular.

There is no one harvest time for manioc. Throughout the year farmers spend time, usually a week or more at one time, harvesting and processing the tubers. Manioc is produced whenever the household needs more or wants to sell some. When farmers make *farinha* they usually spend one or two weeks at the *roça* processing manioc and doing other agricultural chores. A large amount of firewood is gathered and the roots are soaked daily so that a supply of pulp and fuel for toasting the flour is available for each day's work. Men sometimes do this work alone, but it is far more common to find two or more people working together. If the family lives at the *roça* (instead of in town), the entire household will participate in the various tasks of peeling, grating, stirring, and so forth. One researcher calculated that it takes nine hours to produce 140 kilos of *farinha* (Parker 1979). Calculations made for one family group in Santa Terezinha of two men and two women showed that they worked about 19 days to produce 720 kilos of *farinha* and 95 kilos of *tapioca* (another by-product of manioc processing). After reserving several sacks for home consumption and paying the costs of transportation to town, the group sold the remaining *farinha* for 2,910 cruzeiros (US$145.50). Thus, each of the four adults earned a daily profit of 38 cruzeiros (US$1.90) for each day worked in *farinha* production.

A fairly common arrangement in Santa Terezinha is a form of cooperative labor in the production of *farinha* whereby a nonfarmer helps in the processing and receives from one-fourth to one-third of the flour produced. The "guest laborer" usually goes to live temporarily at the fields of the farmer and must bring along his or her own food supply. The worker then works in all phases of the processing. This type of arrangement allows the landless and cash-poor families to lay in relatively large supplies of *farinha*. Women raising families alone frequently obtain manioc flour this way. No money is used in the transaction.

Harvesting of rice differs somewhat from that of all other cultigens. During the two months prior to harvest, rice growers are constantly preoccupied with making sure that there is someone in the fields at all times to scare away birds. Most rice fields are ready for harvesting between April and May, except for the early rice mentioned previously. Another major difference from other crops is that the rice must be harvested all at one time.

A serious problem for farmers is obtaining sufficient labor for the rice harvest. Families and relatives are not always available, and cash to pay workers is usually in short supply at this time of the year. The most common way of obtaining additional rice harvest labor is for the farmer to pay in rice. Workers usually receive from one-fourth to one-third of the bags they harvest. Again, this type of transaction allows landless households to lay in rice supplies without using cash.

Both men and women work as "guest laborers" in the rice harvest. Because the labor requirements occur simultaneously, there is an annual shortage of harvest labor. The farmers I interviewed repeatedly expressed frustration at their inability to find sufficient labor for their rice harvests. Those with small plots were also somewhat unwilling to lose part of the harvest to pay for labor. There were neither cooperative labor parties nor even "trading days" during the rice harvest. The reasons for this lack of cooperation are somewhat unclear. The farmers I interviewed made statements such as, "It's each man for himself. When you win you win, and when you lose you lose." It may be that the brevity of the rice harvest is key to the annual labor shortage.

Another serious problem for many farmers concerns the transportation of rice and the lack of roads throughout the countryside. The majority of farmers interviewed need to transport rice (and other produce) to town to have it cleaned, to store in their town homes, and to sell. Since so few farmers own beasts of burden (only 4 out of 44 households had burros or horses), many producers must hire a vehicle to bring in the produce. Trucks are expensive to hire in Santa Terezinha. Farmers often must pay as much as 200–300 cruzeiros (US$10–15), depending on the distance; or, as occurs more frequently, they pay in rice, usually several sacks. Some farmers stated that they had carried sacks of rice to town on their shoulders. Members of the agricultural cooperative, fewer in number every year, receive a slight discount in price when renting the cooperative's truck.

The many problems with rice production and its commercialization are representative of the major problems of the small farmers of northern Mato Grosso. The entire system of production is quite small in scale and archaic. Very little, if any, capital is invested. Machines and other technological innovations are entirely lacking. Areas under production are necessarily small, and yields are low and highly uncertain. The farmers themselves, however, revealed a tremendous interest in innovation and expansion, as has been observed for peasantries elsewhere (e.g.,

Barlett 1980; Ortiz 1973). Yet the farmers pointed out repeatedly that they needed a source of credit and outside technical help. Unfortunately, no such infrastructural supports exist in Santa Terezinha.

Marketing

The market for local agricultural commodities in Santa Terezinha is primarily one of "selling in the street." There is no marketplace, nor are periodic fairs (*feiras*) held. Most farm families bring small amounts of produce to town and sell it directly from their homes. In daily interactions, people constantly pass information along about who has what for sale. Word will go out, for example, that José just returned from his *roça* and has a supply of *farinha* to sell. Children are frequently sent around to inform neighbors of what their family has for sale, and smaller products, such as onions, are peddled door to door.

Both men and women sell, but women do more because they tend to be home more often. Women carry out most of the smaller sales and are always in charge of selling what they have produced, such as products from their kitchen gardens or their chickens. Larger transactions, such as the sale of a pig or several sacks of rice to a boarding house, are usually arranged and supervised by men.

One important advantage of selling directly from the home is that, in general, farmers can both avoid paying the taxes that are required on commercial transactions and avoid obtaining permits for establishing a commercial establishment. The tax collectors seem to be closing their eyes to the commerce conducted in peoples' homes.

In one survey of 44 households, 25 families provided detailed information on the recent sale of farm products. Almost half of these families insisted that they sold next to nothing and were producing only for home consumption. Five families stated that they engaged in periodic sales of produce from their homes, and 8 families explained that they had recently sold produce to local stores or to the agricultural cooperative.

Most of the local stores are uninterested in buying produce from local farmers. Stores obtain their stock from outside the region. Even items such as beans, coffee, onions, garlic, rice, and *farinha* are imported from southern Brazil. Several of the larger stores occasionally bought *farinha* from local farmers, but most stores simply did not sell *farinha*. Farmers indicated that they liked a bulk sale to a store because it saved them time selling and usually provided a larger lump sum.

The only stores that bought rice from local farmers on a fairly regular basis were the agricultural cooperative and CODEARA's store, called *a planta*. Both of these establishments had rice-cleaning machines and facilities for storage. Most other merchants in town did not even handle rice, although some imported it during the last months of the rainy season when the local price skyrocketed. Furthermore, local rice is commonly considered to be inferior to rice grown elsewhere in Brazil, and most merchants consider local producers to be unreliable suppliers.

The price of rice fluctuates tremendously during the year. For example, at the beginning of the 1978 harvest, in April, a sack of rice was selling for 150 cruzeiros (US$7). By May, the price had reached 200 cruzeiros (US$10), and by June it had risen to 300 (US$15). During the months from September to November, a sack of rice was selling for 400–500 cruzeiros (US$20–25). And by January 1979, when farmers were anxiously waiting for the next harvest, the price had risen to 600 cruzeiros (US$30).

Farmers frequently sold their rice at the low, harvest-time price because they had very little choice. The last months of the rainy season—January, February, and March—are a time of desperation for many families. Both the money earned from dry season employment and stored food supplies are used up. Paid employment at the cattle *fazendas* during the rainy season is very scarce because most work is done during the dry season. Odd jobs in town become hard to find. Local cattle cannot be sold at this time because they are skinny and sickly from inadequate feeding during the rainy season, when flooding decreases the availability of natural savanna areas for grazing. Households pile up debts at local stores until, as often happens, their credit is cut off. Transportation throughout the region and between homesteads in the forest and town are slowed because of flooding. It is therefore not surprising that farmers in great need of cash sell their rice at the time of year that is most disadvantageous to them in terms of price. In many cases, the farmers end up selling not only their surplus rice but also the rice they had planned to retain for home consumption. Rice is used to pay off harvest labor, to pay for transportation, and to settle other outstanding debts. As many of my informants pointed out, Santa Terezinha farmers ironically often end up buying their own rice back from the larger merchants in the months after the harvest at sharply inflated prices.

The agricultural cooperative, mentioned previously, was originally organized by Padre Jentel in the mid-1960s. Apart from the hope that the cooperative would help give the local farmers a better claim on their land, the goals of the cooperative include trying to improve the marketing of local agricultural commodities. It also owns a rice-cleaning machine and a truck, available to members at lower rates. The main method by which the cooperative tries to improve marketing of agricultural commodities is to buy rice at a fixed rate of 260 cruzeiros (US$13) throughout the year. Available to members only, this price is better than the immediate harvest-time price but lower than that of rice at most other times of the year. Accordingly, the advantage of selling through the cooperative appeared marginal to many of the farmers I interviewed. In addition, profits made by the cooperative on rice sales and other activities are supposed to be returned to the members in a form to be determined at the annual meeting. Because this cooperative receives no outside government or other public- or private-sector support, it tends to operate on a very precarious financial basis. Therefore, it is not surprising that any profits realized on rice sales are almost always returned to the operating capital of the cooperative. Local farmers, once initially enthusiastic about the cooperative in its early days, often stated that they saw no direct advantages in belonging to it. Especially in the case of rice, they preferred to take their chances on the open market, hoping to receive a much higher price than the cooperative offered.

The cooperative has a store that sells agricultural commodities, household supplies, and some agricultural and other implements such as knives, hoes, and bicycles. Only cooperative members receive credit at the store; the credit is only for items purchased from the cooperative.

Membership in the cooperative appeared to be declining because of the limited economic power of the organization. Many of the farmers I interviewed expressed disappointment with the cooperative. Only 4 out of the 44 families interviewed in one survey were found to belong to the cooperative. Since nonmembers cannot have credit for purchases, most people shop elsewhere. The reasons for the relative lack of success of the cooperative appear to be interrelated. The cooperative receives no official support of any kind, perhaps because it was founded and still largely run by the Catholic mission, which was viewed as "subversive" by many local and outside government officials. In addition, the decreasing amount of farming activities, the fragility of the local market for locally produced agricultural goods, the total lack of an outside market, and the highly precarious financial situations of members or potential members all contributed to the lack of economic power of the cooperative. As farmers became disenchanted and withdrew, the membership fell, thus further undermining the strength of the organization.

A third major way in which local farmers sell rice is in bulk to some stores and also to some nonfarming households. Boarding-house owners will frequently make private arrangements with a particular farmer to buy his surplus rice at harvest-time prices. One informant and friend, a seamstress named Maria who supported six young sons alone (her husband had abandoned her), purchased her entire year's rice supply from a farmer directly. Maria's rice deal, unfortunately, turned out badly for both parties. The sacks of rice purchased turned out to be moldy because the rice had gotten wet in some unusual May rain. Maria then angrily demanded that the farmer take back the rice and return her money. The farmer complied. His only alternative at that point was to dump the moldy rice. The seamstress, having recovered her money from the farmer, then made another bulk purchase from a different farmer but paid a significantly higher price because several more weeks had elapsed. Maria lost money and the first farmer lost his entire rice profit for the year.

Considering the fragility of the local market for agricultural goods, it is not surprising that most farm families remain oriented primarily toward subsistence production. The farmers' attitudes toward trying to produce surpluses can be viewed as reasonable responses to the conditions of production and marketing. The prices received by farmers for local produce remain low, whereas the prices for almost all other commodities in the frontier rise almost daily. There are many factors, other than a "poverty mentality" or traditionalism, that operate to discourage farmers from trying to expand production.

The entire farming and marketing system operates in a vicious cycle of compounding constraints. Factors such as primitive technology, lack of credit and infrastructure, and an increasing movement of labor from agricultural activities to other remunerative activities contribute to low agricultural productivity. The marginal local market and the lack of outside markets retard all impetus toward agricultural expansion on the part of the small farmers.

Small farmers are sometimes forced out of agriculture altogether when they take a risk that does not pay off, lose family labor, or have an unexpected emergency or disaster. The risk that does not pay off is illustrated by the farmer who lost his investment in surplus rice when unseasonable rain caused it to become moldy and Maria the seamstress demanded her money back. Loss of family labor, especially adult children who want to work in stores or at cattle *fazendas*, is sometimes an insurmountable constraint for aging farmers who simply cannot manage the great physical demands of this kind of farming alone anymore. Emergencies, such as the serious illness of a family member, may also devastate the household economy as the family tries to raise enough money to send the sick person to a hospital outside the region. Land or a home may be sold to pay for airplane rental and medical bills.

Small farmers try to respond to fluctuations in the local market, such as the rice shortage, but they usually cannot benefit from such responses. For example, planting additional *linhas* of rice and a subsequent good harvest will cause the local price of rice to fall again. In addition, it is difficult for local producers to maneuver within the constraints of the local marketing system. Lack of money and credit make waiting for a more advantageous time to sell rice problematic for most farmers. Most farmers also do not have adequate storage facilities and put the sacks of rice in the rafters of their homes where rats can cause considerable

TABLE 4.2
Prices of Some Essential Commodities in Santa Terezinha in 1978 and 1979

Item	Price (Cruzeiros)	Price (U.S. Dollars)
Cooking oil, 1 liter	25	1.25
Salt, 1 kilo	5	.25
Sugar, 1 kilo	10	.50
Green coffee, 1 kilo	100	5.00
Kerosene, 1 liter	12	.60
Powdered milk, 400 grams	40	2.00
Margarine, 500 grams	20	1.00
Crude tobacco, 1 kilo	100	5.00
Tomato paste, 85 grams	8	.40
Spaghetti, 500 grams	10	.50
Garlic, head	5	.25

Prices are averaged prices taken from a variety of stores over a period of several months. The dollar-cruzeiros exchange is being calculated at 1:20, an average for the period.

damage. Farm tenants usually have even less flexibility than owners and must either deliver half the harvest to the owner or leave the field planted with pasture grass. Tenancy arrangements vary, but some of the tenants I encountered seemed little more than employees with little autonomous decisionmaking power.

Consumption

Another important aspect in assessing livelihood patterns is the quality and level of consumption patterns. From what has already been said, it may be clear that very few Santa Terezinha households depend exclusively on farming for their livelihood. Similar to small farmers worldwide, they need to augment even subsistence-oriented production with income-generating activities to purchase certain commodiites they cannot produce, such as kerosene, salt, shoes, and the like. In addition, the fragility of the local market and the generally low prices received by farmers mean that even landowning farmers are unlikely to pursue farming as a single livelihood strategy.

While it was difficult to make calculations because of a lack of records, the informants' reluctance to reveal certain kinds of information, and my dependence on informant recall, the information I collected suggests that most Santa Terezinha households that depend primarily on farming have a monthly income ranging from no money to 1,200 cruzeiros (US$60). The prices of goods in the frontier are often significantly higher than the prices in urban centers. To get an idea of the purchasing power of an average monthly income of 600 cruzeiros (US$30), take a look at the prices of some of the more commonly purchased items in Table 4.2.

Most households also spend money on protein. Beef is considered an extremely desirable food and is purchased as frequently as possible. However, during most of 1978 meat was very scarce because the local small farmer cattle raisers were unable to supply the local market because of production problems, including inadequate grazing areas, diseases, and losses due to excessive and unusual flooding. The cattle *fazendas* refused to sell beef to the town or to any noncompany personnel, saying that it was not economically profitable to do so. The *fazendas'* more punitive attitude toward the local people was reflected in their policy of firing any of their own workers who gave or sold company meat (which is distributed inexpensively to employees) to local people.

Almost all families in Santa Terezinha try to raise some chickens and pigs, but production is extremely marginal—in part because of losses due to disease, inadequate feed, and theft. Chickens as food are usually reserved for special occasions, but most poor families choose to sell rather than eat them because the price at the end of 1978 was 60–100 cruzeiros (US$3–5) per chicken because of scarcity.

Fishing is done by family members during free time, but almost no households sell fish although it is sometimes given away as a gift. The Karajá Indians, reknowned fishermen, sell small quantities of fish in town but mostly to boarding houses and cabarets in the red light district. Fish is also considered by most people to be less desirable than meat. In addition, fish eating is restricted by an elaborate set of folk taboos, which eliminate a large portion of the available fish from consumption.[10] There are also taboos on certain species of wild game, but with the deforestation in the area, the amount of wild game consumed is minuscule.

During most of 1978, the local prices for fish, pork, and beef were fairly reasonable—15–30 cruzeiros (US$.75–1.50) a kilo; but even families with money were often unable to purchase meat or fish because of local unavailability. Butcher shops would be closed for months on end, and a household slaughtering and selling of a pig was a rare event. After the summer of 1978, when local cattle had fattened on the natural savannas, meat became somewhat more available; but the price then doubled in response to rises in national beef prices.

The following case study of the monthly economy of one farm family illustrates some of the basic difficulties of the farming livelihood in this part of the frontier. The family, Dona Luisa and her husband José, was fortunate enough to have received INCRA land. In the reshuffling of locations, however, they lost their place near Santa Terezinha and were given a virgin plot some 12 kilometers from town. When I met them they had been working their new land for four years, and in 1978 José had begun to plant pasture grass again (he had lost pastures upon losing the old homestead). They own no cattle, having sold their small herd in 1974 when they lost their previous place. They also have no work animals. Their children are grown, married, and live in separate homes in Santa Terezinha. The sons and sons-in-law sometimes help José in the fields, but he cannot depend on it.

José, approximately 65 years old, spends most weekdays living and working at the *roça* alone. He commutes between the town and the *roça* by bike, which he also uses to haul cargo. Dona Luisa lives permanently in the house in town and, although she is in her early 60s, works six days a week from dawn to past sundown washing laundry at the river bank; at night she presses the clothes with an iron heated by charcoal. Both stated that the extra income earned by Dona Luisa, approximately 1,300 cruzeiros (US$65) a month, was absolutely essential to the household. They live in a modest brick house and cook on a wood-burning mud stove; their major possessions include two bicycles, a few pieces of homemade furniture, a hand-operated sewing machine, an iron, a watch, and a battery-operated radio.

Though grateful that they received land in the INCRA distribution, they expressed bitterness that they have to begin the work of establishing a farm from scratch once again in their old age. When they first moved to the area in the early 1960s, they purchased the squatters' rights (*posse*) to a homestead on the interfluvial island of Bananal. They worked there for several years but were evicted by the Forest Park authorities. They sold their cattle and again purchased squatters' rights to another homestead near Santa Terezinha, where they worked hard and managed to make some pastures and purchase a few head of cattle. Then in 1974, with the INCRA land distribution, they were required to leave their *roça* near town and begin again at the new lot assigned to them far from town, deep in the forest. Dona Luisa noted sadly that they have never been able to stay in one place long enough to enjoy fruit from the fruit trees they have planted.

The couple also explained that they feel they are too old to do all the work necessary for establishing a farm, which, according to most farm families, takes about ten years. Their adult children are largely unavailable for helping because they have chosen to work for wages in town or at *fazendas*. One son, for example, pumps gasoline at the airstrip for a salary of 1,200 cruzeiros (US$60) a month. Dona Luisa and José constantly urge their children to spend more time farming, but usually these urgings are left unheeded. The grown children do occasionally plant small fields for home consumption needs. But even if they do not plant these subsistence gardens, they usually receive free agricultural staples from their parents. To save face, Dona Luisa and José will sometimes claim that their children work alongside them in the fields and that they are a "united family." However, in less guarded moments

they admit to a great deal of frustration and disappointment that their
children are not more interested in agriculture. The adult children tend
to view farming as a dead-end venture, as backbreaking work with a
very small and unreliable return.

The household economy of Dona Luisa and José illustrates a fairly
typical pattern for the small farming livelihood, even though this family
is slightly better off than others because Dona Luisa works full time
and because they no longer have small children to support. Their income
can be divided into three categories: (1) self-produced provisions, (2)
cash earnings from wages and the sale of produce, and (3) gifts from
relatives and employers. It was impossible to calculate precisely the
amount of farm produce consumed at home because no records are
kept; however, in one month José provided a steady supply of *farinha*,
small amounts of beans, and some rice. The value of farm products
consumed was estimated to be worth 500 cruzeiros (US$25).

The records I kept for the household in October 1978 showed that
Dona Luisa earned 870 cruzeiros (US$43.50) for her laundry work,
somewhat less than normal because of the time she lost to malaria
attacks. José earned 1,521 cruzeiros (US$76.50) from the sale of *farinha*
and two pigs, somewhat higher than normal because of the sale of the
pigs. The estimated value of gifts to the household was 160 cruzeiros
(US$8) worth of items. The total cash income of the family for October
was 2,391 cruzeiros (US$119.50). When the values of farm products
consumed and gifts are added, the household shows a total real income
of roughly 3,051 cruzeiros for the one-month period, or US$152.55.

These figures give an idea of the earning power of a farm household,
although it is important to remember that there can be a lot of variation
from month to month. Dona Luisa's income varies because she can earn
a lot more in the dry season than in the rainy season, when flooding
and cloudy skies make laundry far more difficult and time consuming.
Earnings also fluctuate because of illness. Both Dona Luisa and José
lose many days each year to colds, flu, malaria attacks, and other
infections. They lose income when they stop working. José's earnings
also fluctuate seasonally, and it is not every month that he sells a pig.
One can surmise that José earns more during the rice harvest, but, as
we have seen, farmers' ability to make a profit on rice is far from
assured. The monthly average for farm products alone is more likely
1,000 cruzeiros a month at best, not the 1,521 cruzeiros José made,
including the sale of two pigs. This would average out to 12,000 cruzeiros
or US$600 a year, solely from the farm.

In a town where a new bicycle costs 3,000 cruzeiros (US$150), a
donkey 2,000 (US$100), a set of cooking pots 700 (US$35), and so forth,
one can easily see that farm incomes do not go far. Although poor

TABLE 4.3
Monthly Expenditures of a Typical Farming Household in Santa Terezinha

Item	Price (in U.S. dollars)
Cleaned rice (1 kilo)	.50
Sugar (8 kilos)	4.00
Beef (about 9 kilos)	13.50
Green coffee beans (1¼ kilo)	6.00
Beans (2 kilos)	1.85
Lettuce	.60
Milk (2 liters)	.70
Salt	.45
Tomato paste (1 can)	.30
Black pepper	.20
Kerosene (12 liters)	5.50
Soap	1.25
Cloth	24.25
Scouring pads	.75
Matches	.20
Gifts	5.50
Total Spent on Foodstuffs	28.10
Total Household Maintenance	32.00
Total Expenditures	65.60

Note: The household was composed of only two people, a husband and a wife, and the prices were recorded in October 1978.

families can avoid many expenditures simply by doing without, some purchases are unavoidable. Food and basic necessities such as kerosene and clothing probably account for 90 percent or more of most household budgets. Land taxes on INCRA lots run about 300 cruzeiros (US$15) a year, and many farmers were behind on payments after only four or five years. In addition, most farmers must spend 800–1,000 cruzeiros (US$40–50) to transport their produce from the *roças* into town. Illness, the high costs of drugs and injections, and emergency flights (airplane rentals) to hospitals also often make significant dents in most budgets.

Dona Luisa and José consider themselves to be poor people and feel they cannot afford some of the luxury items desired by frontier families, such as a gas stove, gas lamp, or a kerosene refrigerator. Table 4.3 shows the cash spent by Dona Luisa and José in a one-month period; it also gives an idea of consumption patterns. As can be seen from the table, the couple spent 1,320 cruzeiros (US$66) on food and basic necessities in the month of October. It is also important to note that there were no major nonfood expenditures in this month, such as for tool replacement. If this couple depended exclusively on farm-generated income, they would most likely not have been able to cover their basic cost of living, low as it is—not to mention any additional expenses for emergencies, tool replacement, or savings. Thus, it is only the extra income earned by Dona Luisa that provides this family with a small margin of safety. The couple pointed out many times that, after a lifetime of hard work, they have no rest in their old age.

This case study illustrates that the income level of a farm family is highly precarious, even one that owns 100 hectares of land. Dona Luisa and José manage to create a small surplus because (1) they no longer have children to support, (2) both the husband and wife work full time, and (3) they live modestly and do not purchase luxuries. It is likely that farm families with more dependents, tenants who deliver half the harvest to landowners, and farmers who cannot grow enough to have a surplus for sale or cannot get their produce to market are in far worse shape than the household of Dona Luisa and José. The questionnaire I administered to 44 Santa Terezinha households shows that farm families who depend exclusively on agriculture have cash incomes ranging from zero to about 1,200 cruzeiros (US$60) a month. During the end of the rainy season of 1979, a local man returned from a trip through the forest where he had visited a number of the more isolated farm families. He reported that most of these people had had nothing to eat but *farinha* and boiled green squash for weeks while waiting for the rice harvest.

The insecurity, desperation, and suffering that appear to be an inherent part of the lives of the small farmers in Mato Grosso—and elsewhere in Amazonia as well, for that matter—have become increasingly unattractive to the children of these migratory farmers. In a questionnaire I administered to fourteen schoolchildren, not a single one indicated any interest in pursuing a future occupation in agriculture. Parents, when questioned about their hopes for their children, generally stated that they wanted their children "to learn a profession" so they would "not have to endure this life of suffering." Despite the efforts of the Catholic mission to foster self-help organizations such as the cooperative and to try to protect farmers' rights, young people are increasingly abandoning farming, even when they have access to land through kin. Many of the middle-aged and older couples I interviewed indicated that a lack of family labor was an extremely serious problem for them.

Conclusions

In summary, there are several interlocking factors that contribute to the inability of small farmers to continue farming under current frontier conditions. Most basic is the monopolization of land and other natural resources by the large cattle companies. Moreover, the INCRA land distribution did not change the fundamental situation of increasing concentration of land holdings. Indeed, the majority of migrants to Santa Terezinha were unable to receive INCRA parcels; and, as we have seen in this chapter, even those families that did receive INCRA land have often remained in highly precarious economic situations. Farmers on land held by *posse* or working as tenants are in an even more precarious situation since they are more likely to be forced to leave or to be dispossessed. The increasing unavailability of the natural savannas for grazing cattle has also had a serious negative impact on the farming livelihood because cattle have always been one of the few ways in which the small farmer could save.

The relationship of the region to wider markets has reached stage three, in which there are established links to national markets. However, the main links to outside markets are those of the cattle *fazendas*, which import equipment and foodstuffs and export beef to northern and southern Brazil (and from there into the world market). These types of links have not increased the local or regional market for small farm products. On the contrary, the importation of foodstuffs into the region seriously undermines the market for local products. The cattle *fazendas* have never been interested in purchasing local products. Nor are they at all interested in allowing local farmers to remain as tenants on their vast tracts of land.[11] The rather marginal local market for local goods is relatively unchanged from that which existed in the previous era, despite the population and commercial boom in the town. Increased demands for food products are largely met by importing foodstuffs from southern Brazil. The fragility and marginalization of the local market are further illlustrated by the complete absence of a local *feira* (marketplace), so common in most traditional Brazilian agricultural areas.

The third set of factors that retard and block small farmers are the technological and infrastructural problems previously described. These include (1) lack of access to improvements in agricultural technology and any agricultural expertise, (2) lack of credit for investment, and (3) lack of basic infrastructure such as roads and an adequate transportation system. It seems clear from the previous discussion that neither the very marginalized small farmers nor their fragile self-help organizations are capable of providing the inputs necessary for significant improvements in technology, credit, and infrastructure. Such inputs, one must conclude, could come only from sources outside the region, but there are no current plans to aid the small farmers of northern Mato Grosso. Thus far it has been only the cattle *fazendas* that have qualified for various types of government assistance and development aid.

A number of other factors operate against the small farming livelihood. These include (1) the inability of small farmers to recover from environmental and other disasters, (2) the movement of persons, especially young people, out of agriculture and the concomitant breakdown of the extended family and other forms of cooperative labor, (3) the "pull" effect of short-term benefits perceived in both the movement into other economic activities, such as wage labor or commerce, and the draw of other frontier areas in earlier stages of expansion such as Xinguara and São Felix do Xingu in the state of Pará (Schmink 1980).

In short, the expansion of the economic frontier of the cattle companies into northern Mato Grosso has contributed to the increasing socioeconomic marginalization of the small farmer population of the region. The small farm as a livelihood is swiftly ceasing to be a viable option for most regional inhabitants. Therefore, people continue to seek other ways of making a living. Two of the most important of these are wage labor opportunities and frontier town commerce, both of which are examined in the following chapter.

Notes

1. The timing of the burn must be gauged fairly accurately: Burning too soon leaves a new field open to a rapid invasion of brush, and delaying the burn too long can mean that damp conditions from the rainy season hinder a farmer's ability to obtain a complete burn. Ideally, a farmer burns shortly before the rains begin. Of course, it is sometimes tricky to determine exactly when the winter rains will arrive. The burn simultaneously clears the field and liberates nutrients for the subsequent garden in the form of ashes.

2. Folk beliefs included the idea that anything planted in the time of the new moon would be weak and spindly and bear little fruit. Produce, especially corn and rice, should not be harvested during the new moon either, because it will tend to rot and become pest infested. Wood and thatch for construction should also not be cut at the time of the new moon or it will tend to rot. Almost all Santa Terezhina farmers avoid planting until three days after the beginning of a new moon, and most people prefer to wait at least six days. Manioc, rice, corn, and beans are usually planted during or after the full moon (approximately fourteen days or more into the lunar cycle); it is believed that planting at this time helps to produce healthy, sturdy plants with good yields. However, certain vine plants, such as watermelons, squash, and *maxixe* (gherkins), which should grow long thin vines, are planted shortly after the new moon. These folk beliefs probably have an empirical relationship to variations in the water table and, hence, water content of the land during the lunar cycle. Moon-related beliefs about planting and harvesting have been observed among farmers worldwide.

3. The only type of credit available at the agricultural cooperative is delayed payment for farm implements purchased there. Most other stores in town, however, will give the same kind of credit to reliable customers in good standing.

4. The local farmers reported that weather changes over the previous three years (1976–1978) were causing serious problems for them. In particular, the late arrival of the rains, sometimes a month or two late, and the excessive flooding during the rainy season—as well as the continuation of the rains into months that previously had been dry months—had wreaked havoc with local planting schedules. In 1978, for example, the rain did not arrive until November, and many farmers already had fields full of weak and stunted plants that would never fully recover.

5. The major type used is called *capim colonião (Panicum maimum* var. Colonião). *Capim jaragua (Hyparrhenia rufa* var. Jaragua) and *capim marmelado (Melinis multifolia)*, or molasses grass, were also planted. The price of these special pasture grass seeds in 1978 was about 40 cruzeiros (US$2.00) a kilo.

6. Two types of invading plants cause difficulties for all cattle raisers, large and small: several species of poisonous weeds that kill the cattle that eat them, and a quick-growing wild banana plant with no edible fruit.

7. One highly market-oriented and somewhat exceptional farmer I interviewed reported that he had 60 out of 100 hectares already planted with pasture grass. When asked about the possibility of running out of land to farm, he looked incredulous, waved his arm in a large arc through the air, and declared, "There will always be more land out there." With the increasing difficulty of access to land, rising land prices, and the few remaining squatter areas threatened by the arrival of more companies, this assessment seems somewhat unrealistic.

8. Aside from fruit, people utilize other naturally occurring products in the environment such as palm thatch for roofing material, wood for fires, certain grasses for baskets, and bamboo for fences.

9. Other studies on manioc consumption (see Wagley 1976 and Moran 1974) give similar amounts. Wagley calculated that a family of five consumes more than 2 kilos of *farinha* a day, or somewhat more than 720 kilos a year.

10. Fish are locally classified into two categories: those with scales and those without. Fish without scales, such as catfish, are prohibited to menstruating women for three days and to postpartum women for one year. A number of people interviewed stated that they did not eat fish without scales because they believed they cause diseases.

11. The one exception to this general rule in the area is a Belo Horizonte-based cattle company that is starting a colonization project some 80 kilometers to the northwest of Santa Terezinha. This planned colonization will be located on the planned route of the highway BR 158.

Brazilian government planners, discouraged with the "failure" of the government-sponsored Transamazonian colonization in the early 1970s, are increasingly relying on the private sector to carry out colonization schemes. The advantages of colonization to large enterprises appear to be mainly two. First, since there are legal limits to how much land a company can buy and companies planning colonization are exempt from these restrictions, colonization projects are one way by which companies can arrange to purchase even larger amounts of land. Second, since most of the land acquired by a company speculating in real estate is acquired at a fairly early stage of frontier expansion and at relatively low prices, a company that is willing to wait a longer time for a return on its investment (perhaps ten or twenty years) can realize a good profit from colonization.

The difficulty of obtaining sufficient amounts of land at low prices and of processing the legal titles, which are frequently in dispute for years, discourage companies from attempting colonization. Many companies view their Amazonian investments more in terms of short-term profit. These and other factors contribute to some reluctance on the part of many companies to engage in private colonization.

A former farmer who now runs a small bar.

A woman and her husband quickly construct a wattle-and-daub hut following their arrival in Santa Terezinha after being evicted from a homestead farther south.

This woman and her family are tenant farmers. They transport the manioc roots to their house in town and process them there. She is peeling a manioc root prior to grating and pressing it.

Community groups commonly raise money by holding auctions of contributed foodstuffs such as roast chicken, cake, or passion fruit. This group is making money during the annual celebration of Saint Lazarus's Day to be saved to pay the expenses of next year's celebration.

Fazenda cattle pastures where forests used to be.

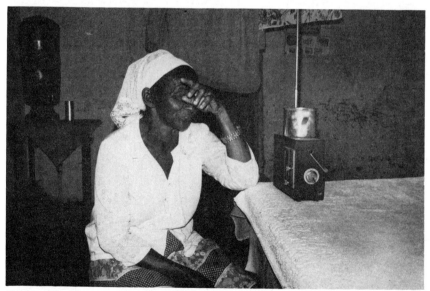

This woman, a farmer and a laundress, is listening to a Vovo Rosa sermon broadcast from São Paulo. The cup of water on the radio will be blessed water after the program and will be used for treating illnesses.

A Santa Terezinha housewife in 1987. Notice (in the rear) the black-and-white television, run on a car battery because the house has no electricity.

This woman is making the lace for hammock fringes. Such crafts are becoming increasingly rare in the frontier, and handcrafted products are replaced by inexpensive industrially produced goods.

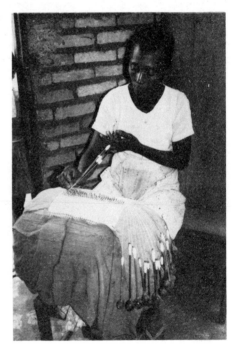

5

Peons and Merchants

Introduction

This chapter examines the other two categories of the folk tripartate division of people into farmers, peons, and merchants. It focuses on the two other main livelihood alternatives available in the frontier: wage labor at the cattle *fazendas* of northern Mato Grosso and commercial activity.

As explained previously, the majority of Santa Terezinha residents, both old-timers and new arrivals, identify themselves as small farmers although many were not actually engaged in farming. For a number of residents, the key issue was access to land. One Santa Terezinha woman explained, "Those who have no land must, of necessity, work for others. We live hunting a job that will provide more money." Another newly arrived former farmer asserted:

> We came to Santa Terezinha because we didn't have a place of our own, and now we really don't have a place! Sure we'd like to have land. Of course we want land. We want it but we don't have any money to buy any. . . . I would prefer the *sertão* (backlands) because one would have land to work, to put in a field and arrange one's life. But we don't have land, so here we stay.

Many former farmers end up working for the cattle ranches, usually as peons on work crews for *gatos*.[1] Most people perceive this kind of work as less a choice than as a last resort for desperate people. For example, another former farmer explained:

> We live running from one cattle *fazenda* to another, and they do with us what they want. We are working for free! I'm unable to find any way out of this fix. I have no resources. If only I had a plot of land and could arrange a bank to help finance my agriculture, I would plant coffee, corn, beans, and soy beans. But I have nothing and live under five palm fronds,

without pleasure in life, without resources. Everything is too expensive
and my money disappears.

Within this context, many attempt to use commerce as a third alternative
and possible escape from transience and poverty. Tiny business enterprises
from kiosks, which sell *cafezinhos*[2] and *cachaça*, to store fronts with one
plank and a pile of tinned goods abound in Santa Terezinha. To become
a successful or "strong" merchant is a frequently mentioned aspiration.

This chapter is divided into two sections, each dealing with a livelihood
option. It completes the picture of the three main kinds of work available
in the frontier. Variations in economic strategies and other survival
techniques—such as diversification, intensification, and mutual aid—
will be explored in Chapter 6.

Wage Labor

The expansion of the cattle *fazendas* into northern Mato Grosso since
the mid-1960s was described in a previous chapter. Most of these *fazendas*
are owned and operated by national and multinational corporations (e.g.,
Volkswagen) with headquarters in either São Paulo or Belo Horizonte.
The ranches are run locally by managers. Private airplanes, usually
company owned and with constant radio communication, enable ranch
managers to maintain continual contact with both the more remote
outposts of a ranch and the usually southern Brazilian corporate headquarters. Higher-echelon management, such as directors and board
members, periodically fly out to the *fazendas* for inspections and meetings.

The cattle *fazendas* try to establish completely autonomous facilities
within the region. One goal is to organize and control the importing
of supplies into the region. For example, CODEARA's store in Santa
Terezinha, which has its own barge system, provides supplies for a
number of companies. *Fazendas* also set up their own "support sectors."
CODEARA, which was one of the older ranches in the region, has its
own airstrip and planes, a sawmill, a carpentry shop, a machine shop,
generators, and supply depots.

There is generally a lot of cooperation between *fazendas*. More established ranches will frequently help out other companies beginning
operations—for example, with loans of equipment or sales of cattle.
However, the *fazendas* do not extend the same kind of cooperation to
frontier settlements, and specifically not to Santa Terezinha because of
its past history of conflict with CODEARA. The sale of CODEARA
lumber, beef, or milk to noncompany persons is strictly prohibited and
punishable by dismissal. Company policy also forbids the loan or sale
of equipment, machine parts, or fuel to noncompany persons. The *fazendas*

justify this policy by asserting that they do not produce enough to have surplus to sell in town and that, in any case, it is not profitable. It is thus that the highly ironic situation of a six-month beef shortage in Santa Terezinha could have occurred in a region dedicated to the production of beef cattle.

The cattle-company managers I interviewed tended to view Santa Terezinha as a backward little town, best known for its whore houses and past history of conflict with CODEARA. *Fazenda* managers generally try to avoid contact with the town or townspeople. They are frequently unaware of local conditions and events. At the same time, the *fazendas* are actively engaged in fencing and guarding their land against invasions by squatters. The *fazendas* and the town constitute almost two entirely different worlds. The major point of intersection between them, apart from land conflicts, results from the labor requirements of the *fazendas*.

Fazendas create pasture in almost the same manner as do the small farmers, although they do it on a much larger scale. Forests are cut, dried, and burned and pasture grass is planted in an area that is then fenced. It is in these forest-clearing operations, which can be carried out only during the dry season, that the *fazendas* have need of large numbers of laborers. Ranches have not yet been able to substitute machinery for manual labor in the deforestation process. Men are also employed, though in much smaller numbers, in pasture maintenance, fence construction, and other tasks.

The cattle *fazendas* obtain labor in two very distinct ways: (1) by direct employment, and (2) by so-called indirect employment. Direct employees are those who are directly hired by the ranch. They are always relatively few in number and consist of management staff and certain specialized workers such as mechanics, truck drivers, cowboys, and office clerks. Although no employees have any job security, direct employees are eligible for benefits as specified in Brazilian labor law. The companies in the region, however, vary quite a bit in their compliance with legal requirements. CODEARA, an older ranch already realizing a profit, provides housing, pumped water, nightly electricity, milk, and inexpensive beef to all its employees above a certain level. Management staff also receive an extra bonus or "hardship pay" for being assigned to such a remote location. Lower-level employees also receive some of the aforementioned benefits. Other ranches in the region, however, provide fewer benefits; informants claimed that some *fazendas* in the region provide none at all.

The majority of the *fazenda* labor force, however, is hired indirectly by labor contractors (*empreiteiros*), similar to crew leaders for migrant farm workers in the United States (Friedland and Nelkin 1971; Goldfarb 1981). The system works as follows. A *fazenda* makes an individual contract with a crew leader to do a certain job in a specific amount of time for a set price. The leader then rounds up his own group of workers, usually referred to as peons (*peãos*). These workers are considered to be employees of the crew leader rather than of the ranch, thus facilitating the *fazendas'* avoidance of protective labor regulations. The crew leaders also "sell" services and often provide transportation to the work site, temporary housing, tools, medicine, and food to workers—charged against their future wages. When a job is completed, workers receive their *saldo* (remaining pay) after the debts to the crew leader have been subtracted. Needless to say, the prices charged for such services are quite high.

The advantages of this indirect labor recruitment system to the *fazendas* are two. First, it enables ranches to avoid compliance with laws and regulations designed to protect rural workers.[3] The ranches do not consider either the crew leaders or their work crews to be true employees of the company. A second important advantage to the *fazendas* is that they entail no further commitment to the workers for future employment. Since the main requirements of the ranch are seasonal and occur during the dry season, the contracting system enables them to shed excess labor during the rainy season. The peons, hired by the crew leader to do only a specific job, have no legal claims on the *fazenda*. In short, this system enables the *fazendas* to obtain large amounts of relatively cheap labor during the season of high demand without incurring any continuing commitment or legal obligations to the workers.

Figure 5.1 shows the organization chart of CODEARA as provided by its resident manager. It appears to be fairly representative of the way cattle *fazendas* in the region are organized, except that the newer ranches do not have support sectors as fully developed. As can be seen from the chart, the only employees of the contract division are the men who supervise the contracts. Crew leaders and their peons are not integrated into the operation.

The pay scale for peons is quite low. It tends to be between 50 and 60 cruzeiros a day, which comes to approximately 1,200 cruzeiros a month or US$60. In fact, the actual wages earned are usually lower than this because from these figures must be subtracted the debts for food, housing, tools, and so forth. According to the workers I interviewed, labor contractors varied in their honesty and treatment of workers. The better crew leaders become known and tend to recruit workers more easily. Sometimes, however, the crew leaders renege entirely on their payments to workers. This may happen when a company delays its payment to the leader or when a leader miscalculates on the costs of a job. A peon waiting for payment or cheated out of his wages has very little recourse.

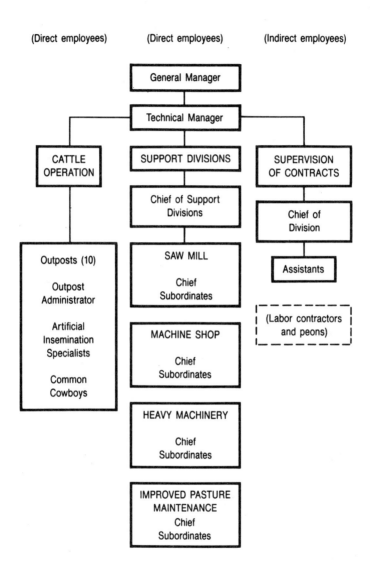

(Direct employees)   (Direct employees)   (Indirect employees)

General Manager

Technical Manager

CATTLE OPERATION

SUPPORT DIVISIONS

SUPERVISION OF CONTRACTS

Chief of Support Divisions

Chief of Division

Outposts (10)

Outpost Administrator

Artificial Insemination Specialists

Common Cowboys

SAW MILL

Chief Subordinates

Assistants

(Labor contractors and peons)

MACHINE SHOP

Chief Subordinates

HEAVY MACHINERY

Chief Subordinates

IMPROVED PASTURE MAINTENANCE
Chief Subordinates

FIGURE 5.1 Organizational Chart of the Codeara Ranch Company, Santa Terezinha (1978–1979)

In the early days after the arrival of the cattle *fazendas* in northern Mato Grosso, during the 1960s and early 1970s, the abuses of the labor contracting system could be seen in their most extreme form. The relatively low population density of the region, together with the local farmers' antipathy toward working for the ranches, forced the *fazendas* to arrange for labor to be imported from other regions of Brazil. Recruiters were sent out to lure workers to Mato Grosso. Judith Shapiro (1967) describes the situation in Santa Terezinha at this time as follows:

> It is the "empreiteiro" (contractor) who has the contract. . . . The workers themselves cannot read and have no individual written agreement as to what is expected of them and what they may expect. Thus, it is very common for workers to be lured from their homelands by "empreiteiros" promising a situation quite different from the one the worker will actually encounter. Such was the case in Santa Terezinha. Some workers had been promised a daily salary of 3,00 cruzeiros, in addition to food, shelter, and tools, which were to be supplied by the company. They were told that medical attention would be provided for them free of charge. Thus, many left work in their own state of Maranhão in the hopes of finding something better in Santa Terezinha. What they found was something a good deal worse: out of this daily wage of 3,00 cruzeiros (a little over a dollar) was to come not only the price of food, but that of the very tools given to the men to do the company's work. No shelters were provided; peons slept out in the open, hanging their hammocks from trees. . . . And the only medical attention for miles around was provided by the priest's nurse. The peons were encouraged to buy on credit from the company store. . . . Thus, most found that, rather than earning money, they were becoming progressively indebted to the company. . . . Even the poor settlers of Santa Terezinha, themselves extremely poor and accustomed to a difficult life, were moved by the spectacle of misery, exhaustion and undernourishment presented by these peons.
>
> Seeing that they had been misled by the "empreiteiros," many peons tried to get away. . . . The peons, however, were not permitted to leave. The company and the "empreiteiros" claimed that there were contracts which committed them to work until a certain date. . . . The company also claimed that the workers could not leave since they were in debt to the company store, which in many cases was true. . . .
>
> Unable to leave freely, the peons began to find ways to escape. In this, they were aided by the local settlers. Indians also participated in this underground railroad.

One peon interviewed in 1979 related the following brief account of how he came to Mato Grosso in 1965. Ademar was born in a German-Brazilian family in the state of Paraná. His parents were killed in a car accident, and he was raised by relatives. He worked various jobs, including that of laborer at a Paraná coffee plantation in 1965. It was there that he began to hear talk about the "good working conditions" in northern Mato Grosso.

Ademar remembered that the crew leader told the men that if they joined the work gang they would receive high wages and that good housing, medical care, and even pool halls would be provided for the workers at the job location. So Ademar left Paraná and traveled with a work crew for days on trucks and boats. He recalled his surprise upon arriving at the work site in Mato Grosso to find that there was nothing there, not even crude shelters for sleeping. Soon the men discovered that they had been deceived. They were told that they were now in debt to the crew leader for their travel expenses and tools. For Ademar this was the beginning of several years of working as a peon in northern Mato Grosso.

Many times during the years he worked in labor crews, he recalled, the men were not paid at all. They were often guarded by gunmen to prevent escape. Many of his fellow workers died, he said, mostly from malaria. Ademar noted that the worst abuses occurred between 1965 and 1970.[4] When asked why he never returned to southern Brazil, he explained that he had never been able to save enough money for the trip and that, in any case, he was too ashamed to return to his relatives and have them see that he was a "broken man."

Many of the peons are single men with no family or relatives nearby. At the end of a job, the workers usually come to frontier settlements like Santa Terezinha, where they stay in boarding houses and sometimes carouse in the red light district. It is not unusual to see broke peons who, after a spree, are selling their last possessions in the street, perhaps a watch or a guitar, to get together some money to tide them over until their next job. The cabaret, known for its sexually transmitted diseases, robberies, and drunken brawls, functions as a short reprieve from the drudgery of the men's usual routines.

More permanent local residents tend to view peons as degraded human beings; although many households contain members who periodically work at the cattle fazendas, they will sometimes deny or try to minimize their connection to ranch employment. The fathers and sons of most Santa Terezinha farm households periodically work for wages, usually as peons in work crews. Landless families, too, are especially likely to seek fazenda employment. Local women find jobs as laundresses, cooks, and domestics at fazenda headquarters and other work sites.

Although the majority of local families had at least one member who sometimes worked at cattle fazendas, the more permanent residents continued to make a distinction between "us" and "them" (peons and outsiders). Single male peons are clearly outsiders and tend to remain so unless they marry a local girl. Peons who arrive in town with their families are somewhat more difficult to classify because, if they remain in town for a long enough time (usually a year), they usually manage to find other livelihood opportunities and become more integrated into the community. The settling down of peon families is relatively rare, however, because the majority are compelled to take another job, usually at a more distant ranch, and often the whole family will move to the work site.

There was a constant movement of people in and out of Santa Terezinha, a flux related to the "boom town" characteristics of the frontier community. As I conducted surveys in the back streets of town, I often encountered the families of peons who had settled temporarily in Santa Terezinha while their menfolk worked at a nearby ranch. Most of these more transient families had backgrounds and histories almost identical to those of the local residents, but they had lost access to land, often by eviction, and were on a constant round of travel from one company job to another. Left alone in town, the wives usually found it extremely difficult to integrate themselves into town life. Most commented to me that the store owners were reluctant to give them credit. They often felt they were paying too much rent for their houses, and they often stated that the people of Santa Terezinha were unfriendly. I tried many times to conduct follow-up case histories of the peon families I encountered during survey work; but in almost every case, when I returned to visit them, they would be gone. Sometimes even the next-door neighbors did not know where they had gone to.

Santa Terezinha residents understand the desperation and misery of these uprooted families, but they are somewhat suspicious of temporary people and new arrivals. Store owners are afraid that the peon families will move away without paying off their accounts. Temporary people are also somewhat immune from the coercive power of community opinion and gossip. And the mere fact of being identified as peons usually implies that they are judged as somewhat morally deficient. It follows that the more temporary households are those most often accused of chicken theft and other antisocial behavior. Local people, who often share access to farmland with their neighbors, are usually unwilling to allow "strangers" to work on their land in any capacity.

Local people do not always clearly distinguish between the various types and levels of *fazenda* employment; indeed, they tend to call all ranch workers peons. The image of the "typical peon" is quite negative. Peons are thought to be spendthrifts who live for today and neglect their social and familial duties. Local families often try to block the marriage of their daughters to ranch workers because they think that peons are unreliable husbands and fear that their daughters will either be abandoned or leave with their husbands for a life of constant roaming from one job to the next. Another point held against peons by the locals is that although the peons often come from farm families themselves, they often lack experience with agriculture and tend to have negative perceptions of farming. Because of parental disapproval of husband choices, many marriages are carried out by elopement.

Local families are quite ambivalent when their menfolk, and especially their sons, go off to work at the cattle *fazendas*. They usually need the cash, but they are fearful that the sons will "become peons" in lifestyle and character. And as frequently happens, the sons of local households, freed suddenly from parental authority and familial duties, away from local gossip, and earning money for the first time in their lives, do rebel against resuming their former roles and obligations. Sometimes they refuse to turn over their ranch earnings to the household, and they may begin spending time in the *cabaret* with other peons. One farm family I often visited was always very embarrassed when their son and son-in-law were home from a ranch job. The afternoon interviews were always punctuated by the groans and retching of the young men who had returned home drunk. There was always a lot of tension in the house during these times. There were arguments about how the young men's earnings should be spent. The parents were also upset by the fact that neither young man put in any time working at the *roça*.

Despite the predominance of the lowly and disadvantageous peon jobs, many young men feel that their best chance for upward mobility lies with cattle *fazenda* employment. One method attempted by many is to try and become a crew leader. There are, however, a number of obstacles in the way of becoming a successful contractor. First, most of the companies give most of their contract work to their regular *gatos;* the established crew leaders have a near monopoly over the better jobs. Second, many fail as crew leaders because they lack the necessary literacy, accounting, and political skills necessary for successful negotiation with the ranches. They need to understand the written contracts and also be able to maintain cooperative relations with company management. Finally, to be a *gato* has negative connotations since it is common knowledge that *gatos* make their money exploiting peons.

Another goal of aspiring workers is to become a direct employee of a *fazenda*. This achievement, while difficult to accomplish, can bring better wages and company benefits. Most of the more desirable jobs, however, require skills and experience, which most men lack. Furthermore, the number of direct employees is always relatively small and most openings occur at the lower occupational levels, such as openings for manual laborers at construction sites or for cooks—positions that are only marginally better than peon-level jobs. Another problem for workers

TABLE 5.1
Monthly Wages at the Codeara Ranch Company

Type of Worker	Monthly Wages (in U.S. dollars)
Administration:	
Manager (Agronomist)	3,500
Manager (Veterinarian)	1,500
Resident Manager	1,000
Accountant	800
Skilled and Unskilled Labor:	
Auto Mechanic	250
Heavy Machine Operator	175
Skilled Saw Mill Operator	150
Driver	120
Experienced Cowboy	87
Manual Laborer (direct)	67
Domestic Worker	50
Office Worker	40

is that because Brazilian labor legislation stipulates that employees receive more benefits for each year worked, many companies periodically fire their employees to prevent them from accruing seniority. In addition, as ranch employees can be fired at any time, anyone thought to be a troublemaker may stand to lose his job.

Table 5.1 shows the average monthly wages of various occupational categories at CODEARA ranch, as provided by the ranch manager. When compared to informants' accounts of wages paid at other ranches, the CODEARA pay looks somewhat higher than average. The monthly salary is generally above the Mato Grosso minimum monthly salary of 1,250 cruzeiros (US$62.50), and workers receive some housing and other benefits. Direct employment at CODEARA can certainly appear to be a step up for many young men.

Very few men, or women, interviewed in Santa Terezinha have managed to secure direct employment with cattle *fazendas*. When they have done so, the employment was usually short term. The lower-level occupations generally provide an average income of 1,200–3,000 cruzeiros (US$60–150) a month; however, since men cannot farm, must purchase food, and frequently have a family to support, this income does not go far. Local men with direct employment at the *fazendas* who live in town do not live significantly better than their neighbors, although their houses do more often contain items such as radios and gas stoves. While the number who secure direct employment remains small, many young people are motivated to try to secure this type of employment.

In sum, the majority of employment opportunities at the cattle *fazendas* throughout northern Mato Grosso continue to be the relatively poorly paid positions of peons on work crews. Younger men entering the region and local people periodically work as peons, primarily during the dry season, to augment their cash incomes. Job security, benefits, and health services are inaccessible to the majority of the ranch labor force. Economic mobility, either by becoming a crew leader or by securing a more permanent position at the company, is relatively rare since the number of openings are few and require more skills. The fact that some advancement opportunities exist, and that wages paid at some ranches are above the minimum wage, motivates and attracts younger people disenchanted with farming to try their luck at the cattle *fazendas*.

Commerce

To become a merchant is the third main livelihood alternative in Santa Terezinha and the one that carries the most prestige. There are approximately eighty-eight commercial ventures in the frontier town. As predicted by Bryan Roberts (1976:106), the town commerce appears to have evolved to meet two major needs related to the presence of the cattle *fazendas*: (1) It serves as a commercial outlet for the sale of imported goods (from southern Brazil), and (2) it provides temporary accommodations for rural migrants. And, indeed, the majority of Santa Terezinha commerce is in the form of stores that sell imported commodities, boarding housing where transients can stay, or bars and places where men seek entertainment. The orientation of the town commerce toward ranch workers is further illustrated by the absence of many businesses normally found in a typical Brazilian town. For example, Santa Terezinha has no restaurants, bakeries, beauty parlors, or car repair shops.

The dependence of the town commerce on cash generated by ranch employment is further underscored by what occurs during the rainy season, when ranches drastically cut back their labor forces. The repercussions in town include a virtual closing down of the *cabaret*, and many bars shut for the season. Money becomes tight and merchants begin to remind their customers of long overdue accounts and sometimes cancel credit. There is a local saying about the seasonality of money: "Cash here has its season, just like oranges or mangoes."

The small farmers of the region never provided much impetus to commercial development. Wagley (1977) reported that in the 1940s the town had only two or three small stores. The sparce population was mostly served by itinerant river traders. The lack of success of the agricultural cooperative is also partly due to low economic density. Originally designed to help provide lower-cost goods, the cooperative today cannot compete with the lower prices offered at the CODEARA store. And although they purchase goods, the small farmers are probably the least important customers of town commerce.

The rapid growth of the town—from 40 houses in 1940, to 140 in 1967, to 380 in 1978—is causally linked to the activity of the *fazendas* in the region. Migrants, evicted from locations within the region by ranches or Forest Park agents, or entering the region seeking land and/ or jobs, continue to arrive in Santa Terezinha. The services and facilities in town, such as the school and rudimentary medical services, also attract people. The growth of the town in turn helps to support the commercial activity. The more people there are who do not grow food, the more there are who will buy imported foodstuffs at the local stores.

Although many people begin small commercial ventures in Santa Terezinha—usually a tiny combination bar and store with a minimal stock of tinned food—most of these establishments are very precarious operations with a tendency to fail. The most frequent response to the question of where the money had gone from the sale of some cattle or a piece of land was that "We used the money to start a shop, but it failed." For a number of reasons, it is not easy to develop a successful commercial venture in Santa Terezinha.

Some of the major problems encountered by merchants in Santa Terezinha include (1) lack of investment capital, (2) lack of direct access to wholesale goods, (3) inability either to extend sufficient credit to attract customers or to withstand the cash shortages of the rainy season, (4) lack of literacy skills and commercial experience, and (5) inability to compete with the many other businesses of the same type in town. Furthermore, anyone opening a business is supposed to secure a permit from the state tax collector and pay taxes on the volume of businesses transacted. Taxes are also paid on all commodities brought in from other states, except by cattle ranches exempted under fiscal incentives.

The more successful, "stronger" local merchants periodically travel to Goiania in the neighboring state of Goiás, where they purchase goods wholesale and supervise the transportation back to Santa Terezinha. As smaller operations usually cannot make these expensive trips, they are compelled to purchase their stock from the larger merchants at a markup. To make a profit, these smaller merchants must then charge a higher price. So the largest stores usually have the lowest prices. Small stores try to compete in terms of convenience, location, and personal relationships with customers. They also try to compete by extending credit to their customers; but, as might be expected, smaller stores are hardly in a position to carry outstanding debt loads. A good number of the smaller merchants manage to keep their stores going by engaging in other economic activities as well. It is not uncommon, for example, to find wives or daughters running the store while the menfolk are away working other jobs.

Only about ten out of the eighty-eight businesses in town are relatively large and successful. Discounting organizational operations—the cooperative and the ranch store—there are about four "strong" stores. The owners of these, along with the sheriff, soldiers, and school teachers, are part of the local elite. All of the more successful merchants have invested in other ventures. They own land nearby and often have herds of cattle on Bananal. They are the owners of most of the local transportation, including vehicles and boats. The strong merchants also generally invest in other commercial ventures in town, opening additional bars or stores, or buying and renting town lots and houses.

Senhor Sebastião is an old-timer in the region and one of the most successful merchants in town. He came originally from northeastern Brazil and as a young man worked many places throughout Mato Grosso and Pará. He has been a farmer, a tenant, a nut gatherer, and a miner and trader in precious minerals and gems. A man of great enterprise, he had started businesses on several occasions; but his really big start came when he married a woman who had inherited a herd of several hundred cattle. Senhor Sebastião used the capital from the sale of the cattle to start a dry goods store in Santa Terezinha. He was one of the first merchants to realize that buying goods oneself directly in Goiania eliminated the middlemen, improved the quality control, and lowered the price.

Today Senhor Sebastião runs the largest dry goods store, a bar, and a dance hall in the *cabaret*. He owns a truck, a motor boat, and the largest of the three electric generators in town. He also owns a number of town properties, houses that he rents to tenants, and a large herd of cattle located illegally in the Forest Park on Bananal. It was difficult to ascertain his holdings because he refused to provide information on his enterprises. Although commonly acknowledged to be one of the richest men in town, Senhor Sebastião is universally disliked because he is unscrupulous and exploitative. He takes advantage of local people, and he always drives hard bargains.

The markup on the prices of most goods sold in Santa Terezinha is between 30 to 150 percent of the price in southern Brazilian urban centers. A certain portion of this, perhaps 25 percent, is due to the cost of transportation and interstate taxes, but the remaining portion appears to be profit. Merchants say that their prices are high because of (1) transportation costs, (2) the supposedly high rate of loss from people reneging on debts, and (3) inflation. Despite these factors, the most powerful merchants apparently make significant profits in the frontier town.

Competition between stores causes merchants to lower prices, usually on a couple of items at a time. In order to take advantage of such "specials," however, a customer would have to walk all over town comparison-shopping and then make many small purchases in various stores. Most local people do not take the time to comparison-shop. More important, many people give most of their business to one store so as to establish a more personal relationship with the merchant and obtain credit. A steady customer can usually count on as much as 300 to 400 cruzeiros worth of credit extended over several months. Given the insecurity of most households' incomes and the seasonality of ranch employment, the ability to shop on credit is often vital to the survival of the household.

The merchants I interviewed could not give a systematic account of the way they made decisions about granting credit to customers. It was quite clear, however, that merchants prefer more permanent residents and dislike taking risks on transients. Thus, relative strangers in town, such as peons awaiting payment or a farm family recently evicted from a forest homestead, have serious problems obtaining even a small amount of local credit.

The two stores with the lowest prices, the cooperative and the CODEARA store, operate mainly on a cash-and-carry basis; therefore, many people cannot take advantage of these lower prices. The cooperative does offer a thirty-day credit period to members and a 10 percent discount on a number of essential commodities; however, the decreasing membership in the cooperative means that fewer and fewer people can use this service. Even the many families who do belong to the cooperative do much of their shopping elsewhere because of personal relationships with other merchants.

To *tocar comercio*, or "engage in business," is the often-mentioned dream of parents for their children or themselves. People hope to have a store where they can make an adequate living without backbreaking labor, with plenty of leisure time in which to talk to customers and sit in chairs in the shade out front. This white-collar goal and lifestyle is a dream for many in Santa Terezinha and Brazil generally (Harris 1971). In response to my repeated questions to adults and children about the most desirable occupation, commerce was always selected. Another frequently mentioned point was that it is considered far better to work for oneself than for others.

People admire the lifestyles of their neighbors who have become rather successful merchants. The more prosperous merchants have better houses, gas stoves, kerosine refrigerators, radios, store-bought furniture, and expensive giant blown-up photographs of their children on the walls of the parlor. If the business is really thriving, the merchant often has a vehicle, land, cattle, and other items of prestige and wealth. Merchants who farm or have tenants, for example, can sometimes circumvent the problems that plague small farmers. They can transport their produce, and they can afford to wait to sell their rice until the price rises. With such a model of success in front of them, it is no wonder that so many frontier people try to get started in commerce.

Little bars, tiny stores, and thatch-covered dance halls have sprung up all over town. Many of these are precarious enterprises run by women whose husbands are away working or who have been abandoned. Most of these smaller businesses do not generate much income, averaging between 500 and 4,000 cruzeiros a month, with major fluctuations depending on the season. Although many of these businesses are marginal, they are often continued not only because the small additional income is deemed worthwhile but also because even the smallest bar or kiosk gives a person a right to call himself or herself a "merchant."

As the *cabaret* is located behind the several small hills, it is somewhat separated from the town proper. It contains a variety of establishments, from tiny bars to large dance halls and boarding houses for prostitutes. Although there is some shame involved in running a *cabaret* business, many try it because there is a lot of cash flowing through the area when ranch workers are paid. I interviewed a number of red light district merchants. One woman ran a bar with a pool table; her husband had abandoned her, and she was supporting her small children. Another woman ran a small bar at night while her husband was away working at the *fazendas*. This woman also did laundry work during the day. A brothel owner came from a family of farmers who had been evicted from their land and arrived in the region too late to qualify for the INCRA land distribution. Still another bar owner in the district was an elderly farmer who owned an INCRA lot but decided to augment his farm income. This older man had recently begun a common-law marriage with an ex-prostitute some thirty years his junior, and she ran the bar while he farmed.

The prostitutes are usually younger women between 15 and 30 years old. The most common story recounted by these women was that they had been dishonored, rejected by their families, and forced to enter the "free life." Apparently, they spend between six months and a year in various towns and cities, and are constantly on the move between red light districts in the states of Maranhão, Pará, Goiás, and Mato Grosso. In Santa Terezinha, the prostitutes live either in the district or in a house in town; most live in the district. In the *cabaret*, the prostitutes are apparently utilized primarily by the male owners of dance halls to encourage customers to consume alcohol and snacks. My informants indicated that most profits were made from refreshments. They explained that the prostitutes set their own prices for sex and do not deliver a portion of their earnings. However, most prostitutes pay between 800 and 2,000 cruzeiros a month for their room and board.

Conclusions

This chapter has demonstrated some important aspects of livelihood options in the frontier. The majority of wage labor opportunities are at the cattle *fazendas*. Most workers participate as peons—temporary, lowly paid, manual laborers with no job security or employment benefits. As persons and families detached from agriculture are dependent on expensive imported foodstuffs, the real income or earning power of most workers remains quite low. Fully proletarianized people are generally on an endless round of migration between short-term jobs at ranches in northern Mato Grosso and southern Pará. Some advancement opportunities—primarily for crew leaders and more skilled workers—exist at the companies; these and the cash earnings attract many young adults. Older people are usually extremely wary of full-time participation in the labor market and try to convince their children to remain in agriculture or enter commerce.

Commerce, oriented toward the dynamics of the cattle *fazendas*, is the main route available for upward mobility. But almost all store owners, large and small, engage in other economic activities as well. Small owners must work at other jobs to make ends meet, and large owners are interested in diversifying their enterprises. Most merchants in Santa Terezinha have come to realize that the boom for town commerce may be short-lived. Upon completion of highway BR 158, located some 100 kilometers to the west of town, it is likely that goods will begin to move on the road system rather than on the river. The center of activities will shift to the towns and villages located along the new road. Many of the wealthier merchants have already bought land in the vicinity of the new road.

In general, one can state that small farming is on the decline in Santa Terezinha. Increasing numbers of people are either becoming wage laborers or entering commerce. In most cases, however, neither option offers a significant improvement of the economic situation of the household. Most frontier households must find other ways to ensure basic subsistence. These other ways, which I call "survival strategies," are the subject of the next chapter.

Notes

1. As earlier noted, *gato* literally translates as "cat" but means a labor contractor or crew leader in local slang.

2. A *cafezinho* is espresso coffee, usually served already sweetened.

3. In his review article on temporary labor in Brazilian agriculture, Saint (1981) makes the same point regarding Brazil as a whole: that increased enforcement of labor legislation designed to protect rural workers has contributed to an increase in the use of temporary workers who are not considered employees and, hence, are not protected by the laws. Saint also notes that in the situation of labor contracting, it is the crew leader who is responsible under the law for the welfare of the workers, but that leaders frequently do not comply with regulations.

4. Ademar claimed that in 1970 the federal government conducted an investigation into the abuses of the labor contracting system in northern Mato Grosso, and that after this investigation companies became more careful about the treatment of workers. I have been unable to find any documentation of this federal action. A slight betterment of the condition of the workers might have resulted from the increased immigration into the region. Given this greater abundance of available labor, companies and crew leaders did not need to resort to debt peonage to obtain and hold onto workers.

6

Survival Strategies

Introduction

This chapter focuses on household survival strategies in the frontier community of Santa Terezinha, Mato Grosso. *Survival strategies* is a term distilled from expressions employed by others, including Larissa Lomnitz's (1976:141) "survival mechanisms used by marginals," Bryan Roberts (1976:114) "informal economy," and Anibal Quijano's (1970:18) "survival structures." It is used here to refer to the patterned activities in which households engage, designed to obtain livelihood and improve social and economic conditions. Since the major livelihood options have already been delineated in Chapters 4 and 5, this chapter focuses on the more indirect, complex, and interstitial kinds of activities not always identified directly as livelihood activities. These include in-migration, intensification and diversification of household labor, mutual aid and patron-client relationships, local organizations, and out-migration.

The term *survival* is specifically used to connote a struggle against almost overwhelming odds. Constraints, including eviction, lack of access to land, frequent illness, limited job opportunities, inadequate infrastructure, little credit, and other factors help to stack the deck against the poor of Amazonia, both the longer-time inhabitants and the more recent arrivals. As noted previously, most spontaneous colonizations such as Santa Terezinha do not usually receive any private or public development support. At the same time, the large-scale cattle ranches have received considerable support such as fiscal incentives.

Within this difficult context, small farmer migrants to Amazonia attempt not only to secure a minimal livelihood but also try to get ahead. In other words, despite many feelings of hopelessness and despair, they do not give up. A common expression often heard in response to the normal greeting query of "How are you?" was *"aqui tudo bom e nada presta,"* which can be translated as "Here everything is great but nothing at all works out right." Nonetheless, people continue to try to work things out, seeking in a variety of ways a betterment of their situations that they sometimes suspect will remain beyond their reach.

Sometimes their efforts involve the sacrifice of short-term benefits for long-term goals. This is illustrated by the farmer who gave up farming his distant lot and moved to town where he worked odd jobs to enable his children to attend the Santa Terezinha elementary school. More often than not, however, pressing subsistence requirements compel families to favor short-term benefits over long-term considerations. Planning for the future is often highly problematic.

The survival strategies presented in this chapter represent a medium level of analysis and abstraction. In other words, while they are sometimes partly described as such by informants, they are also patterns identified by an anthropologist after numerous interviews and observations. These strategies, by no means completely exhaustive in scope, reflect both what people say they do and what they actually do, both what people say they want and what their actions indicate about their goals and objectives. They are an attempt to summarize and make more comprehensible the patterned behaviors of Amazonian migrants in the context of frontier expansion.

In-migration as a Survival Strategy

To understand the dynamics of rural-rural migration in Amazonia, the reader may find it instructive to consider Stanley H. Brandes's (1975:14–15) distinction between "institutional" and "transformational" migration. Institutional migration, according to Brandes, may be thought of in terms of traditional migration patterns—more or less functional solutions worked out to long-standing problems. For example, in a number of countries the out-migration of extra sons because of land scarcity and inheritance patterns contributes to the maintenance of the old, established order of life in the countryside (e.g., Arensberg and Kimball 1968; Friedl 1962; Lopreato 1967). Transformational migration, however, is linked to economic and social changes in a region or a country and, as the name implies, tends to radically transform both the distribution of people and traditional livelihoods. It implies a fundamental change from one way of life to another, for both the actors and the system.

There are many indications that much of the population movement in Amazonia can be legitimately classified as transformational migration. Agricultural economist Ernest Feder (1971:35–36) provides the following description:

One of the telling manifestations of rural unemployment is the forced geographic mobility of the peasantry. This is the outward sign of a deep-seated malaise in rural Latin America, rather than evidence of a dynamic peasantry attempting to improve its economic and social status. By and large, farm people do not wander around in search of better jobs than the ones they have—they just look for jobs. . . . But not all migration within rural areas is seasonal. A good-sized proportion of the labor force is constantly moving from farm to farm, as "professional migrants." Their numbers are probably not recorded in any census or other statistics. . . . All these population movements testify to a continuous, large-scale "milling around" of poor farm people in search of jobs or land, and involve annually several million people in the hemisphere—no doubt the greatest migratory movement in all history. Most people are unaware of this silent march of the poor.

Ultimately, larger policies and forces, often unknown to the migrant, shape and condition this "milling around" in the countryside.[1] My investigation, however, focused on another level of analysis: the migrants' perceptions of their reasons for moving. It is from this vantage point, the migrants' perspective, that in-migration into the Santa Terezinha area may be viewed as a survival strategy.

The detailed migration history data that I collected from Santa Terezinha households showed a pattern of westward movement.[2] The majority of all moves described were between rural locations, and only a very few people interviewed had spent time in provincial or capital cities.[3] Tabulations on the 33 complete migration histories showed that 72 percent (24) of the families had moved on the average of between four and six times previously.

An especially consistent pattern emerged regarding the movement of families into Goiás and from there to Mato Grosso. While only 27 percent of the sample were born in Goiás, 78 percent had lived there. The average amount of time spent in Goiás was 13.8 years. The interfluvial island of Bananal with its savannas for cattle and gallery forests for farming attracted many migrants. Twenty-seven percent of the sample reported having lived on Bananal; the average stay there was six and a half years.

The migration histories support Feder's characterization of the rural migrants as primarily farmers. Ninety-seven percent of my sample had farmed previously, usually in more than one location. Sixty-seven percent mentioned, often reluctantly, periods of employment at cattle *fazendas*. Table 6.1 shows the decades in which the sampled households ceased farming. It is not surprising that almost a third of the families ceased farming in the 1960s, the decade of the arrival of cattle companies.

TABLE 6.1
Decades in Which Farm Families Ceased Farming

Decade	Number of Households
Ceased farming in the 1950s	2
Ceased farming in the 1960s	10
Ceased farming in the 1970s	7
Continued to farm	13
Total	32

First I asked my informants to provide evaluative information on the reasons for each move and the reasons for the selection of each new destination. Ninety-nine of the households interviewed provided 151 such statements regarding their decisionmaking processes. I then divided these statements into three categories: push factors, pull factors, and neutral statements. Push factors were negative aspects of the place(s) or origin, pull factors were positive characterizations about the place(s) of destination, and neutral statements were those showing lack of knowledge or evasion, such as "I don't know why we moved," or "I just wanted to leave that place."

Push statements were mainly of three types: economic, environmental, or familial. The economic reasons the migrants have for moving included eviction from land by landowners or government agencies (e.g., the Forest Park Service), employment problems such as losing a job, inability to find a job, and/or low pay, inability to pay taxes, and failed enterprises of various kinds. Ten percent of the interviewed families had experienced eviction from land at least once.[4] Sixteen percent of the statements could be characterized as environmental reasons for moving. Disasters, specifically droughts in northeastern Brazil and flooding in the Amazon, were the most frequently mentioned. Another 16 percent of the reasons related to the breakup of families, because of either the death of family members or the dissolution of marriages. However, much of the familial instability described appeared to be related to conditions of poverty such as malnutrition, poor health, long separations from working spouses, and so forth. In summary, the basic theme of the push statements, as one might expect, was a constant emphasis on economic constraints on livelihood.

The migrants' descriptions of their decisionmaking processes support the assertion that the root causes of intrarural migration worldwide are rural inequality and poverty (Connell et al. 1976). More specifically, the migrants' descriptions support the larger analysis of the Brazilian agrarian structure as presented by Cardoso and Muller (1978), Davis (1977), and Feder (1971). My research showed that most people intensely disliked moving but perceived that most of the moves were unavoidable. The stated preference of most of the migrants interviewed was to stay settled in one place where they could farm, earn sufficient cash, and become integrated into a community. New arrivals to Santa Terezinha always emphasized the extra difficulties faced by strangers. Migration, then, is a spontaneous choice—but a choice that is frequently perceived as the *only alternative*.

The dominant theme among the positive statements about destinations selected was hopes to improve the livelihood situation. Twenty-seven percent of the statements referred to the desire to find "betterment." Further questioning usually led to more specific statements to the effect that the migrants hoped to find land and/or jobs. Despite much evidence to the contrary, many small farmer migrants continued to nurture dreams about finding land of their own. Another analysis, presented by Dennis J. Mahar (1979), came to similar conclusions:

> The motives behind population movements with a rural destination, however, are not so apparent. After an exhaustive analysis of census data and supplementary studies, M. de Mello Moreira and J. A. Magno de Carvalho conclude that, in spite of the inequitable distribution of land-ownership and generally poor employment possibilities, migrants still move to rural areas because they erroneously believe that land is readily accessible.

My data support this characterization, although I would argue that it is less the case that migrants hold erroneous beliefs than that they cling to even the smallest shred of hope and continue to dream.

Another important pull factor is kin networks in the countryside. Despite the absence of a postal service, telephones, and the like, relatives are often quite successful at keeping track of the whereabouts of scattered family members, even across several states. Remarkably effective contact is maintained through a more informal communication system composed primarily of messages sent through travelers and radio announcements. Sixteen percent of the statements cited "relatives calling them to come" as the reason for selecting a particular destination. The already-settled relative frequently makes promises to share access to land or to try and provide some initial support to newcomers. Thirty percent of the sampled households were composite households, and the additional family members were usually relatives who had been called from another location to come live with the family. These types of kin networks, made up of either relatives or people from the same town, are already described in the literature on rural-urban migration (e.g., Mangin 1970). It seems logical that the same types of networks would also function in relation to intrarural migration as well.

Nine statements referred to the possiblity of cattle *fazenda* employment, and one family interviewed had been brought to northern Mato Grosso by a crew leader. Most migrants, however, are not especially motivated by the opportunities at the cattle ranches, particularly the prospect of working as a peon on a labor gang. Some of the reasons they are uninterested in working as peons concern (1) the insecurity of the jobs, (2) the need to move from one ranch to another to keep working, (3) company policies that discourage workers from bringing their families to ranches, (4) the seasonality of the work, (5) the preference for being self-employed, and (5) company policies that prohibit workers from using land to grow their own crops. Most of the families I interviewed considered *fazenda* jobs either a last resort or a temporary way to generate cash.

Other economic pull statements were made by five informants who cited the desire for land, three who had come to work in mining camps, two who mentioned the commercial opportunities of Santa Terezinha, and one who had come because of a federal job. Few people volunteered statements about land, but further questioning usually revealed a deep desire for it. Some fragments from the interviews demonstrate not only these desires for land but also the migrants' negative evaluations of their chances for obtaining land.

Question: Where would you prefer to live?

Answer: Here in Santa Terezinha will have to do. The *sertão* [backlands] is better. There one can raise animals better. But there is no place to live that we could call our own. Because the *fazenda* threw out all the people.

Q.   Why did you move to Santa Terezinha?

A.   We came here because where we were was very bad and news arrived that here was better. The only way is to try, to keep trying, because really there aren't any more places left to go! Every place is full! Now my son Antonio is working as a peon, doing clearing and weeding work. We have no land to work in the forest.

Q.   Where would you prefer to live?

A.   I'd prefer the *sertão* [backlands] if we had *mata* [forest] to work and live in. We'd have our fields and chickens and pigs. . . . The backlands are definitely better, but since we don't have any land we have to stay here or any other place that suffices.

Most pull statements refer to hopes for improvements in the economic situation of the family. In addition, sixteen statements indicated that the family had selected a place because of the availability of schools. This reason, too, is related to economic betterment because the migrants clearly viewed education as a route to upward mobility.

Finally, one-fourth of the responses were neutral or evasive. Twenty-three informants said that they had moved to accompany their families and/or spouses. Eight stated merely that "they had wanted to," and seven said that Santa Terezinha was as good as any other place.

In summary, repeated migration can be viewed as a survival strategy because people leave places with more difficult conditions and seek out places where they hope to find improved opportunities. The fact that they often do not, in fact, realize their objective of betterment is related more to conditions and constraints in the countryside than to faulty evaluations of destinations by migrants. The migrants also explained, when asked, why they had not tried to move to urban areas. Most observed that they lacked the necessary skills for earning a living in the city and expressed a strong preference for rural life. Their assessment of their chances for improving their livelihood in rural areas was usually tempered by pessimism; however, despite the odds, migration is repeatedly tried in the hopes of ameliorating a difficult situation.

Diversification and Intensification

Most Santa Terezinha households have relatively complex livelihood patterns that feature flexibility and multiplicity, and defy easy categorization; that is, they exhibit the flexibility to adjust to constantly changing conditions and options, and a multifaceted approach to livelihood whereby one's "eggs are always in several baskets at the same time." The following case study illustrates this strategy of intensification and diversification of household labor.

The father, Pedrão, is a tenant farmer on the land of a neighbor who received a plot in the INCRA distribution in 1973. He produces mainly for home consumption but also sells some surplus rice. During the dry season, he sometimes joins work crews at cattle *fazendas* to earn more cash. The eldest son, José, drives a truck for a local merchant and helps his father in the fields. The second son, Adilon, generally works as a peon on work crews at the cattle *fazendas* and is rarely home. The third son, André, helps on the farm, does odd jobs in town, and makes bricks during the dry season. The mother, Antonia, earns money by washing laundry during the day and running a small bar in the *cabaret* at night. The daughter, Francisca, sometimes works as a maid, earning about US$15 a month. During the rainy season, Adilon and André spend months at a time at home, unemployed. Upon the arrival of the dry season in 1979, Pedrão was offered a job tending the cattle of the merchant for whom José works; the herd is illegally located on the savannas of Bananal within the Forest Park. Pedrão's pay will be only every fifth calf born to the herd during his time with the herd. A family decision is reached and Pedrão, José, André, and a female cousin go to live on Bananal to tend the cattle and farm in the forests there. Meanwhile, Antonia stays in Santa Terezinha to continue her work and to take care of the bar and her elderly mother. Adilon is hired on a new work crew and leaves to work at a ranch in southern Pará. A nephew from Maranhaõ arrives, moves into the house, and begins working odd jobs in town.

As an interesting aside, it is unlikely that an unknown person or census taker arriving at the same family's door would be able to ascertain even a fraction of their livelihood activities. Most likely the father would be described as a farmer and the sons as his helpers. Probably there would be no mention of the work at the cattle *fazendas*, nor would the illegal activities on Bananal be brought up. The wife would probably mention her laundry work but might skip her job at the bar in the red light district. In other words, a very incomplete picture of small farm family-livelihood strategies would emerge if such superficial kinds of data were used exclusively. It is in this context that in-depth extended ethnographic participant observation provides a valuable addition to other research techniques.

The majority of frontier households engage in similarly diversified economic activities. Almost all farm families, for example, contain members who work periodically at cattle ranches. Females become maids, washerwomen, cooks, or, if literate, store clerks. Generally all income is used for household subsistence. The transfer of labor from agricultural activities to cash-generating activities often puts a severe strain on the labor requirements for farming. But the short-run need for cash usually overrides these considerations. Although many farm families dislike the fact that many of their members are away working at the companies, they do not deny the importance of the additional income.

Frontier households diversify in other ways. One elderly widow named Maria, for example, had received land in the INCRA distribution. Her sons sold the land and used part of the money to build Dona Maria a sturdy brick house. Dona Maria then lived off the rent of half the house and her laundry job. She also earned some money in her work as one of the town's midwives and by selling chickens occasionally. Dona Maria's brother, Francisco, had also received INCRA land and every year invites his sister to come harvest rice in his fields. Thus Dona Maria obtains her annual rice supplies by harvesting free of charge in Francisco's fields.

From time to time, her sons also give her some money. It is thus that the 62-year-old widow is able to meet her basic subsistence needs.

Another household, composed of Ines and Raimundo and their eight children, used a somewhat different strategy. For several years they had been farmers on INCRA land belonging to Ines's mother. But before the mother died, she decided to sell the land. The reason is that she was afraid her children would not be able to inherit it legally because they lacked birth certificates and other documents. Thus, the family was left landless.

Raimundo began to work at various jobs, such as construction and on work crews at the cattle *fazendas*. Ines began to do laundry and augmented her kitchen garden. The older children began to sell Ines's greens and fried cakes in the streets of town. The eldest daughter, Flora, went to work as a maid at a boarding house. When a traveling rodeo came to town, Ines and Raimundo paid about US$10 to rent a space inside the enclosure so as to sell drinks and snacks during the festivities. By means of a cordial relationship with a local merchant, the family has a source of fairly dependable credit to tide them over when cash is short. And by means of their local network of friends, relatives, and *compadres* (co-godparents), they are often invited to harvest produce in other people's fields at no cost to themselves except the transportation and their own labor. If they need *farinha*, they can go work in another family's *farinha* shed and retain one-third of what is produced. If they are invited to work in the rice harvests of their neighbors, they will earn every fourth sack. In this way, they manage to secure a more or less stable subsistence for their family.

Santa Terezinha men also work at jobs other than the three main livelihoods already discussed. Somewhat exceptional and few in number are the men with special skills—for example, in construction, carpentry, or plumbing. Skilled workers usually earn a better than average living but also tend to diversify their activities. One mason, for example, purchased land and had a tenant farm it; he also sold pelts illegally and was planning to acquire a herd of cattle. Other occupations considered to be skilled include boat pilots, truck drivers, and heavy-machinery operators (at *fazendas*).

Other ways for men to make money include doing odd jobs, such as yard work and well digging, vending drinks and snacks, and brick making in the dry season. A skilled well digger, for example, can earn about 300 cruzeiros a meter. Hired farm workers or yard workers usually earn only 60 cruzeiros a day, and masons' assistants earn about 80 cruzeiros a day. (The masons themselves earn about 180 cruzeiros a day.) Men are also more frequently involved in collecting and selling firewood, whereas the sale of collected wild fruit is usually monopolized by women and children.

Some money-making activities are avoided by men, however—for cultural and economic reasons. No adult male will work for less than about 40 cruzeiros (about US$2) a day, whereas women will and frequently do. Women, as might be expected, tend to predominate in the lower-earning types of jobs, and their economic activities tend to be those that can be more easily combined with home and child care.

The contributions of women and children to household subsistence are more difficult to ascertain because these activities are often not considered by the informants to be economic contributions. Women's cash earnings are often informal and periodic, and cultural values place a premium on presenting an image of the wife as a homemaker. Women's work within the home is considered desirable, whereas women's work for wages or running a business is common yet culturally downplayed. Many households depend on female-generated income, either partly or completely, and there are a number of relatively successful female entrepreneurs in the town. Hence there is a gap between ideal values and reality, such that economic realities are eroding the strength of cultural preferences and values.

Thirty-seven percent of the sampled wives or female household heads indicated that they were engaged in income-generating activities (i.e., work above and beyond normal domestic duties). Housekeeping, laundry, gardening, animal raising, childcare, harvesting, processing manioc, cooking, and the like are all subsumed under the category of domestic work. Fifteen of the sampled households were headed by women. These female-headed households usually resulted either from the death of a spouse or from the increasingly common practice of abandonment on the part of the male. Three of the fifteen women gave their occupations as boarding-house owners, and two were merchants. Two of the women worked for wages, one as a bar girl and the other as a cleaning woman. Female store clerks, office workers, cleaning women, and cooks generally earn somewhere between US$15 and US$40 a month. Frequently these jobs do not provide room and board either. The average monthly wage for women is 550 cruzeiros (US$27.50), which breaks down to a daily earning power of 21 cruzeiros or US$1.05 a day. Few men will work for wages this low, and it is hard to see how a woman could support a household on such earnings alone. Table 6.2 shows the differential earning power of men and women in the frontier town for a random sample of forty-four households.

In a larger sample of ninety-nine households, there were three seamstresses among the women. Sewing for a living has some distinct advantages. The woman has control over the volume of work, and she

TABLE 6.2
Estimated Monthly Cash Income for Household Heads and Spouses, Santa Terezinha (1978–1979)

Monthly Cash Income (in U.S. dollars)	No. of Males	No. of Females
Nothing	2	30
2 to 25	2	5
26 to 50	3	5
51 to 100	7	2
101 to 150	6	2
151 to 250	4	0
More than 250	3	0
Unknown	17	0
Total	44	44

can combine the work fairly easily with her normal domestic duties. The monthly earnings of a respected seamstress average between 1,600 and 3,000 cruzeiros (US$80 to US$150). As most women know how to sew, however, a seamstress must have the additional skills to be able to make special clothing for weddings and special events. Furthermore, the town cannot support too many seamstresses since it is primarily the local elite who use their services. All the seamstresses I knew diversified their economic activities. One woman who sewed for a living was also the cleaning woman for the elementary school and was thinking of opening a snack bar.

The last relatively reliable occupation for women in the frontier town is washing laundry for other households and/or the boarding houses. Ten percent of the sampled women stated that they regularly earned money by doing laundry. Laundry work has some distinct advantages and disadvantages. Again, women in this occupation have more control over time and the volume of their work; they can also more easily combine it with domestic duties. Laundry women usually rise before dawn to do household chores and collect the laundry from their customers. They usually do their cooking and cleaning after they return from washing the clothes at the riverbank, and they generally iron the clothes at night. The major disadvantages of laundry work are that it is very hard work and is poorly paid. A woman must work about twenty-six days a month for six to eight hours a day to earn a monthly income of about 1,200 cruzeiros (US$60). The work is considered obnoxious and tiring, which, indeed, it is. Heavy bundles of clothes, wet and dry, as well as large metal wash basins, soap, and bleach containers must be moved around. Most women wash at the river, which entails a good deal of walking and carrying heavy loads, usually on the head. As the laundry women are wet a good part of the day, skin problems, infections, and arthritis are aggravated. In the rainy season the work becomes ten times more difficult, as women must wade through the mud and water of flooded areas to get to the river and repeatedly put laundry in and out to catch the few moments of sunshine.

In response to my repeated questions to informants about livelihood preferences, laundry work was always mentioned as the most tiring and least rewarding. Many women stop doing laundry as soon as the economic situation of the household improves. Generally the laundresses are much like peasant farmers in that they lack the skills necessary to become employed as clerks or seamstresses—occupations in which younger, more "modern" women predominate.

Women have developed a number of other ways of contributing to household subsistence in the frontier town. Many of these activities, while marginally remunerative, are relatively regular. A few women make manioc and flour rolls and fried cakes to sell in the street and to school children on recess. Others make some money by augmenting their kitchen gardens. Several women were experimenting with and improving their technique of platform gardening, which lifts the garden up off the ground away from some predators. From backyard gardens, small amounts of lettuce, green onions, tomatoes, sweet peppers, and herbs are sold on the street. Women also try to increase the size of their chicken flocks, although they are rarely successful because of inadequate feed, diseases, and theft. It is thus difficult to find either eggs or chickens for sale in the town.

Other home-produced commodities occasionally sold in town are wooden spoons and mortars, acrylic-painted stove and gas tank covers, and baked clay water pots. Only one woman produced wooden implements, and only one produced water pots. More traditional crafts, such as spinning, weaving, hammock making, and lace making (the fringe for hammocks), have become disappearing arts in the frontier zone. Only a few of the older women still know these crafts, but they are producing less and less because they cannot compete with cheaper industrially produced products. A skilled lace maker, for example, can produce about a meter a day for which she can command about one (U.S.) dollar in payment. One of the only women still weaving hammocks in Santa Terezinha found that the only way she could sell her product at a decent price was to sell bingo chances for it, in order to spread the cost.

The same process of substitution of industrial goods for home-produced ones has occurred in relation to a number of other products. In the early days of the settlement, many farmers produced *rapadura* (brown sugar blocks) from sugar cane; today most people buy white sugar from southern Brazil. People used to produce cooking oil from the nuts of the macauba palm; now they assert that the low price for oil makes such enterprises unworthwhile. Many women have continued to make their own soap, but they observe that most people prefer to buy factory-produced scented soap. A number of commodities made at home, such as rendered pig fat, soap, stools and benches, and the like, are not sold at all.

An important way people have of raising money in a hurry in Santa Terezinha is by games of chance such as bingo and *rife*[5] or by auction. Auctions are used primarily to raise money for community events such as saint celebrations or institutions such as the Catholic Church. Residents usually contribute food, which then goes to the highest bidder. Another method of raising money fast is to hold a yard sale where some or all of the contents of the house are sold to passers-by. This method is sometimes used by families in an emergency situation such as a serious illness or by people who have decided to migrate to another location and need cash for traveling expenses.

In summary, it appears that most frontier households respond to economic constraints by developing livelihood strategies that are usually quite diversified and tend to intensify the use of available household labor. When possible, several economic activities are pursued simultaneously to maximize returns and to compensate for sudden failures such as the loss of a job. While farmers and especially small farmers worldwide also tend to diversify income sources and use family labor, the frontier situation differs in terms of the degree to which this is done and the net result achieved. By means of constant hard work on the part of several family members, households such as that of Pedrão and Antonia, who depend on farming, laundry, and other sources of income, can secure a fairly regular though poverty-level existence. The difference on the frontier is not the pattern itself but the extent to which diversification and intensification are exaggerated and the low level of material well-being achieved. Most income of all kinds is generally used for basic subsistence; saving and credit are almost nonexistent. A family that does manage to get ahead will tend to invest in cattle, another classic peasant strategy.

Many households are compelled to choose short-term and immediate benefits, such as wage labor at the cattle *fazendas*, over planning for the long term. Women and children frequently become involved in remunerative activities. The ways in which additional income is earned are varied and sometimes imaginative, but they are restricted by conditions of local demand and limited local cash resources both for capital investment and potential customers. Money-making activities are also shaped by cultural values and customs. Male and female work spheres remain sharply differentiated. Survival strategies thus reflect both the socioeconomic realities of the frontier and cultural values and preferences.

Mutual Aid and Patron-Client Relationships

The focus of this section is on the types of mutual aid prevalent within families and extended families and on the exchanges between households and individuals in the frontier community. On the whole, I found that the traditional Latin American emphasis on family—respect for family, loyalty, and mutual aid—remained an important value among frontier households. Two exceptions to this pattern, which appear to be increasingly common, were abandonment by husbands of their families and the rebellion of sons working at the cattle *fazendas.* Both of these behaviors in turn seem to be linked to the rapid socioeconomic changes occurring in the frontier; however, the majority of inhabitants continued to follow traditional patterns.

The types of mutual aid extended and the kin networks activated are quite varied, both synchronically and diachronically. Survival strategies in the frontier, as mentioned previously, tend to be highly flexible and subject to a great deal of variation and change depending on shifting circumstances. On the whole, the extent of loyalty and mutual aid diminishes as one moves from the residential unit of the nuclear family, to the extended family located in other houses, and then to relatives who are more scattered in other parts of the state or even in other states. Newly married couples favor the establishment of an independent nuclear family unit, and the first loyalty is usually to this unit.

The second most important claim on loyalties is generally to one's parents. Families, even on the edge of economic survival, will usually do all they can to provide for the care of elderly parents. I saw repeated examples in Santa Terezinha of families that had brought elderly parents to live with them. Adult children living elsewhere often sent their parents money and sometimes asked them to join them in a new location. Adult children who could do so sometimes set their parents up in new livelihoods. For example, one man brought his parents from Maranhão and gave them a boarding house to run. Farm labor, child care, and other types of labor are frequently exchanged. In times of illness, adult children are expected to do all they can for their parents.

The small farmers Dona Luisa and José, discussed in Chapter 4, can serve as an example. One of their sons, Manuel, lives directly behind his parents' house. Manuel pumps gas at the airstrip but also periodically helps José in the fields. Manuel's wife, Nadi, spends a good deal of time with Dona Luisa; the two women cooperate in many chores and are company for each other when the men are gone. The younger couple frequently receive agricultural products from the parents. The second son, João, lives in a house that is ten minutes walk from the house of Dona Luisa and José. He had previously worked with José in the fields, and his wife Maria visits and exchanges with her in-laws. Since Maria's family also lives in town, she spends more time with her own parents. Joáo had begun to farm with his father-in-law, a fact that distresses José. Delmina, Luisa and José's daughter, lived with her family only five minutes walk away. Delmina works with her mother every day, washing clothes at the river bank. Their customers are different but they help each other out, picking up laundry for each other and even doing the other's work in times of illness. Delmina's husband works at the cattle *fazendas* and sometimes helps José in the fields. Delmina's adolescent children are sometimes recruited to do chores and errands for the two women.

The last son, Jaime, had left town several years previously. He had gone to Goiás, where he eventually became the owner of a small ranch. When rising property taxes influenced him to sell his ranch, he brought his herd to the island of Bananal and purchased some land to the north of Santa Terezinha near his parents' land.[6] In 1979, Jaime asked his sister Delmina and her husband to become caretakers (*vaqueiros*) of his herd on Bananal, and they agreed. They lent their house in town to another family and left with their children to live on Bananal for an extended period.

It is thus the case that many frontier families remain linked together in terms of mutual aid and multiple exchanges. Siblings cooperate, as can be seen from the above examples; but the pivotal link is frequently the parental household. Despite loyalties and exchanges, not all parties are satisfied—as is often the case among families. José and Luisa, for example, are disappointed that their children are not more actively involved in the family farm. If they could persuade one or more of their adult children to live at the forest homestead with them, it is very likely they would leave town and live at that homestead. The children, however, prefer to remain in the town, where they can pursue other livelihood activities. Luisa does not like the idea of living "all alone" at the *roça* far from neighbors, so she remains in town near her children and José commutes by bicycle between the *roça* and the town. The older couple are not sure what will happen to their land when they die. Depending on the relative success of their adult children, Luisa and José may some day be able to "retire" with a little security; but Dona Luisa, always the pessimist, thinks it is more likely that she and José will be hard at work until the day they die.

Single male peons, prostitutes, and newly arrived migrants are the ones who generally have no kin in the area, although a certain proportion of the new migrants come precisely because they do have relatives in Santa Terezinha. People without relatives often mentioned that this was a major handicap. The importance of the help people receive from their kin networks can be contrasted with the acute discomfort of people without such networks. Newly arrived migrants with no relatives in town frequently made such statements as "People in this town are the strangest I have ever encountered" or "No one helps each other in this town."

One very newly arrived family I interviewed was composed of a husband, wife, and three small children. They had just been evicted by a cattle *fazenda* from their small farm in the Porto Alegre area of northern Mato Grosso. When I encountered them, they had been in town about one week and were rapidly depleting the compensation money they had received from the *fazenda* for leaving their place. The husband was looking for work and wanted to farm on someone's land. When asked about how he planned to arrange this, he stated, "I have relatives everywhere because I know how to make friends fast." When I returned to visit the same family about a week later, they were already gone. The neighbors reported that they had indeed managed to become tenants on a local farmer's land. Not all new arrivals, however, were as successful in making contacts and finding work as this resourceful man from Porto Alegre.

Brazilians in general, and the frontier inhabitants in particular, place a high priority on having, raising, and caring for children. While the acute situation of poverty and desperation in Brazilian urban areas has resulted in the problem of literally millions of abandoned children in the streets, there were no abandoned children in the countryside, at least in the region I researched. In the various cases that I investigated involving dissolved marriages, subsequent remarriages, deaths of parents, or the needs of working mothers, the children either were placed more or less permanently with relatives or were temporarily cared for by relatives. Indeed, I often encountered households that included children from a previous marriage, children of dead parents or siblings, or grandchildren. A home was always found for children who needed care.

Such adopted children are sometimes referred to in Brazil as *crianças de criação* (raised or adopted children). While many middle- and upper-class Brazilians tend to treat such adopted children as servants (usually the children are from rural areas and sent to families in the city), the frontier households were not motivated by the desire to obtain cheap domestic labor. Permanently adopted children were usually treated in much the same way as biological children. For that matter, it was often difficult to get informants to specify the exact nature of their relationship with each child in the household. Only with additional probing would an informant finally explain that the child in question was really a nephew or a grandchild or simply adopted. In most of the cases I observed, children moved through the consanguineal or affinal kin networks and were not given to friends or strangers. Giving a child to a casual acquaintance or a stranger, as sometimes happens in poverty-stricken regions of Brazil, is viewed as the last desperate resort of a person in the most extreme circumstances.

Both relatives and neighboring women frequently provide child care for one another. Child care is generally a service for which payment is not expected. If a woman cannot find a relative near enough or available for child care, she will usually depend on either her *compadres* (co-godparents) and/or more trusted female neighbors. In the short run, the additional burdens of extra child care might be seen as a drain on household resources; in the long run, however, the result is the defense of the young, whereby almost all children gain access to a home, emotional and physical nourishment, parental guidance, training, and a family unit with which to identify.

Hence, while more than two-thirds of the frontier households are composed of nuclear family units, in actuality the households of related people are usually involved in myriad and multifaceted exchanges and mutual aid of varying kinds. One might even consider several cooperating houses as one functional household. One advantage of establishing separate residential units seems to lie in the maximization of flexibility in terms of cooperation. Much like other frontier survival strategies, the cooperation patterns between households are characterized by flexibility over time; the maintenance of separate abodes allows the families to participate more or less depending on their needs and circumstances. In other words, it facilitates the fusion and fission of cooperating units, which can more easily respond to changing conditions.

Composite households in Santa Terezinha generally consist of some form of extended family. In one survey of forty-four homes, nine contained siblings of the heads of household, three contained grandparents, and two had cousins; only two contained friends, while one included an employee. Often a grandparent in the home was widowed. Sometimes children are sent to live with a widowed relative, because living alone is considered a terrible thing. Siblings, cousins, nephews, and others who join family units are often from outside the town itself. Children of farm families who live at the *roça* are frequently sent to live with relatives in town so they can attend school. Siblings and other relatives may arrive from outside the region and live for several years with relatives until they marry and/or become permanently established in their own homes. Because it is relatively easy to construct a hut, and because some of the land in town is still beyond the legal control of the municipal authorities, most families can and do build and move into their own dwellings as soon as possible. As controls over town lots tightened in 1978–1979, some of the more recent arrivals began to construct houses in the backyards of their kin.

To ascertain patterns of reciprocity and mutual aid, I often asked informants a series of "what if" questions such as the following:

- If you were very ill, who would take care of your children?
- If your family had an emergency, such as a serious illness and you needed to raise money in a hurry, who would you turn to for help?
- If your husband lost his job, what would you do then?
- If you decided to begin farming again, to whom would you go to gain access to land?

The answers to these and other questions revealed some consistent patterns of mutual aid. As expected, informants generally stated that they would rely first on their nuclear families. After that, they would rely on other relatives, such as parents, in-laws, and siblings. As a third alternative, they would appeal to those they considered to be either their good friends (*amigos*) or their *compadres* (co-godparents). The fourth alternative was patrons, and the fifth and last resort was persons considered friends but classified as only acquaintances (*conhecidos*).

Another factor that influences the decision as to whom one can appeal for help is the type of help required. Help that can most often be obtained from relatives includes relatively free room and board, child care, assistance with domestic and agricultural chores, assistance in preparation of special events such as weddings and funerals, advice and information about a myriad of subjects, reciprocal exchanges of goods and services such as "trading days" of labor, loans of equipment such as bicycles and work animals, and access to farm land and/or *farinha* making or rice harvesting.

Most of these types of exchange move along relatively symmetrical or horizontal lines. That is, the exchanges are between parties of almost equal socioeconomic status. This is not to say that some households do not have more of some item than others. Some families, for example, have received INCRA land while others did not or arrived too late. Many of the farmers with INCRA land, however, then allowed relatives and close friends to use (farm) their land, usually for no payment at all except a promise to help with taxes, if necessary, and a pledge to never press squatters' claims against the owner either to obtain land or to force the payment of compensation. Usually the recipient of a favor also looks for other ways of "paying back" the benefactor.

Most of the people I interviewed also mentioned the important role that "good friends" play in their lives. Good friends are often but not always further bonded by means of ritual godparenthood. The two most important and common ways of establishing the co-godparenthood relationship in the frontier in order of importance were (1) by asking someone to be the godparent of your child's baptism, and (2) by jumping over bonfires together at the festival for São João. In the baptism, the critical relationship is that between the *compadres*—that is, between the parents and the godparents. In the ceremony of the bonfire, the critical relationship is the one established between the two people who jump over the fire together.

Not all persons who stand in a *compadre* relationship are considered good and trustworthy friends, and not all good friends are *compadres*. In part because of the frequent moves made by households, many people have not been in one place long enough to build up the knowledge, trust, and connections for this type of fictive kinship, or they may have established *compadres* in a half-dozen different places only to lose contact with the people involved. The concept of a "good friend" whom one trusts and to whom one can easily appeal for help was clearly articulated by informants and often contrasted with the concept of acquaintance. Often people who considered each other good friends did not feel it was necessary to augment the tie through fictive kinship. Thus, one may conclude that in the context of the frontier where so many people are transient, the institution of co-parenthood seems to be diminishing and has been partly replaced by the less formalized and ritualized bonds of friendship.

Considering the rather precarious situation of most households, it is not surprising that the list of mutual obligations between friends or *compadres* provided by informants was usually short. People commented that godparents should always bless their godchildren and, if possible, help cover the costs of school books or uniforms. Godchildren were expected to visit their godparents regularly to ask for their blessings and to heed their advice. Informants *never* mentioned that godparents would take full responsibility for godchildren in cases of emergencies, and the relationship between the *compadres* (i.e., the adults) was downplayed. When informants were questioned further on these points, they usually stated that both *compadres* and good friends were expected to provide help, but to help only within reason. Since the majority of these relationships are relatively horizontal ones between frontier families in economically marginal circumstances, it makes sense that the informants would assume that their friends and *compadres* would, most likely, be unable to help them in major ways. Another facet of such close relationships stressed by the informants was that good friends do not have to be asked for help but that they simply perceive the need and act to fulfill it. Generally, people view direct requests for help as humiliating, especially when the request is addressed to an equal. Requests to social "superiors" are also considered humiliating but more justifiable.

I observed that the flows of goods and services between close friends and/or *compadres* often resembled the exchanges between relatives. As noted, people tend to avoid rigid definitions about such mutual obligations and instead favor a more flexible and shifting series of exchange configurations. One such "favor" between *compadres* was observed. A male neighbor stopped by briefly and left several kilos of fresh beef, rare and hard to obtain, on the woman's kitchen table. It turned out that this neighbor, who was a butcher, was a *compadre* of the family and had used his position to help the family obtain some meat before it went on sale and rapidly sold out.

The relationship of friendship is structured by the participating parties in the form and style that best suits their circumstances. For example, I formed several close relationships during the year in which I lived in Santa Terezinha. Whereas I contributed store-bought goods or medicines to my friends, I usually received in return goods and services that the frontier people could more easily provide, such as a few eggs or fruit, and, of course, the time and patience of informants for research purposes. Even in such a relatively asymmetrical relationship, most people were careful not to make excessive demands on me; indeed, they often waited patiently, giving only a few hints as to what it was they needed that I could help with.

In the context of agricultural activities and access to land, the same generalizations hold true as were made for other kinds of mutual aid. The persons or households given free access to land, participating in "trading days" or working in the *farinha* shed or rice harvest, tended to be, first, the nuclear family, then relatives, and then good friends and *compadres*.

In many cases there is the crucial element of time—the time necessary to get to know and trust one's neighbors and acquaintances in order to establish friendships and other ties. Indeed, I observed that the more years a family had spent in the community, the more ties and other mutual aid networks it could rely on. But because of the continuous migration occurring in many parts of Amazonia, the frontier people also tend to speed up the formation of critical relationships. Not all people, however, are equally skilled at manipulating and maneuvering their interpersonal relationships. The close attention that people give to the opinions of others and the avoidance of *vergonha* (shame) are traditional Brazilian concerns that take on added significance in the frontier, where interpersonal relationships are often utterly crucial to peoples' chances for access to basic resources and livelihood opportunities.

Thus, in terms of community social constraints and control, the frontier town simultaneously manifests two divergent tendencies. On the one hand, the many transients and workers who carouse in the red light area enhance its urbanity and contribute to a sense of anonymity that is consistent with the more stereotypical images of a wild and rowdy frontier town where there are fewer social restraints on behavior. In other respects, however, the social constraints on behavior are even stronger and more conservative in the frontier town, partly because it is only by following the social rules that newly arrived people and families become integrated into the community and its networks. Even for old-timers, public image remains vitally important and helps determine access to networks and, hence, availablity of mutual aid. Thus, in a sense, a frontier town such as Santa Terezinha is at once two com-munities—or, perhaps, one community with two very different faces. One face is the wild frontier town, and the other is trying to be a rural Brazilian community like almost any other throughout the interior regions of the country. This bipolar dynamic has generated an underlying tension and sense of confusion that some would say is inherently characteristic of frontier "boom" towns.

Frontierspeople also naturally try to cultivate exchange relationships with people more powerful than themselves. The patron-client rela-tionships in Santa Terezinha are, however, rather rudimentary. This is the case in part because the most powerful figures in this section of the frontier, the cattle *fazenda* managers and directors, studiously and carefully avoid establishing any relationships with local people other than employer-employee relationships. They generally do not allow themselves to become involved with locals or workers in the more traditional Brazilian plantation system, where landlords have long op-erated by the rules of *noblesse oblige*. They refuse to become closely involved with their workers, the community, or the region. Rather, they have a more "factory mentality."

This aloof attitude on the part of the cattle company officials confuses and distresses the small farmers who find it hard to understand how the rich can refuse to acknowledge their traditional obligations to the poor. Relationships between workers and the cattle companies are fundamentally "economically rational." For example, the discovery of any wife of a company employee to be either selling or even giving away company beef to noncompany people (a common but secret practice) will cause the immediate firing of her husband.[7] The really powerful figures in the frontier—company owners, managers, labor contractors, or crew leaders, and even the various government officials passing through—do their best to sidestep any attempts by local people to initiate patron-client relationships. The once-common arrangement by which large landowners allowed tenants to farm part of their lands does not pertain in the frontier, where companies actually patrol their borders to make sure no farmer enters or begins working on company land. One informant summarized the situation this way: "What we need here are men with conditions [wealth] to notice us. Here the rich take from the poor and do not help us."

Similar to the Brazilian police who are routinely rotated to new communities every few years to reduce their local loyalties, most cattle *fazenda* managers usually do not spend more than about five years in one location. In addition, they tend to believe that the regional inhabitants and small farmer migrants are worthless, ignorant, and backward peasants who are periodically "stirred up" by radical agitators to make trouble for the *fazendas*. Company managers therefore generally pursue a policy of avoidance. The following example illustrates this.

A middle-aged couple arrived in Santa Terezinha from another river town some 60 kilometers to the north. They came because they hoped to return to their former farm nearby, which they had fled six years previously during the period of violent confrontations with CODEARA, the neighboring cattle company. The couple, intimidated by the violence, had stayed downriver for the past six years. The husband then went to the CODEARA headquarters one day and managed to talk to an administrator of the company who was briefly visiting from São Paulo. This official, perhaps a kindly man, listened to the farmer's story and then "promised" him that he would get his old homestead back. The administrator then left the region.

Afterward, the farmer made several trips to the CODEARA headquarters to see the resident manager and to try to obtain written proof of the company's intention of giving him back his farm. The manager repeatedly refused even to see the farmer. The farmer and his wife, explaining the situation to me, said, "We will indeed get our land back because the 'owner' [sic] told us that we could have it." As the weeks passed, the family began to get suspicious. Planting time was approaching. In an interview during that time with the CODEARA manager, I inquired about pending land claims against the company. The manager told me that CODEARA had already given out all the land that it intended to distribute and that no more land would be released unless the claimant had a document proving possession. The farm family had no documents. This family then began planting at the site of their former farm, but the probability that they would come under eviction pressure in the future, as had happened six years previously, seemed quite high. Needless to say, their chances of another meeting with the kind ranch administrator from São Paulo were remote.

Hence, most of the more vertical relationships established in the frontier are with other local people, primarily with members of the local elite. This elite, while not as powerful as the multinational companies or southern Brazilian banks that own the cattle *fazendas*, do have some limited powers and access to strategic goods and resources. Certain needs of many poor families that cannot be met by horizontal contacts but can be facilitated by vertical contacts include (1) access to strategic resources such as land or a job; (2) access to valuable services such as transportation, communication, medical care, or free military flights; (3) access to social welfare benefits such as retirement payments; (4) access to various types of credit and/or loans of capital or equipment; (5) help in dealing with officials and legal paraphenalia such as deeds, permits, taxes, school requirements, and other documents; (6) help during major emergencies; and (7) general information of all kinds.

Some of these needs can be met through horizontal exchanges. Certain families, for example, have obtained access to land through relatives or friends. But many others are compelled to obtain access to land by becoming tenants for a wealthier local person. Many families also undergo periods during which they need credit at the local stores. Thus, many households must at various times depend on people more powerful than themselves.

While some of the local elite do cultivate exchange relationships with their poorer neighbors, like the cattle company officials they generally try to avoid them. Why do the local elite tend to avoid traditional patron-client relationships? First, a good deal of their business is oriented toward people who are largely transient and they prefer not to "invest" in these relationships. Second, many merchants are in relatively precarious situations themselves and simply cannot afford to do much for their neighbors. Finally, the more well-to-do of the local elite have already diversified their economic activities. As most of them raise food crops and cattle, they have little need for what the poor have to offer by way of exchange—namely, loyalty, labor, or agricultural products.

The same reluctance to enter into patron-client relationships could be seen among the local elite who receive their pay from outside the region, such as school officials, tax collectors, and police. Persons paid from outside rarely have the same vested interests as other community members. Most of these people, with the major exception of the missionaries, apparently saw little social or economic advantage in cultivating exchange relationships with their poorer neighbors.

Not only do better-off people resist entering exchange relationships but, when they do participate, they often carefully limit the demands and/or requests that can be made. The following example illustrates the fairly marginal types of exchanges that one rather successful Santa Terezinha entrepreneur engages in with neighbors, employees, customers, and even *compadres.*

Dona Clara, a woman in her late 40s, runs the most successful boarding house in Santa Terezinha. She and her husband Joaquin have lived in town for seven years. They had purchased the squatters' rights (*posse*) to 60 hectares of land in the Chrisoste to the north of town, where Joaquin farms and raises cattle. The couple's background is similar to that of most other families in town. Although they are doing well, they consider themselves to be "poor people."

Dona Clara is indeed a shrewd businesswoman, but she is also known for her generosity to friends and acquaintances. Despite some reluctance on her part, she became the godmother to children of five different local families, all of whom were far poorer than she. Her generosity, however, generally takes the form of giving small gifts such as a can of cooking oil, some tomatoes, or a piece of cloth. Sometimes she gives free meals or cups of coffee from the boarding-house kitchen. She makes no effort to seek out her less fortunate *compadres* to find out how they are doing, but if they happen to stop by the boarding house, she makes sure that they receive some refreshments; and if they hint at a small request for a godchild, she may provide aid if she does not consider the request excessive.

Dona Clara is active in community affairs and donates electricity from her generator to the Catholic Church for several hours a night. Most of the people with whom she maintains a semi-patron-client relationship, however, are aware that there are narrow limits to the help they can expect to receive from her. For example, her laundry woman, Dona Luisa, accepts small gifts from Dona Clara, such as a bar of soap, but has had a difficult time convincing Dona Clara that she ought to pay a better wage for the laundry service.

Not surprisingly, the vertical links to her "clients" were of less importance to Dona Clara than her horizontal and sometimes vertical exchanges with her socioeconomic equals and superiors. What Dona Clara and Joaquin receive from their subordinates is primarily the "good opinion" of the community. Their most important "friends" in town, since they had no relatives there, were two quite successful fellow merchants and their families. To become *compadres*, Dona Clara had jumped over the São Joao fire with the wife of one of these men, and her daughter had jumped over the fire with the wife of the other merchant. The three families are very close, and exchanges of goods, services, and information occur daily. One of these merchants had provided Joaquin and Clara with the original capital loan to purchase the boarding house, which had then generated enough money for investment in the cattle that they eventually used to pay off the debt. Clara and Joaquin had been instrumental in the start of the other merchant, who had been in town for only four years. He, in turn, often provided them with free transportation in his truck and so forth. They also maintain exchange networks with a series of "useful" people in town such as the butcher who sets aside meat for them. They maintain socializing relations with other "important" people as well, some of whom, such as the sheriff and the tax collector, have been their political opponents. I once saw Dona Clara run next door to another merchant's home and borrow 2,000 cruzeiros, the equivalent of a month and a half's earnings for a laundry woman, to send her daughter on a plane trip for an eye examination in Gurupi (Goiás). Needless to say, Dona Clara's credit for such requests was excellent.

Thus, it is frequently the case that subordinates cultivate patron-client relationships but the superiors discourage them, and many needs of the poorer families remain unsatisfied. More recent arrivals and those with few relatives in town tend to have serious problems with both horizontal and vertical linkages. It is not surprising, then, that many of the worse-off families often decide to leave town. Whenever I conducted surveys in the backstreets of town, I always found that the majority of the most desperate families were gone when I revisited later. Thus, it was very difficult to obtain complete data on any of these most marginalized households.

Despite the reluctance of the local elite to engage in patron-client relationships, many actually provide some important commodities and services to their less fortunate neighbors. Help from a superior, such as typing a document or a lift in an airplane, is either "sold" or "given"— but the former is more common. In horizontal relationships, noneconomic exchanges predominate; and in vertical relationships, economic exchanges, especially payments in cash, predominate. Sometimes, however, wealthier people simply donate a few essential services or commodities to the poor because such actions bolster their public image as outstanding community members.

In summary, the more traditional forms of patron-client relationships are more attenuated in the frontier. Lack of choice and consumer power, the transience of many people, desperate need, and other factors operate to discourage the formation of ties. Loyalty and favors from the poor are less desirable to the local elite than cold cash. Most customers or clients are not so valuable that they have to be "courted." The representatives of the cattle companies attempt to sidestep local obligations altogether. Some of Santa Terezinha's local elite have tried to form relationships with *fazenda* personnel, but with minimal success.

Therefore, the predominant form is mutual aid between more or less socioeconomic equals. But even the horizontal ties seem less formalized and less stable in the frontier context. Flexibility characterizes most relationships, and informal arrangements (e.g., friendship) are increasingly favored over formal relationships (e.g., co-godparenthood). These patterns are not due to the farmers' cognitive orientation of the limited good, as has been suggested by George Foster (1965); nor are they the result of a "poverty mentality" (Crist and Nissly 1973). Rather, the constraints of rural poverty compounded in the frontier by development strategies that favor corporate cattle projects have influenced the ways in which farmers and their families try to obtain basic subsistence and improve their situations. The more attenuated and casual forms of mutual aid are better understood as a function of the constraints of frontier life— lack of access to basic resources, poverty, and migration—rather than as some kind of cultural mindset characteristic of the Brazilian small farmer.

Institutions and Organizations

The most important and active organization in Santa Terezinha is the Catholic mission. It was the mission, under the leadership of Padre Jentel, that helped establish the town in its present site, built and staffed the first elementary school and health clinic, and was the driving force behind the creation of the agricultural cooperative. Later, the mission played a crucial role in the struggle between the local farmers and CODEARA, the neighboring *fazenda*. While hundreds and perhaps thousands of similar land conflicts have occurred relatively unnoticed and sometimes unrecorded throughout the Brazilian Amazon, the Santa Terezinha conflict and the imprisonment of Padre Jentel received publicity that led to the INCRA intervention.[8]

As stated previously, the ideological commitment of the local Catholic mission falls within the framework of liberation theology. The missionaries' goal is to act as advocates for the poor, disinherited, and oppressed people of Amazonia. As such, they have been a vocal force both in shaping events in Amazonia and in bringing outside attention to regional issues. A complete report and analysis of the local mission within the context of the liberation theology movement in Brazil and Latin America would require a study in and of itself and is beyond the scope of this book.

Although a number of mission projects, such as the cooperative and the health clinic, have been transformed into "community run" organizations, the mission support and leadership have remained vital to the continued existence of these organizations. The mission was also pivotal, during 1978–1979, in helping form two other local organizations—the "Committee for the Emancipation of Santa Terezinha," which sought to make Santa Terezinha the seat of its own municipality separate from Luciara, and a branch of the federally controlled Rural Workers' Union. The elementary school, originally staffed by the mission, was taken over by state educational officials in 1973; the ideology, curriculum and administration of the school were issues of conflict in town from that point on. An informant wrote me in 1981 that these disagreements in educational philosophy had actually led to a school strike on the part of students and their parents.

It is quite remarkable that the local Catholic mission, with its small staff of a priest and several lay workers, manages to have such a major impact on so many areas of regional life. However, it is linked to a larger network within the church dedicated to the same goals. Philosophical discussion aside, it is clear that no other organization, particularly during the years of Brazil's military dictatorship, has done so much to promote the social, economic, and physical well-being of the less powerful inhabitants of Amazonia. Unfortunately, the mission, at the time of my study, was considered subversive and had come under surveillance. The missionaries themselves seemed uncomfortable with the idea that a foreign anthropologist wanted to observe and record their activities. In accordance with their preferences, I did not attempt to document their organization or its activities. However, an in-depth study of the grassroots activities of liberation theology groups is needed. My treatment here is limited because of the aforementioned constraints.

Representatives of other institutions in the town—the state employees at the school, the state police, the tax collector, the municipal councilmen, and the vice-mayor—carry out certain functions but are considered by most inhabitants to be ineffective and rather useless. For example, one of the first actions of the town councilmen was to tighten control over town properties. This action, together with the fact that the councilmen managed to obtain prime lots for themselves, was extremely unpopular. Criticism was organized by means of the diocese regional newsletter, under the auspices of the Catholic mission. One councilman used his political connections to secure lucrative buildings contracts, and the vice-mayor is best known as a trucker of peons to distant cattle *fazendas*. Apart from a very few sinecures and some control over access to free Brazilian Air Force flights, such officials are viewed locally as unable or unwilling to provide much aid, either through community organizations or to needy individuals. It is far more likely that a person or family seeking to process documents or looking for medicine or help with other problems will go directly to the Catholic mission or to mission-related organizations. For example, during the heavy flooding of the rainy season of 1978, it was the mission, not the town government, that arranged emergency housing for ten destitute families whose homes had been washed away.

Other religious groups present in the town include the Pentecostals, the Baptists, and Vovo Rosa (see Chapter 2). The Baptist Church was founded in 1979, and its congregation includes about three adults and ten children. The Pentecostal Assembly of God received its first minister from the outside in 1979 but had existed in the town for twenty years. The congregation is composed of a group of about four better-off families and some others totaling approximately thirty people. Their church, with its strict rules, attracts many; but few remain adherents for very long. Pentecostals pay a tithe to the church and provide some services to members. Most of the members' free-time activities focus on the church rather than on other community organizations or issues. Pentecostals also tend to avoid political involvement.

The Vovo Rosa sect is a kind of fundamentalist Catholic religion preached over the radio from Saõ Paulo. There are fifteen converts in town, primarily made up of washerwomen. They are not yet organized, although they occasionally meet in one person's home to listen to the radio sermons together; occasionally, small groups plan religious outings to Cazeara or other cities. Although the Vovo Rosa sect is critical of current Catholic practices and actions, it also largely refrains from any kind of political or community involvement. Both the Pentecostals and the Vova Rosa sect stress acceptance, hard work, self-discipline, and support for the status quo.

The great appeal of these and other religious movements and groups in the frontier is an interesting and complex topic. It appears that these religions offer potential solutions and alternative ways of dealing with the realities of frontier life. For example, some participants feel that important needs are being met when they accept various kinds of faith healing. The Vovo Rosa adherents place a glass of water on the radio during sermons and believe that this blessed water cures illnesses. There are also economic factors such as the cooperation exhibited by the Pentecostals. It would be interesting to compare the dynamics of folk religion and various types of popular movements in Amazonia with similar groups and dynamics already well described for northeastern Brazil (e.g., Queiroz 1977).

The Catholic Church, in contrast to the Protestant and fundamentalist groups, has fewer rules and procedures for adherents, at least in terms of daily life. Most Brazilians, both rural and urban, rarely become involved in the church except for purposes of baptism, marriage, and death (Wagley 1971). Although the local Catholic mission personnel are closest to a smaller group of the active participants in their church and

organizations, they also extend their services—religious and otherwise—
to all regional inhabitants including Indians. Their focal point has been
the rural poor, particularly the small farmers (*posseiros*). In 1979, they
appeared to be reevaluating their target populations because their activities were increasingly reaching out to the transient workers at cattle
ranches as well.

Because there are so many needy people in the region, and because
Catholic mission personnel and resources are limited, the mission sometimes disappoints people requesting help. In other words, the mission
is so well thought of that people have very high expectations of what
it will do for them. The mission has tried to shift some of its activities
to the members of organizations it has helped create, but these transfers
of responsibility have not been especially successful. Many initially
enthusiastic members thus become discouraged and frustrated when the
self-help organizations do not meet their expectations.

For example, the health clinic, which is really only a pharmacy with
a couple of beds in a back room, operates under some serious constraints.
Because of the rising costs of drugs and transportation, a low profit
margin, and an overworked staff, the clinic, according to many informants,
continues to raise membership dues annually while the quality of services
provided deteriorates. For example, although it was previously the case
that the payment of dues in the clinic entitled a family to up to four
home visits form the clinic nurse, the number of free visits has been
cut to one and people now complain that it is hard to get the staff to
come to their homes at all. The mission health clinic, with its staff of
one practical nurse and several helpers, still sells medicines at close to
cost and extends credit. It has more members than any other community
organization in town. One-fourth of the ninety-nine households surveyed
belong to the clinic; four other households previously belonged but
terminated their memberships.

Although all members are eligible to come to policy and planning
meetings, most of the meetings are sparsely attended. Few volunteer
for committee work and the like. It is thus not unreasonable to assume
that while almost all frontier households want and need medical services,
very few can afford the time and energy to make significant voluntary
contributions. People always note that their family obligations come
first. In theory, most of the informants I interviewed agreed that such
community organizations and a general "unity among poor people"
were necessary and crucial; however, they often concluded that "we are
too disunited for that here." The reasons for this disunity appear to be
linked to the already-stated requirements for flexibility, multiplicity, and
intensification necessary for survival in the frontier. Even mutual aid
between close relatives rarely takes the form of a stable long-term

arrangement. People generally favor short-term, temporary, and dyadic arrangements over long-term group efforts.

Therefore, while most of the Catholic mission's activities are designed to promote regional and community self-help organizations, there are powerful forces working against the success of such endeavors. The survival strategies themselves are often antithetical to long-term planning, commitment, and group projects. Some of the most active participants in mission-supported organizations are not the poor but, rather, some of the better-off households, such as Dona Clara the boarding-house owner. Although the survival strategies described above seem to be functional for short-term goals, they are not always appropriate for the sustained efforts needed for larger-scale organizations.

Out-migration

Many of the small farmer migrants to Santa Terezinha leave the town as they have left so many places before. Generally, the shorter the period of residence and the more insecure the livelihood, the greater is the likelihood of continuing migration. Some leave temporarily, some leave with ideas of returning in the future, and others know they will never return. Out-migration, like in-migration to the area, is less a free and "spontaneous" choice than an alternative dictated by limited options. The primary concerns and impetus are livelihood and survival. The push factors in this case are the constraints already described and analyzed for Santa Terezinha.

Since it was problematic to obtain data on people who had already left the town, I used as a sample a total of 79 adult children living outside of the 44 surveyed households. Of these 79, 9 were actually children under the age of 16 and 70 were adults. Of these 70 adults, 20 had not come to Santa Terezinha with their parents but either remained in a previous location or had selected a different destination. Sixty percent of these adults who had never migrated to Santa Terezinha with their parents were located in major urban centers, and their parents reported that they had reasonably secure occupations. Twelve were in Brasília, Goiania, Terezinha (Piaui), or Fortaleza (Ceará). They worked as soldiers, office workers, bakers, butchers, hotel clerks, garage mechanics, and employees of trucking firms and government agencies. Two were students who lived with employed siblings. The remaining 8 adults were located in Goiás, Pará, and Mato Grosso. Three had remained in Luciara working as wage laborers, 2 were in São Miguel (Goiás) working in carpentry and cattle transportation, 1 was a tenant farmer in Goiás, and 2 females were thought to be prostitutes in unknown locations in Pará.

The remaining 50 adults had either been born in Santa Terezinha or accompanied their parents when they moved there. Slightly fewer than 40 percent of these adults continued to live in or near Santa Terezinha. The occupational profile of this 40 percent who remained was comparable to that of the rest of the population, as described in previous chapters. Approximately 60 percent of these adult children, however, had left Santa Terezinha more or less permanently. Where did they go, and how have they made out?

Only 4 of the 30 who had left ended up in major urban centers: 3 in Brasília and 1 in Goiania. The 3 in Brasília came from small farm families; 1 was trying to make a career in the army, and 2 were students. One student lived with her grandmother and the other worked as a maid in a middle-class home. These data, together with other observations and conversations, suggest that for the frontier inhabitants rural-urban migration is relatively rare. Other Santa Terezinha residents known to be residing in either Brasília or Goiania were all students—children of the more well-to-do town families. It does not appear likely that these students will later choose to return to live in Santa Terezinha.

The majority of the adults who left Santa Terezinha, however, ended up in Mato Grosso, Pará, or Goiás. Approximtely one-third (12) of the adults were in Mato Grosso: 3 in São Felix do Xingu, 2 in Luciara, 1 in Xavantina, and the rest in rural locations such as farms or large cattle *fazendas*. Their occupations break down as follows: 5 *fazenda* workers, 2 cattle tenders, 1 tenant farmer, 1 small ranch owner, 1 teacher, 1 employee of the Catholic mission in São Felix do Araguaia, and 1 unknown. Nine Santa Terezinha adults had moved to Pará, where 6 worked at cattle *fazendas* (5 peons and 1 crew leader), 1 was farming his sister's land, 1 worked as store clerk, and 1 was unknown. Six had moved to the state of Goiás, where 1 was a farmer who was being evicted from his farm, 1 was farming his sister's land, 1 was a tenant farmer, 1 was a cattle tender working for his godmother, and 2 were unknown. In sum, the occupational profile of people migrating away from Santa Terezinha is quite similar to those who remain. Why migrate, then?

Since I was not able to interview people who had already left the area, my interviews were conducted with people getting ready to move in 1978–1979. The major motivation they mentioned for the move was the search for economic betterment. Information and rumors about "better places" were fairly common in Santa Terezinha. For example, during 1978–1979, five families I knew moved to a place in Pará called Entrucamento, one of the latest "boom" spots where people were going because of the completion of some roads, a rumored INCRA land distribution, and wage labor opportunities at several cattle *fazendas* in the early stages of installation. One man about to leave for Entrucamento explained that he thought it would be a good place for new businesses. This man, whose married sister and parents lived in Santa Terezinha, had sold his squatters' rights (*posse*) to about 80 hectares of land for about 10,000 cruzeiros (US$500) and was planning to open a house of prostitution in the new location.

Another woman seen selling all of her household goods in the street explained to me one day that her husband had already gone ahead and secured a job at a cattle company in southern Pará. Other families, often located on the perimeters of town, frequently mentioned that they would be leaving Santa Terezinha soon. They did not state this as a choice but, rather, indicated that they felt they had no alternative but to stay on an endless round of travel from one cattle *fazenda* to another.

In summary, one may observe that the same forces that bring people to Santa Terezinha also operate to pull people away. Most of the population movement was not to urban or even provincial urban centers but, rather, to other frontier locations in earlier stages of frontier expansion. The increasingly limited opportunities in Santa Terezinha contributed to the out-migration of more than 60 percent of the sample of adults. This out-migration was an attempt to achieve economic betterment and can also be considered a survival strategy.

Yet, again as with the other survival strategies examined here, the potential for success appears to be quite small. Many frontier people, for whom migration has become a way of life, simply move continually from frontier areas in later stages of expansion to frontier areas that are just beginning to be opened up. Furthermore, over the last two decades the cycle of these frontier stages appears to have been speeded up as national policies have actively directed Amazonian development efforts. There is also a pattern of continual movement of labor to each successive location of the installation of capitalist enterprises in the Amazon. Since so many of the corporate projects, such as cattle raising, require significant labor only in the initial stages, it is not in their interests to encourage the formation of a landed peasantry that could function as a permanent supply of periodic labor. Therefore, the small farmer migrants end up competing with capitalist enterprises for control over local basic resources. The small farmers rarely win in this competition.

Small farmer migrants to frontier areas in the later stages of expansion, such as Santa Terezinha, face enormous obstacles and economic constraints such as greatly decreased access to productive resources. The survival strategies described above, then, must be viewed as rational attempts to obtain livelihood and progress within a situation of acute constraints. But to point to either the logical or the rational quality of the farmers' survival strategies is not to say that they are more than marginally successful. With almost any measure, one must conclude that, on the average, people's efforts bring them little more than bare survival. In fact, these survival strategies, in the final analysis, yield little better than a "holding action" of people swimming against increasingly strong currents. In addition, the multiplicity, flexibility, and maximization of short-term goals are often incompatable with or dysfunctional for long-term planning and organizing.

The final point that needs to be emphasized is that frontier household survival strategies "make sense" within the context of frontier socio-economic constraints. Therefore, solutions to the acute problems of the rural poor in Amazonia should not begin with efforts to change the small farmers' attitudes or values. These are not really the problem at all. Nor would technological or even infrastructural change help very much, unless the fundamentally dichotomized structure of frontier expansion is recognized and changed.

Notes

1. See Cardoso and Muller (1978), Davis (1977), Feder (1971), and Foweraker (1981) for analyses of the larger forces that influence migration in the countryside.

2. Only 33 out of the 81 migration histories collected were sufficiently complete and detailed to allow for comparison. The generalizations based on this small sample, however, are also supported by other data derived from participant-observation and interviews.

3. Mahar (1979:49) reports that of the total population movement in the Amazon, 40.9 percent was urban-to-urban, 30 percent was rural-to-rural, 14.6 percent was rural-to-urban, and 14.5 percent was urban-to-rural.

4. Part of the reason more evictions were not reported relates to the tendency of the small farmers to move voluntarily before eviction occurs. As eviction is considered to be highly humiliating, many farmers who anticipated eviction moved *before* action was taken against them.

5. *Rife* is a chance game.

6. The land that Jaime purchased near Santa Terezinha was part of a 100-hectare lot distributed by INCRA to a local family. Many families have already sold part or all of the land that they received from INCRA. Disputes over this land will occur later, however, because most deeds processed by INCRA stipulate that the land is not to be sold for a certain period of time, usually ten to fifteen years. Local farmers are unaware of these regulations. When they sell parts of the INCRA lots, it is unclear as to whether the buyer or the seller actually does the legal paperwork necessary for a legal transfer of the deed. In 1979, there were already rumors circulating in Santa Terezinha that INCRA planned to take back land that had already changed hands. It was impossible to either confirm or deny these rumors.

7. The CODEARA *fazenda* sold beef to its employees once a week for half the normal market price. The availability of this beef was more important than its reduced price because of the six-month meat shortage in the town.

8. One indication of the "fame" of the Santa Terezinha conflict is that Shelton Davis (1977) devoted an entire chapter of his book, *Victims of the Miracle,* to events in Santa Terezinha.

7

Santa Terezinha Revisited: 1987

Returning to Santa Terezinha

It was with considerable anticipation that I climbed down from the little plane at the Santa Terezinha airstrip one hot afternoon in early November 1987. It was almost nine years since I had sold my hut, packed my fieldnotes, and left the town. During the intervening years, I had received only a handful of letters with scant news from informants; but this was not surprising given the general lack of literacy and the absence of postal service in the region. I wondered what I would find now.

When I had left in 1979, it was very difficult to be optimistic about the future of Santa Terezinha. The cattle *fazendas* were clearly dominant in the region, and their relations with the local population could best be described as a "cold war." Small farming seemed destined to continue to decline given the multiple constraints of land scarcity, lack of technical or credit support, absence of infrastructure such as roads, a minimal market for agricultural products, and many young adults seeking other livelihood alternatives. Despite legal stipulations to the contrary, many recipients of INCRA land were selling it, often to meet immediate cash needs because of a serious illness or other emergency. The status and future of the small farmers in the squatter areas—the *posseiros* of Lago Grande, Antonio Rosa, the Crisoste, and elsewhere—seemed precarious, the ownership of the lands uncertain.

The service-center functions of the town also seemed threatened. As cattle *fazendas* completed formation of their pastures, deforestation activities would slow, thereby eliminating most of the jobs available at the ranches. In addition, a new road, the BR 158, was being constructed some 80 kilometers inland to the west of the Araguaia River. It seemed likely that this road would make river transportation obsolete. Thus, Santa Terezinha's role as a hub for imported goods and a way station for the regional workers would be undermined. In 1979, many local merchants were already discussing the possibility of leaving Santa

Terezinha to relocate at a proposed new settlement along the BR 158. Neither the agricultural nor commercial future of the town appeared promising.

With this negative prognosis in mind, I braced myself for disappointment as the taxi lurched down the dirt road toward town that November afternoon. However, I would soon be pleasantly surprised. The Santa Terezinha of 1987, I saw immediately, was both reassuringly familiar and also larger and more established looking than ever. The first thing I noticed were the poles, electric wires, and street lights along the road. The road itself, while still dirt, was ploughed into two lanes, with drainage ditches and a neat row of young trees planted down the center strip. Soon we passed the Santa Terezinha postal and telegram office, identified by a metal plaque, and then a deafeningly noisy power station. Next to it was a water pumping station. High atop one of the town's central hills was a tall tower with a dish receiver for Santa Terezinha's one telephone. Even before arriving for an emotional welcome at an old friend's *pensão* on Rua do Comercio, I was overwhelmed by the signs of change apparent everywhere.

During my first week back, I spent almost all my time visiting old friends and cataloguing the more obvious differences from 1979. Apart from improved streets, electricity, piped water, a telephone, and postal service, I found new municipal buildings, including a garage for trucks and machines, a civil registry office, two banks, a second large primary school and a second cemetery, and three municipal projects under construction: a new *praça*, a municipal sawmill, and a row of federally sponsored *casas populares* (subsidized low-income housing units). In 1980, Santa Terezinha had won its battle to secede from Luciara and had become the seat of its own municipality—a political victory of considerable significance. Although I was later to learn that the CODEARA *fazenda* continued to represent what the Santa Terezinha mayor called a "parallel power structure" in the region, CODEARA, from 1980 onward, was located within the municipality of Santa Terezinha instead of Santa Terezinha being within CODEARA, as had been the case for the previous fifteen years.

Another startling change was that the *cabaret* (red light district) had completely disappeared; only some overgrown ruins marked the place where the nightclubs had once so successfully captured the wages of ranch workers. The residential streets were expanded on both sides of town, and while neither electricity nor piped water extended into the back neighborhoods, all streets had been renamed and the houses numbered. The entire urban area had been surveyed and divided into lots and, after some initial confusion between the first and second municipal administrations, all residents had gained the right to one free lot. (To prevent speculation, however, the title was delivered only after five years in residence.)

The BR 158 had been completed, and Santa Terezinha was linked to it by a feeder road. A new city, Vila Rica, had grown up north of the intersection between the feeder road and the BR 158, some 80 kilometers from Santa Terezinha. A daily bus ran between Santa Terezinha and Vila Rica, three hours in the dry season and four or more during the rainy season, and from Vila Rica one could catch buses north to Redenção, Marabá, or even Belém in the state of Pará, or south to Cuiaba, Goiania, or Brasília. Vila Rica had initially been formed by a private Banco do Brasil colonization project in the early 1980s. By 1987, many southern Brazilian colonists were farming there in what were reputed to be superior soils. At first, Vila Rica had been within the municipality of Santa Terezinha, but several years later it too gained its independence and became a separate municipality. Santa Terezinha residents concurred in their general dislike of Vila Rica's transient boom-town atmosphere, criticizing it as too hot and dry and too full of southerners whom they found rather strange and foreign. However, almost everyone I spoke to had been there at least once, to shop at the "real supermarkets," to catch a bus to somewhere else, or, most important, to use one of the two hospitals there. (The medical services in Santa Terezinha were still woefully inadequate.)

Perhaps one of the greatest surprises of all my first days back was to see the CODEARA bus, referred to as the *colectiva* or collective bus, picking up workers in town every morning and delivering them home in the early evening. No one paid any particular attention to this bus, and local people often hitched free rides on it to various settlements within CODEARA. But to someone who remembered the general perception of CODEARA as the powerful enemy of Santa Terezinha, this evidence of peaceful town-ranch coexistence was truly remarkable. References to the changed relations with the *fazenda* emerged in conversations from the very first day, when I mentioned the bus and was told that "good jobs" were available at CODEARA these days. What jobs, I asked? Jobs in rubber, I was told. What about the peons, I inquired? The days of the peons were over, people said. What about the times of hostility between the *fazenda* and Santa Terezinha? Those days are finished, they explained, adding that local people often went to the CODEARA hospital to be treated and that the *fazenda* now sold beef to local butchers. Clearly, a great deal had changed in the past nine years.

Changes

People pointed proudly to the growth of the town, and indeed, I was surprised to find that the population had increased from 1,930 in 1979 to approximately 3,350 by the end of 1987. Not all of this increase can be attributed to natural population growth; therefore immigration, into the urban area at least, had continued.

Business growth was not as dramatic. The total number of businesses had increased from 88 in 1979 to 96 in 1987—only 9 percent more. What I found most interesting about the commercial activity was not so much its growth (which seemed against the odds) but, rather, the kinds of businesses now present. While the bulk of businesses continued to be little stores and bars, most revealing was the disappearance of the *cabaret*, clearly linked to the decrease in ranch workers, and the reduction in the number of *pensões* (boarding houses) from six to two—again pointing to a decrease in transience. There were more of the kinds of businesses one might find in any "normal" Brazilian interior town—banks, restaurants, garages, gas stations, and the like.

The municipality itself, once an incredibly vast one encompassing the entire northeastern corner of Mato Grosso, was much reduced in size because of the formation of other municipalities. Parts of Luciara bordered Santa Terezinha to the south and west, with Vila Rica to the northwest and another new municipality, Porto Alegre, to the southwest. The current municipality of Santa Terezinha, approximately 14,000 square kilometers, still included several *fazendas* (such as CODEARA) and the squatter farmer areas to the north as far as Lago Grande near the border with Pará. Rudimentary roads and wooden or barge bridges now connected most of the interior settlements to town, including the INCRA areas to the west (renamed Palestina, Roça Grande, and Nova Esperança). Northward, the *posseiro* area (Gleba Presidente) now contained five nucleated settlements: Antonio Rosa, Colonia São José, Colonia São João, Lagoa de Arroz, and Crisostomo (also known as Crisoste). The SUCAM malaria spray teams estimated the total municipal population at approximately 9,000 persons.

By 1987, some 50 percent of the INCRA distributed land had changed hands, much of it purchased by local merchants. The estimated population of the northern *posseiro* area was approximately 200 families. At the beginning of the rainy season in 1987, the Gleba Presidente (land belonging to the estate of the heirs of the former president of Brazil, João Goulart) was being surveyed by an agrarian reform team in preparation for eventual land distribution to local residents. The responsiveness of the national agrarian reform ministry (Ministério de Desenvolvimento e Reforma Agrária, or MIDRA—formerly INCRA) to the formal request from Santa Terezinha for regularization of this area can be linked to the 1985 passage of a reformulated agrarian reform law by the new civilian government of Brazil.[1] A census and the formal distribution of land would likely take another one or two years; and because of ambiguity in the new law, it was unclear whether the *posseiros* would gain titles or usufruct to their land. The concern was that giving title to the MIDRA distributed land would lead to land speculation, as often occurs in Amazonia.

Santa Terezinha was especially fortunate in the timing of its political emancipation, which coincided with the national transition from military to civilian government but predated the subsequent national economic crisis by several years. Shortly after Santa Terezinha became a municipality, control of the state government of Mato Grosso passed to the control of the political party formed from the previous opposition movement (i.e., the Partido de Movimento Democrático Brasileiro, or PMDB)—the same party that was in power in Santa Terezinha. State funds and resources began flowing to Santa Terezinha as never before, and many of the public improvements I had noticed upon my return dated back to this particularly flush period. Apart from the previously mentioned projects, important municipal activities included road construction and maintenance, low-cost public transportation between interior settlements and the town, a short-lived municipal farmers' market, an educational program including the construction of seventeen rural school houses, a health education program, and an agricultural development project.

Although the state government was responsible for the town elementary schools, the municipality took the initiative to build and staff the seventeen rural schools; usually with young farm wives. The rural schools allowed farm families to remain at their *roças* without forgoing educational opportunities for their children. Transportation of people, produce, and animals from the *roças* to town was facilitated by a municipal truck that serviced a different settlement each week. The passengers shared fuel costs, thereby reducing the cost of a trip to town to under a dollar.

The most uniformly criticized aspect of municipal services was health care, which even the Santa Terezinha mayor regretfully described as "a disaster." Low salaries and difficult living conditions discouraged highly trained medical personnel from working for the municipality, and the Mato Grosso health post still provided little more than basic vaccinations. Since the Brazilian Air Force doctors had stopped visiting the town, and the cooperative UNICA pharmacy dispensed mainly drugs and advice, basic medical services remained highly problematic. As a 1986 report from the Santa Terezinha Department of Health stated

> The health conditions of the municipal population of Santa Terezinha are extremely precarious. Various factors contribute to this situation: a deficient and inadequate diet which is a function of the low income of the population and dietary taboos; a lack of adequate hygienic practices and basic sanitation; and an almost complete lack of medical treatment.

> Malaria is endemic in the region, and the incidence of Hansen's disease [leprosy] is alarming. Worms infest 100 percent of the adults and children.

Most people either visited the hospital at CODEARA, which was open to everyone on a fees-for-service basis, or traveled to the private hospitals in Vila Rica. The municipal health program, severely limited by financial and human resource constraints, concentrated on preventative health education. This included lectures and demonstrations on basic sanitation and hygiene, treatment of garbage, dental hygiene, use of water filters, avoidance of worm infestations and the like. The only instruments available were two microscopes used for the identification of types of malaria and worms. In December 1987, however, these microscopes were stolen in an apparent attempt to further discredit the current municipal government in upcoming elections in 1988. The nurse in charge of the municipal Department of Health was actively seeking funding to establish a series of rural health posts, to be linked to the rural school houses. In addition, there was the possibility of a state and federally sponsored health center at some time in the future. But in 1987 the available medical services were minimal, and local inhabitants still often sold everything they owned, including land and animals, to pay for transportation and treatment for serious illnesses or accidents.

The situation of Dona Flora and Francisco, in the late 1970s, described in Chapter 2, may serve as an example of the serious consequences of inadequate health services. The reader may remember that this family, which had lived in the region for several generations, had received an INCRA land allocation in the early 1970s in Palestina, the area farthest from town. When I last saw them in 1979, they were in the late 40s, struggling to establish their new farm and trying hard to encourage their adult children to participate more fully in agricultural activities. Dona Flora also washed laundry at the river for extra income.

When I arrived at their house in 1987, Francisco was sitting quietly on a homemade stool in an almost empty living room. He explained that about a year ago, at age 57, he had started having chest pains. The couple then sold one-fifth of their land in order to raise money for a trip to Vila Rica for a medical examination. Francisco was told to stop working in the fields because of a serious heart condition requiring surgery. The family knew of no way they could afford the necessary operation.

Within a half-hour, Dona Flora arrived home from a firewood-gathering expedition. Looking considerably older and dispirited, she did not recognize me until her husband told her who I was; in fact, her eye sight had continued to deteriorate, and she had no glasses. She then explained that since she could not run the farm without Francisco's help, the family, now consisting of the couple and their youngest daughter, now 11, had abandoned the farm and moved permanently back to town. Beginning to weep, she told me of their two adult sons: One had died recently "from fevers," and the other was working at a gold rush town in southern Pará. Their two grown daughters lived in Santa Terezinha, but one had been abandoned by her husband, and the other son-in-law worked full-time as a manual laborer for the municipal government. After making coffee for us all, the 11-year-old daughter started to make the bread that she sold daily to the elementary school children during recreation time.

Dona Flora had a cold. When she smiled, I could see only one remaining tooth in the front of her mouth. Her hair, still drawn back into a tight bun, had greyed considerably. I inquired how the family was going to survive. She explained that they were currently living on stored rice and manioc flour from the previous year's harvest. Nothing was being planted this year, and it was unclear how they would manage to feed themselves in the future. We also discussed the possibility that they might rent their remaining land to a tenant farmer, but they were very afraid of losing the land to a squatter's claims. They had failed to convince more trusted friends to farm at such a remote location. The farm in Palestina was also less desirable because the new municipal agricultural program, which Dona Flora and Francisco would have liked to participate in, was being targeted to the neediest farmers, the *posseiros* of the Gleba Presidente to the north. As we continued to discuss what the family could do, it soon became clear that what they perceived to be their only realistic option was to sell the remaining four-fifths of their land. If successful, this sale might raise enough money for Francisco's surgery; but there was still a question as to how this farm family would earn a livelihood after the cash was spent. Having surmounted considerable obstacles in their lifelong struggle to make a decent living at farming, the family faced a final blow—ill health—from which they will probably never recover.

One of the most positive directions of change was the relatively new municipal agricultural development program headed by a dedicated Italian ecology buff who had originally started working in Amazonia eight years before in the Italian equivalent of the Peace Corps. Linked to a regional ecology movement, MEPA,[2] he stated that his goal was to promote appropriate and sustainable agricultural development by encouraging high cash value and low-risk perennial crops suitable for continuous production in the *capoeiras* (secondary growth areas). To this end, he had carefully researched all crops ever grown by regional inhabitants and formulated a program focused on sesame production for sale to natural food/macrobiotic stores in urban centers in Minas

Gerais, Goiás, São Paulo, and elsewhere. Other products under consideration and being encouraged included *urucu* (*Bixa orellana*), the fruit of the perennial annatto tree from whose pulp is extracted a red dye; azuki beans, favored by macrobiotic consumers; cashews, another high cash value perennial; a variety of rice favored by natural food and macrobiotic consumers (*Arroz catitinho*); *rapadura*, the crude brown sugar blocks made from sugar cane; and honey from the "killer bees" now so common throughout Amazonia. All but the cashews were familar to most farmers.

The basic goal of the agricultural program was to help "fix the small farmer to the land." Basic elements included the following:

1. A concern for ecological sustainability—especially in terms of slowing the rate of deforestation in the slash-and-burn cycle by encouraging continuous cultivation of the *capoeiras;*
2. An emphasis on high cash value, low-risk crops to help raise farm family incomes while simultaneously encouraging diversified agriculture and particularly the continuation of basic food crops for home consumption (manioc, rice, etc.);
3. Selection of target crops already familiar to local farmers, and the suggestion of relatively minor modifications in cultivation practices to facilitate learning and adoption;
4. Selection of target crops for commercialization that were neither already vertically integrated into large firms (e.g., cocoa) nor especially amendable or attractive for large-scale, mechanized production, in order to minimize outside control and future competition;
5. Emphasis on low-cost methods, with shared use of any needed agricultural machinery (e.g., tractors) for which payment could be made in sesame or rice, thus avoiding loans; and
6. A linkage to relatively small and independent outside buyers (in this case, natural food/macrobiotic firms) willing to undertake the additional costs of doing business with small producers in relatively distant locations.

There was talk in 1987 that one natural food company was willing to invest in preliminary processing plants in the region. In addition, there were plans being made for a sesame oil plant in Santa Terezinha, a cashew plant in São Felix, and a dried banana chips plant in Canarana.

The Italian, instrumental in formulating these plans, had come to work for the municipal government of Santa Terezinha in 1985, from a previous post in São Felix. Prior to his arrival, the municipality had made a half-hearted attempt to encourage local farmers to plant more *mamona*, or castorbean (*Ricinus comunis*), as had been suggested by some government agricultural experts. But the low prices received for the castor oil beans, together with a general disorganization and lack of coordination of marketing, led to rapid disillusionment with this project. The agricultural cooperative, founded in the mid-1960s by Padre Francisco Jentel, closed its doors in the early 1980s, mainly because of falling membership and inability to collect on bad debts. Jentel's successor, Padre Canuto, attempted some socialist experiments in encouraging collective farming (*roça comunitaria*), but these never generated much enthusiasm among the majority of the small farmers.[3] The Italian thus faced a certain amount of cynicism on the part of local farmers about any efforts to improve their situation.

Yet the Italian was quite experienced in working with regional farmers. He started out quite modestly by encouraging only small-scale and experimental planting of sesame, previously grown in very tiny amounts for home consumption. He provided free seeds and guaranteed purchase of any surplus, paying the farmers in money, rice, or corn. In addition, he organized a demonstration "field" by planting sesame all around the borders of the Santa Terezinha airstrip. By the planting season of 1987, almost half of the approximately 1,000 farm households in the municipality had plans to cultivate surplus sesame, according to the Santa Terezinha Department of Agriculture.

Although it is still too early to evaluate the merits of the sesame project (1987–1988 was the first year of extensive planting), it appears that the prognosis is more positive than for any previous project. Without ever labeling or categorizing his program, the Italian's project closely follows the outlines of a farming systems research and development approach, given its concerns with farmers' actual goals and constraints, its attention to the environmental and sociocultural contexts, and its emphasis on low-risk, minimal investment, farmer involvement, and adoptibility.[4] The attention to and choice of linkages to urban natural food markets is especially noteworthy, inasmuch as the marketing of surplus had always been a major obstacle in all previous projects. Most of the farmers I interviewed in 1987 expressed knowledge of and interest in what was commonly referred to as "the sesame project"; and many, even those skeptical about possibilities for success, reported plans to plant larger areas of sesame.

Thus, the formation of Santa Terezinha as an independent municipality influenced many changes. However, other forces and events were also affecting the region. Two of the most important variables for understanding regional change were the cattle *fazendas*, especially CODEARA, and the new roads, particularly the BR 158.

In general, the cattle *fazendas* of northern Mato Grosso were in serious financial trouble by the mid-1980s. Although all official Amazonian development plans since 1979 have supported large-scale cattle projects, other factors—expiring fiscal incentives, closer supervision, less abundant credit, environmental problems with pastures, misspent investment monies, poor performance records, and a worsening national economic crisis—have taken their toll. Most analysts concur that the Amazonian cattle *fazendas* have largely been economic failures. Many of the predicted ecological consequences resulting from deforestation and the subsequent replacement with pastures have occurred. The ranch officials I interviewed reported major problems with weeds, thus necessitating extensive and expensive restoration of pasture and the increased use of fertilizers and pesticides.[5] There was much discussion of the misappropriation of investment monies, and several ranch managers reported that only about half of the previously projected infrastructural and development plans had been realized. Cattle production was far less than anticipated. One *fazenda* manager I interviewed stated that "these *fazendas* have become what you might call white elephants."

The CODEARA *fazenda*, however, had fairly early on begun to anticipate many of the problems the other ranches were having and had taken a variety of steps to avoid them. CODEARA's strategy was markedly distinguished from those of neighboring *fazendas* by four components: the structural reorganization into eight separate firms; significant attention to research and development in plant and animal breeding; the diversification of economic activities beyond cattle; and, as of 1986, a private colonization project designed to sell off 65 percent of the *fazenda's* vast holdings.

By 1987, CODEARA was actually a conglomerate of eight companies, each engaged in different but related activities. This organizational fissioning was useful in many respects, including the fact that, by forming new companies, each entity would again become eligible for SUDAM fiscal incentives. In general, Amazonian projects received only six to eight years of SUDAM support and incentives, with no renewals of projects. Although in recent years the fiscal incentives package had become less generous, SUDAM support was still advantageous and new firms could qualify as new projects. Since CODEARA had begun its initial project in 1966, the oldest firm, named Codeara, no longer qualified for fiscal incentives.

The eight firms of CODEARA included Codeara, Nova Codeara, BCN-Moto-Mechanização Rural, BCN-Agro-Pastoral, BCN Sementes, Plamex-Serraria, Araguaia Hervia, and Colonizadora Codeara. Cattle production, the original *raison d'être* of the company, was split between Codeara, which focused on cattle raising and breeding, and BCN-Agro-Pastoral, which, because of its location closer to the BR 158, concentrated on fattening and finishing the animals just prior to marketing. Codeara, with 139 regular employees, also grew corn, beans, and irrigated rice for ranch consumption and sale. The oldest of the CODEARA companies, Codeara, was also the site of one of the two new rubber plantations.

The first rubber plantation, Araguaia Hervia, was a joint venture with Goodyear Rubber Company, begun in 1983. Although local farmers were skeptical about the project (inasmuch as rubber trees do not occur naturally in this drier transitional zone of the Amazon Basin), the CODEARA managers and Goodyear technicians were optimistic. There is both a domestic and an international market for rubber since Brazil, ironically, imports almost 70 percent of its rubber from abroad. The project with Goodyear was not without problems, and the initial planting of the trees in cleared pastures did not work well. About one-ninth of the rubber trees planted were lost to a variety of problems. By 1987, some 2,500 hectares (approximately 1 million trees) had been planted. The oldest trees at Araguaia Hervia were five years old; since they do not start producing for six or seven years, the future success of the project is still uncertain. CODEARA, however, was sufficiently enthusiastic about its future with rubber that, once its managers had learned Goodyear's technological innovations and management practices, they began their own independent rubber plantation at Codeara. By 1987, the Codeara rubber project encompassed 1,000 hectares, or approximately 400,000 trees.

The second new agricultural activity was a water buffalo project at Codeara Nova. Begun in 1984 with SUDAM support, it had a herd of 1,200 head by 1987 and required only four employees. Buffalo meat is sold as a lower-grade beef in Brazilian cities. BCN-Agro-Pastoral, near the new road, employed 79 full-time people. Apart from finishing cattle, it included a ceramics factory that manufactured several kinds of tiles. Plamex-Serraria, a separate firm operating at the headquarters of BCN-Agro-Pastoral, had 9 employees who ran a large sawmill, a small furniture workshop, and a power plant fueled by wood. Deforestation activities had slowed down considerably since the 1970s, when the initial pastures were created. In 1987, the CODEARA firms and other regional cattle *fazendas* were concentrating on restoring old pastures rather than on creating new ones. The relative absence of peons in Santa Terezinha was a direct function of the cessation of forest-clearing operations. Some cutting of virgin forest continued, however; to prepare areas for rubber tree planting and to obtain high-cash-value woods (selectively cut).

An innovative aspect of CODEARA's strategy was its emphasis on research and development. At Codeara, managers were quite optimistic about a new breed of cattle they had developed, *Raça Codeara* (Codeara Race), which is better adapted to regional conditions. They planned to begin selling the new breed to other *fazendas* in 1988. As of 1983, another new firm, BCN-Sementes, was formed for research and development of pasture grasses and cultigens. Headed by an agronomist and staffed by three other employees, it directed its major efforts to finding pasture grasses better suited to regional environmental conditions. The two main types of grass previously planted, *capim colonião* (*Panicum maximum* var. Colonião) and *capim jaragua* (*Hyparrhenia rufa* var. Jaragua), were considered unsatisfactory because of their high nutrient demands and their tendency to be invaded by weeds. The CODEARA firms stopped using these two types in 1985. Instead, Codeara and BCN-Agro-Pastoral now use the new types tested and produced at their own research unit, BCN-Sementes. These new varieties included *andropogon* (*Andropogon guayanus*), a grass especially resistant to dry conditions and weeds; *humicola*, also called *quicuio* (*Brachiaria humidicola*), a grass with low nutrient requirements that is very resistant to humid conditions and weeds; and *brachiarão*, also called *marandu* or *brizantão* (*Brachiaria brizantha* var. Marandu), another grass with low nutrient requirements used to fatten cattle. BCN-Sementes produced these grass seeds not only for CODEARA firms but also for sale to other *fazendas*.

BCN-Sementes conducted some research on other cultigens as well, including cotton, beans, rice, corn, soy beans, sorghum, sunflowers, and peanuts and other legumes. In particular, it tested their suitability to local conditions. Researchers rejected cotton as too demanding of soil nutrients, soy beans because of pest and disease problems, and peanuts because they require too much hand labor and pose difficulties with respect to marketing. Sorghum and sunflowers were also found unsuitable. Twenty-three varieties of corn are being tested with no definite conclusions as of yet.

In addition, BCN-Sementes had begun experimental fields of coffee, black pepper, and *urucu* (annatto). These were being grown with fertilizers, pesticides, and piped irrigation from a nearby river. Relatively little research was being carried out on these crops. The main goals of the project were to set up demonstration fields for potential colonists coming to the CODEARA colonization and to provide seedlings for sale to colonists. The agronomist recommended specific varieties of coffee and pepper thought to be optimal for regional conditions. He included the *urucu* and also recommended sesame on the basis of his observations of the Santa Terezinha agricultural project.

These activities, together with the animal breeding program, indicate the new direction of many of CODEARA's activities. The research and development were clearly designed to make CODEARA a supplier of high-quality agricultural inputs to other *fazendas* and regional farmers. Together with the rubber and water buffalo projects, they show a definite trend away from cattle production as the economic mainstay of the operation.

The last "new" firm was BCN-Moto-Mechanização Rural, which shared its headquarters with BCN-Sementes. This firm, which employed 113 people, controlled and serviced all machinery and equipment used at the seven CODEARA firms, including all vehicles, trucks, tractors, and heavy equipment. The other firms leased vehicles and equipment from BCN-Moto-Mechanização. The operation included garages, a large parts inventory for repairs, and machine shops.

Whereas the buffalo project employed only 4 people, the Araguaia Hervia project had 74 full-time employees and many temporary workers. The labor needs for rubber trees included planting, weeding, fertilization every three months, application of pesticides, and eventually harvesting. For the relatively lighter work, many women and children were temporarily employed both at Araguaia Hervia and the Codeara rubber fields, often being trucked over daily from Santa Terezinha. The majority of full-time rubber workers resided with their families in *fazenda*-constructed villages near the fields. Given the approximately 100 full-time and many temporary jobs created by the two rubber projects, the townspeoples' comments about the relative abundance of jobs in rubber at CODEARA were indeed accurate. Meanwhile, the other *fazendas* in the region had continued their primary emphasis on cattle production, employed far fewer people, and provided little temporary work.

The structure of labor at CODEARA, because of its diversification, had changed radically over the past decade. Whereas a large proportion of ranch labor had once been peons (the temporary workers hired indirectly by crew leaders) by 1987 only about one-fifth of CODEARA's labor force were hired in this indirect way. CODEARA claimed to have 422 full-time employees at all eight firms and only 100 or so peons (with some seasonal fluctuations).

The extent to which conditions for *fazenda* workers can be considered to have improved is debatable. Still, the scandalous conditions of debt servitude in the 1960s and the deplorable conditions of the peon crews in the 1970s set such a low standard that current conditions are better if only by comparison with this earlier era. In the late 1970s, the majority of the ranch labor force were peons, who were usually completely disenfranchised from worker benefits of any kind. Therefore, becoming a "regular" ranch employee, with possible access to benefits such as worker housing and ostensible protection under worker rights laws, was viewed as a more desirable position by local people. The options in 1979, when I left the region, were basically two with respect to *fazenda* employment: working as a peon for crew leaders, or working as a full-time employee of the ranch.

The labor situation in 1987 was more complicated. There were essentially four kinds of workers. Within the context of direct employment by the ranch, there were full-time regular employees as well as the many people hired on a temporary daily basis during busy seasons. These temporary workers were local people, usually women and children, and were not referred to as peons because they were not organized by crew leaders. Within the context of indirect employment, there were again basically two kinds of work being contracted out. One resembled the old system of peonage in that crew leaders brought outside workers, usually from northeastern Brazil, for specific jobs and limited time periods to work at the *fazenda*. Whereas it had once been relatively common for these migrant workers to have entered the region with their families, the currently diminished peon workforce was generally made up of men who had left their families in the northeast, hoping to bring their earnings home with them at the end of their time in Mato Grosso. The second kind of indirect or contracted work was a variant on the idea of the work crew. Local people had discovered that contracting for a specific job for a specific amount of money was sometimes more lucrative than working directly for the ranch. Therefore, a certain number of jobs, on which CODEARA did not provide data, were contracted out on a piece basis either to very small groups of men, usually locals who formed a far more egalitarian "crew," or to single individuals with special machinery of their own. (The system is referred to as "custom work" in the United States.)

Thus, the highly dichotomized structure of the *fazenda* workforce was more diffused, and the distinctions between direct and indirect employment, with direct employment as a desired goal, were far less clear. The migrant worker crews were still utilized by the ranch for work in clearing and preparing fields, pasture restoration, fence-making, and some planting work. The total number of functioning crew leaders was much reduced, to approximately twenty. Four devoted themselves exclusively to rubber, and an undetermined number were local people organized into more egalitarian groups resembling partnerships. These locals asserted that they could make more money working on a contract basis than as direct ranch employees. The CODEARA officials admitted that the existing laws designed to protect both temporary and contract (indirectly hired) workers were still largely unenforced, but they were proud of the fact that they now checked all their contractors to make sure they were registered to pay taxes.

Direct employment as a full-time *fazenda* employee was viewed as a less attractive option in 1987 than in 1979. According to my calculations based on CODEARA's own data, the full-time employees at all eight CODEARA firms made less money in real terms in 1987 than they had in 1979. This is probably due to a variety of factors, including the spiraling Brazilian inflation (approximately 1,000 percent annually), the opening of the region, which diminished the need to "lure" skilled workers to such a remote place, and the relative abundance of a larger and somewhat more stable local population. Some examples illustrate this trend. Whereas a highly skilled vehicle mechanic at CODEARA made about US$250 a month in 1979, the same position in 1987 paid US$227. An experienced cowboy earned US$87 a month in 1979 but only $75 in 1987. While some error in the calculation of salaries may result because of major fluctuations in inflation and currency conversion rates, particularly in 1987, there was a general downward trend in real earnings. Counterbalancing this, however, was a more attractive benefit package for regular employees, including improved *fazenda*-provided housing, some health care, and elementary school facilities at the majority of the worker villages. The quality and amenities of *fazenda* housing, as before, were sharply stratified by level of position.

Two contrasting households made up of *fazenda* employees illustrate the range of benefits and quality of life at CODEARA. A manager of one of the firms, a southern Brazilian married to a local Santa Terezinha woman, had a house with electricity, piped water, and screens. He enjoyed a variety of other in-kind earnings such as access to company vehicles and a substantial allocation of land on which he had grown rice for sale and turned a good profit. The family had a maid and traveled to Santa Terezinha weekly for shopping and socializing. This relatively comfortable standard of living can be compared to the household of Ines and Raimundo, the family described in Chapter 6. Raimundo and Ines and their eight children had been farmers until 1976, when Ines's mother sold her INCRA land allocation because of her misunderstanding that her children would be unable to inherit it. By 1979, Raimundo was working periodically as a peon at *fazendas* while Ines washed laundry and sold greens and cakes in the streets of the town. When I returned to Santa Terezinha in 1987, I found Ines and Raimundo and their younger children living at the worker village at Araguaia Hervia. Raimundo was the supervisor of the rubber workers, earned one of the higher salaries of US$106 a month, and worked eleven hours a day. Their concrete house lacked electricity, piped water, and screens. Ines, ill with diabetes and its complications, kept house and raised some chickens and fresh vegetables in the backyard.

During a one-day interview with the family, Ines explained that her husband had worked for the ranch but had later quit and formed a small, more egalitarian work crew with some neighbors in Santa Terezinha. The group had been relatively successful in getting contract jobs at the ranch. Because the *fazenda* managers admired Raimundo's organizational and supervisory talents, they had asked him to return to full-time direct employment as the supervisor of rubber workers and promised that his salary would be higher than what he was earning as an independent contractor. After almost a year of direct employment at Araguaia Hervia, however, the family was disappointed. Ines asserted that Raimundo was actually earning less than he had by contract work, and she described at length why she hated the dreary row-house ranch village so far from town and her other relatives and friends. For their transportation to and from Santa Terezinha they took the usually overcrowded CODEARA bus, whose seats were mostly allocated to ranch employees who lived in Santa Terezinha and commuted daily. In sum, for Raimundo and Ines, even with a somewhat improved job in the ranch hierarchy, the advantages of full-time work at CODEARA were marginal. After less than a year at Araguaia Hervia, they were already considering quitting and returning to contract work.

Yet there can be no doubt that relations between Santa Terezinha and CODEARA not only changed but improved over the past nine years. To begin with, the general perception of the *fazenda* as "the enemy" was being replaced by a more benevolent and almost paternalistic image of a company providing a variety of benefits for the region and its inhabitants. This shift in the *fazenda's* role can be attributed partly to the Japanese-Brazilian manager who ran the operation for several years in the early 1980s. This particular manager, a southern Brazilian, had lived in the region for almost twenty years. He had innumerable friends and acquaintances in Santa Terezinha and sent his children to school in the town. He initiated many cooperative gestures, including opening the ranch hospital to regional inhabitants, selling *fazenda* beef to Santa Terezinha butchers, and helping out the new municipal government with machinery repairs and parts. Given the history of CODEARA in the region and its previous policies, these were radical departures from its former role.

The economic diversification strategy of CODEARA also altered what might have been the expected course of regional involvement and labor needs of the ranch. If CODEARA had continued its exclusive emphasis on cattle production, as many other regional *fazendas* have done, the number of jobs available would have steadily decreased. The number of people needed to run an animal operation is minimal, as demonstrated by the water buffalo project, which required only four employees. While many CODEARA employees (particularly those at the management level) still come from outside the region, a significant portion of the labor force is local. The mayor of Santa Terezinha estimated that about 70 percent of the urban population were employed by CODEARA. CODEARA managers, on the other hand, estimated that only about 20 percent of regular employees and 20 percent of contract workers (about 17 percent of the town's households) were local. In all likelihood, the true percentage of Santa Terezinha households containing someone working for CODEARA is probably 20 to 30 percent. It is interesting to note that the municipality itself also employed some 110 people, which represents 16 percent of Santa Terezinha households.

Resentments and frustrations between CODEARA and Santa Terezinha remained despite the warming trend between town and ranch. The municipal government viewed the *fazenda* as a "parallel power structure." The mayor considered them secretive about many of their activities, especially the colonization program, and not as helpful and forthcoming as he would like. Especially surprising was the very tiny amount of agricultural information exchanged, particularly with the respect to the research and development being carried out at BCN-Sementes. I was interested to discover, for example, that the secretary of agriculture of Santa Terezinha and the agronomist in charge of BCN-Sementes had never met or exchanged information. This lack of communication was particularly telling considering that the agronomist had married a local girl and spent a lot of time at his in-laws' home some five doors away from the home of the secretary of agriculture. An exchange of information would have been mutually beneficial, since the agronomist tested cultigens and varieties, and the secretary of agriculture worked with small farmers similar to the kinds of colonists CODEARA wished to establish in its new colonization project. The secretary of agriculture maintained the attitude that there was little to learn from the model of large-scale agricultural enterprises as typified by CODEARA. The agronomist felt that his job was not to be a regional extension agent, although he stated he was willing to help anyone who came to him for assistance. Ironically, the agronomist seemed to have learned more from the Santa Terezinha agricultural project than the reverse; he admitted that the idea of encouraging new colonists to plant *urucu* and sesame came from the project.

An interesting recent development at CODEARA was its new colonization program, Colonizadora Codeara, initiated in 1986. Since the *fazenda* was using only between 48,000 to 50,000 hectares of its total holdings of 350,000 hectares, the main goal of the project was to sell off approximately 225,000 hectares, or 65 percent of the land. To this end, large portions of the *fazenda* had been marked off into lots with plans for feeder roads and eventual health and educational facilities. The goal was to attract "farmer colonists" from southern Brazil.

CODEARA officials considered the Santa Terezinha residents to be unsatisfactory potential colonists. One manager explained that local people generally lack agricultural know-how and did not have a work ethic, and that when they became disgruntled they simply picked up and left to go fishing. Southerners, he asserted, would make far better colonists because they had superior agricultural knowledge and practices, were oriented toward surplus production, and really liked to work hard. When I asked if he was familiar with the relative success rates of colonists from various regions of Brazil in other government and private colonizations in the Amazon, he said no. However, he was completely convinced that southern Brazilians were the best colonists.

CODEARA had three main goals with respect to the projected colonization. These were to sell excess land holdings, to attract superior-quality farmers to form a labor pool for periodic work at the *fazenda* projects, and to increase the value of their own lands through increased regional development. In its plan to attract southern Brazilian farmers, the *fazenda* was anticipating the labor requirements of rubber harvesting and processing.

Because of this emphasis on attracting Southerners, the colonization land sales had been entrusted to real estate brokers in southern Brazil, primarily the state of São Paulo. CODEARA's first strategy was to try to attract farmers with some resources and money to buy land. Since the average price of farmland in southern Brazil was about 50,000 cruzados a hectare (US$758), compared with 6,000 cruzados per hectare (US$91) in the CODEARA colonization project area,[6] they confidently expected many enthusiastic colonists. Initial arrangements to sell lots were indeed brisk at the beginning of 1986, but the growing national economic crisis and Plano Cruzado introduced later that year caused most of the potential buyers to change their minds. When land sales did not pick up, CODEARA decided to change its strategy. An attempt was made to attract smaller farmers of more modest means by allowing them to pay for land in kind. The new plan was to have colonists make a 10 percent cash down-payment, with the remaining payment to be made in rice over a period of four years. For a lot size of 100 hectares, this entailed a cash down-payment of 60,000 cruzados (US$909) and an annual delivery of 270 sacks of rice for the next four years. It was expected that colonists would take out bank loans for their down-payments, equipment, and other agricultural inputs.

By the planting season of 1987 Colonizadora Codeara had sold land to three families, although only two families had arrived to start farming. Both families were from rural São Paulo, and they were already extremely nervous about the possibilities for success in the forests of northern Mato Grosso. Saddled with bank loans, unfamiliar with local environmental conditions, disappointed in the lack of infrastructural supports (e.g., schools and health care facilities), and worried about their distance from roads, the new colonists were already beginning to think about giving up. One family, interviewed extensively, made it clear that they had little agricultural experience, having lived previously in a provincial town where the husband had worked as a wood cutter. The wife repeatedly told me that she "hated Santa Terezinha" and "wanted to go home to São Paulo as soon as possible." Both families were planting rice and corn and had not yet even begun to consider the *fazenda's* recommendations to produce coffee, black pepper, *urucu*, or sesame. One family had purchased a house in Santa Terezinha so their children could continue school. The prognosis for the colonization project did not appear promising.

Previous research on the relative success rates of Amazonian agricultural colonization has shown that previous agricultural and especially managerial experience tend to be far more critical to frontier farming success than region of origin.[7] Yet the myth of the superior southerner remained. Some farmers from southern Brazil, particularly those from Vila Rica northwest of Santa Terezinha, did have more experience with animal traction and managing bank loans than the local farmers. However, most of the southerners' supposedly superior agricultural practices, as cited by the CODEARA manager, were practiced by locals as well, including raising chickens and pigs, planting vegetable gardens on raised platforms, and women working in the fields along with men.

Apart from questions about the qualities of the colonists themselves, other considerations for successful colonization include attention to key infrastructural components (such as feeder roads) and marketing arrangements. While Colonizadora Codeara had much of this planned out on paper, the majority of its plans—for projects ranging from roads to rural health posts—were not yet realized. This placed the new colonists in a very vulnerable position, something they were quick to point out when interviewed. It is also important to remember that while CODEARA had developed plans to sell colonists the needed inputs for coffee, black pepper, and *urucu*, almost no research had been done on the suitability of these crops for regional environmental conditions. Nor did it seem likely that the impoverished southern Brazilian farmers, who practiced slash-and-burn agriculture, would have the sophistication and financial resources necessary to duplicate CODEARA's demonstration fields with their piped irrigation system and use of fertilizers and pesticides. In sum, the deck seemed stacked against the CODEARA colonists from the start.

Because many aspects of CODEARA strategies for the 1980s—from rubber to water buffalos to colonization plans—seemed not only a reasonable response to the constraints of cattle ranching but also relatively beneficial for the regional economy, I asked officials of other regional *fazendas* if they had or were planning similar agricultural diversification or colonization. The answer to this question was a uniform no. When asked why not, the managers explained that CODEARA was in an especially fortunate situation because of its proximity to both the BR 158 and Santa Terezinha. They pointed out that the infrastructure already in place—Santa Terezinha with its schools and other facilities, an improved regional road system, and a convenient pool of labor—facilitated CODEARA's rubber projects and colonization scheme. Although this argument may ignore the other factors involved, such as corporate policies, in general it underscores the growing symbiotic relationship between Santa Terezinha and CODEARA. An uneasy relationship in many ways, it has nevertheless proved to be of some mutual benefit to both groups.

The diversification of CODEARA also helped diminish the negative impact of the BR 158 on Santa Terezinha. Whereas Santa Terezinha had once been the regional hub through which almost all goods passed, by 1987 it was a *cul de sac* at the end of a feeder road to the BR 158. Although a more functional road system facilitated the movement of goods throughout the region, the new settlements along the BR 158, particularly Vila Rica, captured the lion's share of the commercial activity. Yet Santa Terezinha's commerce did not decrease as much as might have been expected; indeed, it shifted away from the frontier to the commercial sector of a more established provincial town. The reasons for this appeared to be several. First, Santa Terezinha continued to be the central place for its own hinterland, including numerous rural settlements and Indian posts on both sides of the river. Second, with a somewhat more diversified economy and increased numbers of CODEARA agricultural workers, municipal employees, and state officials (such as teachers, tax collectors, and police), there were people with paychecks to patronize local stores. Third, CODEARA personnel, including managers and other professionals, increasingly used Santa Terezinha's stores and services, and some even lived in or near town and sent their children to school in Santa Terezinha. CODEARA had dismantled its own company store, Planta, in town and had allowed local merchants concessions to set up stores and cafeterias at *fazenda* villages.

Complaining bitterly about Vila Rica's "theft" of their commerce, local merchants and CODEARA were strongly in favor of a projected new road that would cross Bananal Island and connect Santa Terezinha directly to the Belém-Brasília Highway. If constructed, this new road would catapult Santa Terezinha into a key position on a superior transportation route and lessen the distance that goods would have to be transported. CODEARA was extremely eager to see this new road built. It would facilitate CODEARA's marketing of rubber and reduce the cost of inputs—including that of lime purchased near the Belém-Brasília, which now had to be transported by a more indirect and expensive route. There were many in Santa Terezinha who firmly believed that the Transbananal road would be the "miracle" that would revitalize the town and municipality.

Opposing the new road for various reasons was a camp consisting largely of Catholic mission personnel and some municipal officials. There was some concern about the potential impact of the road on the Karajá Indians whose reservation was located on the southern two-thirds of the interfluvial island of Bananal. A related concern was the possible effects of the road and subsequent development on the Forest Park in the northern third of the island. One partial resolution suggested was to allow the Karajá to charge a toll for every vehicle crossing the island. According to municipal officials, the tribe accepted this proposal. Another reason had to do with the accelerating effects on regional development because of the road. Although municipal officials clearly recognized that this overland route would facilitate the marketing of local products and stimulate municipal commerce, they were also worried about the effects of the road on regional land values. The road and subsequent development would likely increase the desirability and, hence, the value of land in the municipality. This in turn would put pressure on small farmers to sell. Eviction pressures on *posseiros* (squatters) would also increase. It was generally believed that the road should be delayed for several years to allow regional small farmers time to reap the benefits of the new agricultural development program and, hence, be in a stronger and more financially stable position when development pressure increased.

The final outcome on the Transbananal road is uncertain, but as of December 1987, political pressures had brought the project to a halt. How long it will be delayed is unclear. CODEARA has continued to lobby in favor of the road. Many Santa Terezinha residents expressed resentment against the municipal government for "blocking the way to progress" and found it very difficult to understand why the new road was being opposed. It is a tribute to the municipal officials' deep concern and commitment to more equitable regional development that they took such a politically unpopular position on the road.

Is It Progress?

When one is a witness to development, there is always the question of whether the changes constitute progress. Social scientists tend to ask questions about the social and environmental consequences of development; in other words, what are the costs? Anthropologists in particular have always tended to be highly conservative about endorsing development schemes because of their acute awareness of the often hidden or obscured social and ecological costs, such as the deculturation of indigenous groups or the deforestation of tropical forests.

Ironically, the "answers" to some of these larger questions were more obvious in the late 1970s than in 1987. During what might be called the second stage of regional development in northern Mato Grosso, the largely negative social and ecological effects of government-supported large-scale cattle projects were readily apparent. The displacement, marginalization, and poverty of most regional inhabitants and the acute suffering of migrant workers and families caught up in the peonage system, as documented in this book, constitute one of the most powerful and convincing arguments against this type of development strategy.

By 1987, however, the situation in the region was far more complicated. Benefits as well as costs in the shifting regional equation can be attributed to the effects of the BR 158, CODEARA's changing strategies and policies, the formation of the municipality, the projected regularization of the *posseiros'* farms, the municipal development programs, and, in the future, the private colonization and the Transbananal road. Santa Terezinha had not, as expected, become a "hollow frontier."

But the question still remained as to how much life had really improved for regional inhabitants. At first glance, the Santa Terezinha of 1987 appeared to have experienced "progress." I myself was initially very favorably impressed by such material indicators as the electrification, postal service, improved roads, and a telephone. Evidence of municipal activities was everywhere, and, as my informants had noted, there are many jobs in rubber. However, as I continued to conduct interviews and visit homes and farms, I began to suspect that much of the "progress" was more illusory than real, and that many of the benefits of change were very unevenly distributed among the regional population. Some of the worst abuses of the early period had indeed ended, such as the open war between the *fazenda* and the town and the debt peonage resembling slavery at the ranches; but the current situations of many inhabitants were hauntingly similar to what I had observed in the late 1970s.

The situation of Dona Rosa and her husband Joaquin serves as an example of this lack of progress. Although they had migrated to the region in the 1960s, they had not received an INCRA land allocation because they had fled Santa Terezinha for several years in the early 1970s, during the time of violent confrontations between the ranch and townspeople. By the time they returned to Santa Terezinha in 1974, they had missed the land distribution. When I interviewed them in 1978 and 1979, Joaquin was working both as a tenant for a neighboring merchant (who had received INCRA land) and periodically as a peon on work crews at the cattle *fazendas* in the region. Dona Rosa earned extra income making hammocks, which she sold at bingo games. Their two sons and only daughter were still in school.

When I returned to their home in 1987, it was immediately obvious that the family was not doing well. Their modest brick house was little changed since 1979, and the only evidence of the modern conveniences now available in Santa Terezinha was a single light bulb hanging from an exposed wire in the livingroom. Lunch that day consisted of rice and manioc flour flavored with some broth obtained by boiling beef bones. Dona Rosa did not even have coffee to make, which caused her considerable embarrassment. As another sign of bad times, Dona Rosa's older brother, a recent widower who had just moved to Santa Terezinha from a ranch further south, stopped by for lunch and tried to talk me into adopting his 13-year-old daughter and bringing her to the United States. This was quite startling: Although conditions had become very difficult in the late 1970s, very few people were desperate enough to try to give away their children.

It turned out that, after two decades of trying, Dona Rosa and Joaquin had finally acquired some land in 1985, when their daughter's husband (a truck driver for the municipality) purchased a small parcel for them in Nova Esperança, the closest INCRA area to town. Joaquin, however, had always had back problems; by 1987, he was unable to do heavy fieldwork. The two sons were unavailable to help their parents because, like many other local adult children, they had moved away from the area. One had gone off to southern Pará to seek his fortune in gold mining there, and the other worked as a clerk in a warehouse at a distant *fazenda*. Joaquin had hired a man to clear an area for a fresh field but discovered too late that the work had not been done. Since the clearing, drying, and subsequent burning of a new field must be done in the proper sequence just prior to the rainy season, Joaquin was out of luck by September. Only by means of some fast talking was he able to convince his former landlord, the merchant, to give him permission to sharecrop a portion of the merchant's already-cleared fields. However, as the merchant's fields were located in Roça Grande, Joaquin had to ride his bicycle two hours each way when he went to do fieldwork.

Dona Rosa had aged considerably since I had last seen her in 1979, when she had been chubbier and more cheerful. Although she was only in her early 50s, she had a variety of physical ailments including seriously deteriorating eyesight and painful arthritis. She was no longer able to do the fine work of weaving hammocks and had disassembled her loom. This was a serious loss of income to the family. Apart from her domestic duties, Dona Rosa now often cared for her grandchildren and earned tiny amounts of money making folk remedies for ailments from medicinal plants she cultivated in her backyard.

While no one family can be said to perfectly illustrate the consequences of the social and economic transformations occurring in the region, the story of Dona Rosa and Joaquin underscores the so-called human costs of development. For them, the compounding factors of lack of access to productive resources, chronic ill health with almost no medical services, and out-migration of their adult children seeking better opportunities elsewhere have resulted in a decreased quality of life. For them, the municipal small farmer sesame program came too late. It is very likely that they will ultimately give up entirely on farming and become dependent on work in rubber for low wages.

Returning to our consideration of Joseph Foweraker's (1981) three-stage model of Amazonian frontier expansion discussed in Chapter 1, we may conclude that Santa Terezinha has entered stage three, the capitalist stage. This stage is reached when the capitalist enterprises become the dominant form of production. It is characterized by rising land values, further institutionalization of private property, and concentration of landownership. The relations of production are mainly characterized by a free labor market in which the workers are engaged in wage labor. This stage does not preclude other continuing types of production; in particular, small farmers may be allowed to remain if they serve as a convenient labor pool for the periodic needs of the capitalist enterprises.

There is now a certain uneasy symbiotic relationship between CO-DEARA and Santa Terezinha. The municipality derives a series of benefits from the *fazenda*, including increased wage labor opportunities, use of the company roads, access to its health care facilities, and benevolent policies such as the sale of meat and assistance with machinery parts. This more cooperative stance makes sense because CODEARA is also dependent on Santa Terezinha in more ways than its officials would like to admit. The formation of the municipality gave CODEARA access to resources for infrastructural development that, in the form of roads and so forth, also benefit the *fazenda*. The town serves as a convenient labor pool for the ranch, and Santa Terezinha figures prominantly in the promotional literature distributed by the CODEARA colonization project. The proximity of Santa Terezinha, with its festivals, commerce, banks, and schools, is of considerable importance to potential colonists. Thus, there is a certain inevitability to the warming trend of relations between the *fazenda* and the town.

However, CODEARA as a corporate entity is not interested in the objective of more socially equitable regional development. Indeed, it is clear from the managers' comments that they hope to bring in "superior" settlers who will ultimately usurp the roles now filled by locals at the company's projects. Nor is the *fazenda* altruistic in its colonization project. Its goals in that respect are to rid the ranch of excess land, increase land values, and create a convenient pool of agricultural workers. If these activities create further development pressures—including rising land values, which will likely contribute to the displacement of local small farmers—so much the better as far as the *fazenda* is concerned. CODEARA's reasons for supporting the new Transbananal road are quite different and distinct from the reasons for which local Santa Terezinha merchants support the road. Indeed, the potential displacement of locals and the development of a successful colonization barely enter into the conscious calculation of the merchants. They just want to usurp Vila Rica's favored position on the transportation routes.

Meanwhile, the regional small farmers, while often still skeptical, largely recognize that it is the municipality alone that is working to create programs to improve their standards of living. The sesame project and the projected sesame processing plant are the most optimistic elements in the entire regional development scenario, at least when the criteria of social equity and ecological sustainability are applied. Because most regional inhabitants understand this at one level or another, and because those with agricultural interests still outnumber those who depend exclusively on commerce, the current political party, despite its opposition to the road, will likely win the next election.

Ultimately, one's evaluation of whether the changes in Santa Terezinha constitute "progress" depend on the criteria used to define development. To a large extent, what one sees in the Amazonian frontier is a duplication of traditional Brazilian agrarian structure whereby the powerful few control the majority of productive resources, such that a trickle-down effect has allowed millions of peasants to eke out impoverished livelihoods as tenants, sharecroppers, agricultural workers, and small landholders. Displaced agriculturalists, particularly from northeastern and southern Brazil, continue to flood into the nation's urban centers where, as a recent newspaper article concluded, they can make more money begging than from the low wages paid in the countryside (Riding 1988).

Within the context of Amazonian development policies favoring large-scale enterprises and the current national economic crisis characterized by nearly 1,000 percent annual inflation, Santa Terezinha emerges as neither a development success story nor a failure. A combination of factors, including the *fazenda*'s shift away from cattle production and a municipal government committed to more equitable and sustainable development, allow for a certain measure of optimism for the future of Santa Terezinha and, in particular, for the futures of the regional small farmers.

The sesame project appears to have the potential for raising the standard of living of regional farmers, thereby countering some of the pressures that will be generated by the colonization and the new road. Although it is little spoken of, there is also a possibility for cooperation and mutual aid between arriving colonists and local farmers, especially given the colonists' greater experience with animal traction and agricultural machinery, and the local farmers' greater experience and knowledge of regional environmental conditions. At present, such cooperation is difficult to predict because the colonization is in such an early stage and is being carried out quite separately from municipal development efforts. If the first two colonist families are any indication, however, subsequent colonists may very well end up turning to the municipality for assistance and support in a variety of areas.

In the final analysis, the future prognosis for Santa Terezinha certainly appears less grim now than it did in the 1970s. The diversification of CODEARA agricultural activities has fundamentally shifted the head-on collision course between the *fazenda* and the municipality; it has also created some spin-off benefits for regional inhabitants. The future welfare of Santa Terezinha, however, cannot—and, indeed, should not—be totally dependent on its becoming a "company town." To the broader goals of a more just development, the as yet untried and untested municipal programs appear to be the key.

Notes

1. See Schmink (1986) for a discussion of Brazil's 1985 agrarian reform.

2. MEPA, the Movimento Ecologico de Porto Alegre, encompasses a regional ecological movement in the municipalities of Porto Alegre, São Felix, Santa Terezinha, and Canarana. It is likely that this group was linked to the Workers party (Partido Trabalhadores, or PT) which has a very strong and active ecological commitment.

3. See Branford and Glock (1985) and Esterci (1985) for details regarding the attempts to encourage collective farming in Santa Terezinha.

4. See Shaner, Philipp, and Schmehl (1982) for a more complete description of the farming systems research and development approach.

5. These observations are supported by scientific research, reviewed by Hecht (1983, 1984).

6. In 1986, during an economic crisis, Brazil changed its money from the cruzeiro to the cruzado.

7. See Moran (1981, 1983) for a thorough discussion of the factors involved in colonists' success.

References

Anthropology Resource Center
1981 Bulletin Number 8 (September). Boston: ARC.

Amin, Samir
1974 Modern Migrations in Western Africa. London: Oxford University Press.

Arensberg, Conrad, and Solon T. Kimball
1968 Family and Community in Ireland, 2nd ed. Cambridge: Harvard University Press.

Baldus, Herbert
1960a The Tapirapé: A Tupi Tribe of Central Brazil. New Haven, Conn.: Human Relations Area File Translated Source (originally published in 1944).
1960b The Tribes of the Araguaia Basin and the Indian Service. New Haven, Conn.: Human Relations Area File Translated Source (originally published in 1948).

Barlett, Peggy F.
1980 Adaptive Strategies in Peasant Agricultural Production. Annual Review of Anthropology 9:545–573.

Bennett, John
1976 The Ecological Transition: Cultural Ecology and Human Adaptation. New York: Pergamon.

Brandes, Stanley H.
1975 Migration, Kinship, and Community. New York: Academic Press.

Branford, Sue, and Oriel Glock
1985 The Last Frontier: Fighting Over Land in the Amazon. London: Zed Books Ltd.

Bunker, Stephen G.
1979 Power Structures and Exchange Between Government Agencies in the Expansion of the Agricultural Sector. Studies in Comparative International Development 14(1):56–76.
1980 Colonization, Rural Development and the State: Settlement Along the Transamazon Highway. Latin American Symposia Series, Gainesville, Center for Latin American Studies, University of Florida.

Butler, John
1985 Land, Gold, and Farmers: Agricultural Colonization and Frontier Expansion in the Brazilian Amazon. Ph.D. Dissertation, University of Florida, Gainesville.

Butterworth, Douglas, and John K. Chance
  1981   Latin American Urbanization. New York: Cambridge University Press.
Cardoso, Fernando H., and Enzo Faletto
  1979   Dependency and Development in Latin America. Berkeley: University
         of California Press.
Cardoso, Fernando H., and Geraldo Muller
  1978   Amazonia: Expansão do Capitalismo. São Paulo: Editôra Brasiliense.
Casaldáliga, Pedro
  1971   Uma Igresa da Amazônia em Conflito com o Latifúndio e a Margin-
         alização Social. Mato Grosso (manuscript). Cited in Victims of the
         Miracle, by Shelton H. Davis. New York: Cambridge University Press.
  1978   Questão Agrária, Uma Questão Politica. *In* A Amazônia Brasileiro Em
         Foco, edited by Comissão Nacional de Defesa e Pelo Desenvolvimento
         da Amazônia. Rio de Janeiro: CNDDA.
Chambers, Erve
  1977   Public Policy and Anthropology. Review of Anthropology 4(6):543–
         554.
Chilcote, Ronald H.
  1974   Dependency: A Critical Synthesis of the Literature. Latin American
         Perspectives 1(1):4–29.
CIDA (Comite Interamericano de Desenvolvimento Agricola)
  1966   Reports on Land Tenure Conditions and Socio-Economic Development
         in (1) Argentina, (2) Brazil, (3) Chile, (4) Colombia, (5) Ecuador, (6)
         Guatemala, and (7) Peru. Washington, D.C.: Pan American Union,
         Organization of American States.
CNBB-CEP
  1976   Pastoral da Terra: Posse e Conflitos. São Paulo: Edições Paulinas
         (Conferência Nacional dos Bispos do Brasil; Comissão Episcopal do
         Pastoral).
CNDDA
  1978   A Amazônia Brasileira Em Foco. Rio de Janeiro: Comissão Nacional
         de Defesa e Pelo Desenvolvimento da Amazônia.
Connell, John, Biplap Dasgupta, Roy Laishley, and Michael Lipton
  1976   The Evidence from Village Studies. Bombay: Delhi; Oxford University
         Press.
Cotler, Julio
  1976   The Mechanics of Internal Domination and Social Change in Peru. *In*
         Peruvian Nationalism: A Corporate Revolution, edited by David Chap-
         lin. New Brunswick, N.J.: Transaction Press.
Crist, Raymond E., and Charles M. Nissly
  1973   East from the Andes. Gainesville: University of Florida Press.
Davis, Shelton H.
  1977   Victims of the Miracle. New York: Cambridge University Press.

Ehrenreich, Paul
  1965   Contributions to the Ethnology of Brazil. New Haven, Conn.: Human
          Relations Area File Source (originally published in 1891).
Esterci, Neide
  1985   Conflitos No Araguaia. Peões e Posseiros Contra a Grande Empresa.
          Ph.D. Dissertation presented to the Department of Social Sciences,
          Universidade de São Paulo.
Feder, Ernest,
  1971   The Rape of the Peasantry: Latin America's Landholding System. Garden
          City, N.Y.: Doubleday and Co.
Forman, Shepard
  1975   The Brazilian Peasantry. New York: Columbia University Press.
Forman, Shepard, and Joyce F. Riegelhaupt
  1970   Market Place and Marketing System: Toward a Theory of Peasant
          Economic Integration. Comparative Studies in Society and History
          12:188–212.
Foster, George
  1965   Peasant Society and the Image of Limited Good. American Anthro-
          pologist 67:293–315.
Foweraker, Joe
  1981   The Struggle for Land: A Political Economy of the Pioneer Frontier
          in Brazil from 1930 to the Present Day. New York: Cambridge University
          Press.
Frank, Andre Gunder
  1969   Capitalism and Underdevelopment in Latin America: Historical Studies
          of Chile and Brazil. New York: Monthly Review Press.
Friedl, Ernestine
  1962   Vasilika: A Village in Modern Greece. New York: Holt, Rinehart and
          Winston.
Friedland, William H., and Dorothy Nelkin
  1971   Migrant Agricultural Workers in America's Northeast. New York: Holt,
          Rinehart and Winston.
FUNAI
  1976   Relatório de Lavantamento Socio-Economico Realizado Nos Postos
          Indigenas da Ilha do Bananal. Brasília: Fundação Nacional do Indio
          (mimeographed manuscript).
  1978   Transcript of Interviews Conducted at FUNAI (author's private file).
Gamst, Frederick C.
  1974   Peasants in Complex Society. New York: Holt, Rinehart and Winston.
Goldfarb, Ronald L.
  1981   A Caste of Despair: Migrant Farm Workers. Ames: Iowa State University
          Press.
Gomes, Mércio
  1977   The Ethnic Survival of the Tenetehara Indians of Maranhão, Brazil.
          Ph.D. Dissertation, University of Florida, Gainesville.

Gross, Daniel, and barbara A. Underwood
   1971   Technological Change and Caloric Costs: Sisal Agriculture in North-
          eastern Brazil. American Anthropologist 73:725–737.
Harris, Marvin
   1971   Town and Country in Brazil. New York: W. W. Norton.
Hebette, Jean, and Rosa Acevedo
   1979   Colonização Para Quem? Belém, Pará: Nucleo de Altos Estudos Ama-
          zônicos.
Hecht, Susanna
   1983   Cattle Ranching in the Eastern Amazon: Environmental and Social
          Implications. *In* The Dilemma of Amazonian Development, edited by
          Emilio F. Moran. Boulder, Colo.: Westview Press.
   1984   Cattle Ranching in Amazonia: Political and Ecological Considerations.
          In Frontier Expansion in Amazonia, edited by Marianne Schmink and
          Charles H. Wood. Gainesville: University Presses of Florida.
Hutchinson, Harry W.
   1957   Village and Plantation Life in Northeastern Brazil. Seattle: University
          of Washington Press.
Ianni, Octavio
   1978   A Luta Pela Terra. Petropolis: Vozes.
IBDF/MEC
   1978   Atlas da Fauna Brasileira. São Paulo: Instituto Brasileiro de Desen-
          volvimento Florestal; Ministério de Educação e Cultura.
IBGE
   1977   Geografia do Brasil—Região Centro-Oeste. Rio de Janeiro: Instituto
          Brasileiro de Geografia e Estatística.
INCRA
   1978   Transcript of Interviews Conducted at INCRA, Brasília headquarters
          (author's private file).
Johnson, Allen W.
   1971   Sharecroppers of the Sertão: Economics and Dependence on a Brazilian
          Plantation. Stanford, Calif.: Stanford University Press.
Jones, James
   1980   Conflict Between Whites and Indians on the Llanos de Moxos, Beni
          Department: A Case Study in Development from the Cattle Regions
          of the Bolivian Oriente. Ph.D. Dissertation, University of Florida,
          Gainesville.
Kimball, Solon T.
   1978   Anthropology as a Policy Science. *In* Applied Anthropology in America,
          edited by Elizabeth M. Eddy and William L. Partridge. New York:
          Columbia University Press.
Kleinpenning, J.M.G.
   1977   An Evaluation of the Brazilian Policy for the Integration of the Amazon
          Region. Journal of Economic and Social Geography 67(5):345–360
          (Netherlands).

Kleinpenning, J.M.G., and Sjoukje Volbeda
  1985   Recent Changes in Population Size and Distribution in the Amazon
         Region of Brazil. *In* Change in the Amazon Basin Volume II: The
         Frontier After a Decade of Colonization, edited by John Hemming.
         Manchester and Dover, N.H.: Manchester University Press.

Krause, Fritz
  1966   In the Wilderness of Brazil: Report and Results of the Leipzig Expedition
         of 1908. New Haven: Human Relations Area File Source (originally
         published in 1911).

Leclau, Ernesto
  1979   Politics and Ideology in Marxist Theory. London: Verso Editions.

Lipkind, William
  1963   The Carajá. *In* Handbook of South American Indians, edited by Julian
         Steward. Washington, D.C.: Smithsonian Institute.

Lisansky, Judith
  1979   Women in the Brazilian Frontier. The Latinamericanist 15(1):1–3.

  1980a Santa Terezinha: Life in a Brazilian Frontier Town. Ph.D. Dissertation,
         University of Florida, Gainesville.

  1980b Bandeira Verde: A Revitalization Movement Among Amazonian Peas-
         ants. Paper presented at the annual meeting of the Florida Academy
         of Sciences. Tampa: University of South Florida.

  1981a Peasants and Post-Peasants in the Brazilian Frontier. Paper presented
         at the annual Southern Anthropological Society meeting, Fort Worth,
         Texas (April).

  1981b Survival Strategies in the Brazilian Amazon. Florida Journal of An-
         thropology 6(1):15–32.

  1983   Functions and Dysfunctions of a Brazilian Frontier Town: A Structural
         Analysis. Paper presented at the Middle Atlantic Council of Latin
         American Studies meeting, Williamsburg, Virginia (April).

Lomnitz, Larissa
  1976   Migration and Network in Latin America. *In* Current Perspectives in
         Latin American Urban Research, edited by Alejandro Portes and Harley
         L. Browning. Austin: Institute of Latin American Studies at the Uni-
         versity of Texas at Austin.

Long, Norman
  1977   An Introduction to the Sociology of Rural Development. London:
         Tavistock Publications.

Lopreato, Joseph
  1967   Peasants No More: Social Class and Social Change in an Underde-
         veloped Society. San Francisco: Chandler Publishing Company.

Mahar, Dennis J.
  1979   Frontier Development Policy in Brazil: A Study of the Amazon. New
         York: Praeger Publishers.

Mangin, William, ed.
  1970   Peasants in Cities: Readings in the Anthropology of Urbanization. New York: Houghton Mifflin Company.
Margolis, Maxine
  1973   The Moving Frontier: Social and Economic Change in a Southern Brazilian Community. Gainesville: University of Florida Press.
  1977   Historical Perspectives on Frontier Agriculture as an Adaptive Strategy. American Ethnologist 4(1):42–67.
Martins, José de Souza
  1975   Capitalismo e Tradicionalismo: Estudos Sobre As Contradições da Sociedade Agrária No Brasil. São Paulo: Livraria Pioneira Editôra.
Meggers, Betty
  1971   Amazonia: Man and Culture in a Counterfeit Paradise. Chicago: Aldine-Atherton.
Miller, Darrel
  1979   Transamazon Town: Transformation of a Brazilian Riverine Community. Ph.D. Dissertation, University of Florida, Gainesville; Ann Arbor: University Microfilms.
Miller, David Harry, and Jerome O. Steffen, eds.
  1977   The Frontier: Comparative Studies. Norman: University of Oklahoma Press.
Miller, Linda
  1982   Schools, Community and Change: The Role of Educators in the Development of Muitaspedras. Ph.D. Dissertation, University of Florida, Gainesville.
Mintz, Sidney
  1974   Worker in the Cane. New York: W. W. Norton.
Morães, Clodomir
  1970   Peasant Leagues in Brazil. *In* Agrarian Problems and Peasant Movements in Latin America, edited by Rodolfo Stavenhagen. Garden City, N.Y.: Doubleday.
Moran, Emilio
  1974   The Adaptive System of the Amazonian Coboclo. *In* Man in the Amazon, edited by Charles Wagley. Gainesville: University of Florida Press.
  1975   Pioneer Farmers of the Transamazon Highway: Adaptation and Agricultural Production in the Lowland Tropics. Ph.D. Dissertation, University of Florida, Gainesville.
  1981   Developing the Amazon. Bloomington: Indiana University Press.
  1983   Government-Directed Settlement in the 1970s: An Assessment of Transamazon Highway Colonization. *In* The Dilemma of Amazonian Development, edited by Emilio F. Moran. Boulder, Colo.: Westview Press.
Ortiz, Sutti R. de
  1973   Uncertainties in Peasant Farming: A Colombian Case. New York: Humanities Press, Inc.

Panagides, Stahis S., and Vande Lage Magalhães
1974   Amazon Economic Policy and Prospects. *In* Man in the Amazon, edited by Charles Wagley. Gainesville: University of Florida Press.

Parker, Eugene Philip, ed.
1979   Personal communication.
1985   The Amazon Coboclo: Historical and Contemporary Perspectives. Studies in Third World Societies 32 (June).

Perlman, Janice E.
1976   The Myth of Marginality: Urban Poverty and Politics in Rio de Janeiro. Berkeley: University of California Press.

Picchi, Debra S.
1979   The Fate of Small Farmers in Mato Grosso, Brazil (mimeographed manuscript).
1982   Energetic Modeling in Development Evaluation: The Case of the Bakaiçi Indians of Central Brazil. Ph.D. Dissertation, University of Florida, Gainesville.

Pitt, David C., ed.
1976   Developments from Below: Anthropologists and Development Situations. The Hague: Mouton Chicago.

Pitt-Rivers, J.A.
1969   The People of the Sierra. Chicago: University of Chicago Press.

Poats, Susan Virginia
1975   Kilometer 42: A Transamazon Highway Community. Master's thesis, University of Florida, Gainesville.

Pompermeier, M.
1979   The State and the Frontier in Brazil. Ann Arbor: University Microfilms.

Portes, Alejandro, and Harley L. Browning, eds.
1976   Current Perspectives in Latin American Urban Research. Austin: Institute of Latin American Studies of the University of Texas at Austin.

Prado, Caio Jr.
1971   The Colonial Background of Modern Brazil. Berkeley: University of California Press.

Queiroz, Maria Isaura Pereira de
1977   O Messianismo No Brasil e No Mundo. São Paulo: Editôra Alfa-Omega.

Quijano, Anibal
1970   Redefinizacion de la Dependencia y Marginalizacion en America Latina. Santiago: Centro de Estudios Socio-Economics, Universidad de Chile.

Redfield, Robert
1941   The Folk Culture of Yucatan. Chicago: University of Chicago Press.
1963   The Little Community and Peasant Society and Culture. Chicago: University of Chicago Press.

Reis, Arthur Cesar Ferreira
1974   Economic History of the Brazilian Amazon. *In* Man in the Amazon, edited by Charles Wagley. Gainesville: University of Florida Press.

Riding, Alan
  1988   In Brazil's Northeast, Misery Molded by Man and Nature. New York
          Times (May 3):1, 4.
Roberts, Bryan R.
  1976   The Provincial Urban System and the Process of Dependency. *In*
          Current Perspectives in Latin American Urban Research, edited by
          Alejandro Portes and Harley L. Browning. Austin: Institute of Latin
          American Studies, University of Texas.
  1978   Cities of Peasants: The Political Economy of Urbanization in the Third
          World. Beverly Hills: Sage Publications.
Roosevelt, Anna
  1980   Parmana: Prehistoric Maize and Manioc Subsistence Along the Amazon
          and the Orinoco. New York: Academic Press.
Saint, William S.
  1981   The Wages of Modernization: A Review of the Literature on Temporary
          Labor Arrangements in Brazilian Agriculture. Latin American Research
          Review 16(3):91–110.
Santos, Theotonio dos
  1968   El Nuevo Caracter de la dependencia. Santiago: Cuadernos de Estudios
          Socio-Economicos (10), Centro de Estudios Socio-Economicos (CESO),
          Universidad de Chile.
Sawyer, Donald R.
  1977   Peasants and Capitalism on the Amazon Frontier. Paper presented at
          the annual meeting of the Latin American Studies Association, Houston,
          Texas.
Schmink, Marianne
  1977   Frontier Expansion and Land Conflicts in the Brazilian Amazon: Con-
          tradictions in Policy and Process. Paper presented at the annual meeting
          of the American Anthropological Association, Houston, Texas.
  1980   São Felix do Xingu: A Sociodemographic and Economic Profile (mim-
          eographed manuscript).
  1982   Land Conflicts in Amazonia. American Ethnologist 9(2):341–357.
  1986   The Rationality of Tropical Forest Destruction. Paper presented at a
          conference on Management of the Forests of Tropical America: Prospects
          and Technológies, San Juan, Puerto Rico (September).
Schmink, Marianne, and Charles Wood, eds.
  1984   Frontier Expansion in Amazonia. Gainesville: University of Florida
          Press.
Shaner, W. W., P. F. Philipp, and W. R. Schmehl
  1982   Farming Systems Research and Development: Guidelines for Developing
          Countries. Boulder, Colo.: Westview Press.
Shapiro, Judith
  1967   Notes from Santa Terezinha (mimeographed manuscript).

Shoemaker, Robin
1981   The Peasants of El Dorado: Conflict and Contradiction in a Peruvian Frontier Settlement. Ithaca, N.Y.: Cornell University Press.

Smith, Nigel J. H.
1982   Rainforest Corridors: The Transamazon Colonization Scheme. Berkeley: University of California Press.

Stack, Carol B.
1974   All Our Kin. New York: Harper and Row.

Stavenhagen, Rodolfo
1974   The Future of Latin America: Between Underdevelopment and Revolution. Latin American Perspectives 1(1):124–148.

Steward, Julian H.
1955   Theory of Culture Change. Chicago: University of Illinois Press.

Stocks, Anthony
1978   The Invisible Indians: A History and Analysis of the Relations of the Cocamilla Indians of Loreto, Peru, to the State. Ph.D. Dissertation, University of Florida, Gainesville.

Strickon, Arnold
1965   The Euro-American Ranching Complex. *In* Man, Culture and Animals: The Role of Animals in Human Ecological Adjustments, edited by Anthony Leeds and Andrew P. Vayda. Washington, D.C.: Publication No. 78 of the American Association for the Advancement of Science.

SUDAM (Superintêndencia de Desenvolvimento da Amazônia)
1978   Transcript of Interviews Conducted at SUDAM (author's private file).

Tavener, Christopher
1973   The Karajá and the Brazilian Frontier. *In* Peoples and Cultures of Native South America, edited by Daniel Gross. Garden City, N.Y.: Natural History Press.

Thompson, Stephen I.
1973   Pioneer Colonization: A Cross-Cultural View. An Addison-Wesley Module in Anthropology, No. 33.

Turner, Frederick Jackson
1961   Frontier and Section: Selected Essays of Frederick Jackson Turner. Englewood Cliffs, N.J.: Prentice-Hall (originally published in 1891).

Van Es, J. C., Eugene Wilkening, and João Bosco Guedes Pinto
1968   Rural Migrants in Central Brazil, Research Paper No. 29. Madison, Wisc.: Land Tenure Center.

Velho, Otavio Guilherme
1972   Frentes de Expansão e Estrutura Agrária: Estudo de Processo de Penetração Numa Area da Transamazonica. Rio de Janeiro: Zahar Editôres.

Visão
1978   Mínimo Vs. Nutrição. Visão. Julho–Agosto:69–72.

Vollweiler, J. Georg
   1979a Colonia Fritz: Migration and Social Mobility in a Brazilian Frontier
          Community. Florida Journal of Anthropology 4(2):18–43.
   1979b Colonia Fritz: Danube-Swabian Pioneer Farmers in a Southern Brazilian
          Frontier Community. Ph.D. Dissertation, University of Florida, Gaines-
          ville.
Wagley, Charles
   1968   The Latin American Tradition: Essays on the Unity and the Diversity
          of Latin American Culture. New York: Columbia University Press.
   1971   Introduction to Brazil, revised ed. New York: Columbia University
          Press.
   1976   Amazon Town: A Study of Man in the Tropics. New York: Oxford
          University Press.
   1977   Welcome of Tears: The Tapirapé Indians of Central Brazil. New York:
          Oxford University Press.
Wagley, Charles, ed.
   1974   Man in the Amazon. Gainesville: University of Florida Press.
Waibel, Leo H.
   1955   As Zonas Pioneiras do Brasil. Revista Brasileira de Geografia 17(4):391–
          392.
Willems, Emilio
   1975   Latin American Culture: An Anthropological Synthesis. New York:
          Harper and Row.
Wilson, John
   1985   Ariquemes: Settlement and Class in a Brazilian Frontier. Ph.D. Dis-
          sertation, University of Florida, Gainesville.
Wolf, Eric
   1966   Peasants. Englewood Cliffs, N.J.: Prentice-Hall.
Wood, Charles H.
   1980   Structural Change and Household Strategies: An Integrated Approach
          to Rural Migration in Latin America. Paper presented at the annual
          meeting of the Population Association of America, Denver, Colorado.
Wood, Charles H., and Marianne Schmink
   1979   Blaming the Victim: Small Farmer Production in an Amazon Colo-
          nization Project. In Changing Agricultural Systems in Latin America,
          edited by Emilio Moran. Special Issue of the Journal of Third World
          Studies. Williamsburg, Virginia.